The Doles
Unlimited Partners

Bob and Elizabeth Dole

with Richard Norton Smith

SIMON AND SCHUSTER

NEW YORK • LONDON • TORONTO • SYDNEY • TOKYO

Copyright © 1988 by Robert Dole and Elizabeth Dole
All rights reserved
including the right of reproduction
in whole or in part in any form
Published by Simon and Schuster
A Division of Simon & Schuster Inc.
Simon & Schuster Building
Rockefeller Center
1230 Avenue of the Americas
New York, New York 10020
SIMON AND SCHUSTER and colophon are
registered trademarks of Simon & Schuster Inc.
Designed by Edith Fowler
Manufactured in the United States of America

10 9 8 7 6 5 4 3 2 1

Library of Congress Cataloging in Publication Data

Dole, Robert J., 1923–

   The Doles: Unlimited Partners/by Robert and Elizabeth Dole.
p.   cm.
   Includes index.
   1. Dole, Robert J., 1923–   . 2. Dole, Elizabeth Hanford.
3. Legislators—United States—Biography.   4. Cabinet officers
—United States—Biography.   5. United States. Congress. Senate
—Biography.   I. Dole, Elizabeth Hanford.   II. Title.
E840.6.D64 1988   *87-32032*
973.927'092'2—dc19   *CIP*
ISBN 0-671-60202-0

To all those who serve the public,
and who make government the public's servant

Contents

Prologue

ELIZABETH

Not every debate in Washington takes place in public. Some of the most intensive are also among the most personal. By the summer of 1987, I was quietly grappling with a uniquely difficult decision: whether to leave a challenging job I loved in President Reagan's Cabinet to hit the campaign trail full time for my husband. Bob hoped to succeed President Reagan in the Oval Office, and as he drew nearer to a formal declaration of candidacy, things were moving fast in the polls and in Bob's campaign organization.

By then I had served four and a half years—longer than anyone else—as Secretary of Transportation. I had always put the department first. If for any reason I could not continue to do so, then my choice would be inescapable. That time was rapidly approaching. From Bob himself came not a hint of pressure. "It's your call, Elizabeth," he told me, in words that echoed through my head for months.

Of course, there were people in his campaign organization who wouldn't mind having me on the road straight out, especially in my native South. Better yet, some would like me to open a North Carolina office geared toward "Super Tuesday" and Dixie's first regional primary. I was flattered—and torn. It was time for some quiet soul-searching. But quiet was hard to come by.

My opportunity finally came on a lazy Sunday afternoon in August. Bob was a couple of thousand miles away, debating the future of Central America with Daniel Ortega. My internal debate was waged in very different surroundings. Leaving our apartment, I drove up Wisconsin Avenue in the direction of the Washington Cathedral. I sat on a bench in the shadow of the cathedral's twin spires, not far from the entrance to the Bethlehem Chapel. I couldn't help but remember the day in December, 1975, when Bob and I were married in the chapel, as well as the other special experiences that had crowded my life ever since.

Thanks to Bob, I had gotten to know America as few people ever do, and it was my privilege to give back something of this country's gifts to me. I had spent the better part of a lifetime arguing that women should be able to make their own choices, to define their own contributions to society. During that period, I had seen a transformation in the role played by women in American politics.

So it came as no surprise when some people, men as well as women, questioned my decision to leave DOT. Why should I have to quit my job, they asked, just because my husband was running for President? I didn't see it that way at all. The choice was mine and mine alone, and I made the choice that was right for me. Not because I *had* to, but because I *wanted* to. I was setting aside one important cause to take up another, to play a significant part in the drama of national politics and in the selection of the leader of the free world, the person who would sit across the table from Mr. Gorbachev.

There was more to it than that. No person is fully defined by a résumé. Besides the speeches given, the bills introduced and the tough problems solved, a public figure has a private dimension rarely if ever captured in the day's headlines. As Bob Dole's wife, I could introduce voters to a man I knew better than anyone else. I could describe a leader who draws his strength from a lifetime spent in overcoming adversity, whose compassion comes from a deep well of human sympathy. All this and more went through my mind as I contemplated, there on the Cathedral grounds, that August afternoon. Gradually, the choice defined itself. I couldn't campaign as Bob deserved and run the Department of Transportation as my own conscience dictated. A hundred yards from the scene of our wedding, everything came clear.

Having reached a decision, I then had to consider how and when to reveal it. A couple of weeks went by. While Bob was in Iowa, addressing a statewide gathering of Republicans, I was on the phone—to him, to my family and to members of my staff. Something in the sound of Bob's voice when I told him my plans reaffirmed the good feelings I had about it all.

Around six o'clock that evening, I telephoned President Reagan to inform him that I would be resigning my post effective October 1, and to request an appointment for Monday morning. Before visiting the President, I had a warm, emotional meeting with my senior staff in the tenth-floor office where together we had charted transportation policy since the spring of 1983.

"As you can imagine," I wrote in my formal letter to the President, "I have not reached this decision lightly. Only a compelling reason—the need to elect a successor who can build on your Administration's remarkable record of achievement—has persuaded me to leave office at this time. . . . I learned long ago that public life is full of private choices. I have chosen to devote all my time and energies to my husband's campaign for the presidency, not only because Bob needs me but because I believe the American people need Bob."

In accepting my resignation with deepest regret, President Reagan recalled that I had been part of his Administration since January, 1981, a charter member of the team that launched America's "New Beginning." He noted my subsequent efforts to make transportation both safer and more competitive, to declare drugs and alcohol off-limits in American transport and to lead the Federal government in privatization—whereby Federal assets are transferred or sold to ensure more efficiency at less cost.

"No one knows better than I the challenge of making government respond to the conservative mandate of 1981," declared the President in his official response. "Elizabeth, I will miss you at the Cabinet table and in the inner councils of government. But I understand your decision to leave and believe the reasons behind it will strike a chord with everyone who values the very human emotions that underlie public life at its finest."

While I was in the Oval Office with the President, Bob was just outside in the West Lobby, calling my mother in Salisbury to assure her that everything was okay. Then we went out on to the North Lawn, to be greeted by a large crowd of reporters. I reminded them that when Bob had first run for the presidency back in 1979, I had left the Federal Trade Commission in March, a full year before the primaries. This time around, I was waiting until the September before the first caucuses and primaries that were just about four months away.

I'm not sure I convinced Sam Donaldson.

In the parking lot between the White House and the Executive Office Building, a stone's throw from my old office in Public Liaison, Bob and I embraced. Neither of us said anything. We didn't have to; the moment was too special for words. I knew I had done the right thing, and for the right reason. If I could help make a difference for Bob, then together, Bob and I could help make a difference for America.

September 13, 1987 was not an ending for me. It was a beginning.

BOB

Whoever said you can't go home again didn't know Russell, Kansas.

It is my home, my roots, and my constant source of strength. And a wellspring of wisdom and all-American common sense.

If you're from Russell, you can get an education just by looking at life around you. When I was a boy, I doubt we knew the names of our congressmen or senators. But we were blessed in having friends and neighbors who knew and cared for one another. When times were tough, people were tougher.

On November 9, 1987—on a crisp, brilliant blue-sky day —I came home once more. In front of the people who know me best, I came home to announce my candidacy for President of the United States.

Speaking from a platform in the middle of Main Street, I saw the people who have always accepted me and believed in me. I saw, too, the faces of long ago—faces of the good people of Russell, who put quarters they couldn't spare in a cigar box to help a wounded World War II veteran named Bob Dole get the medical treatment he needed but could not afford.

Of course, caring for your neighbor does not stop at Russell's city limits. It extends from coast to coast; from town to town; from person to person—it's the heart and soul of America.

No doubt about it, the people of Russell made a big difference in my life. I would like to give something back—not only for my neighbors, but for all Americans.

I want to lead America into an even greater era of opportunity for our people and security for our nation. I offer a lifetime of experience and a record that shows not merely where I stand, but the hopes and dreams of a lifetime rooted in Russell. I offer a willingness to work hard, to hang tough, to go the distance. I offer the strength and determination—molded in America's heartland and tempered during a career of public service—to bring common-sense answers to the complex problems facing America in its third century.

America's great heartland presidents were plain-speaking men whose clear-eyed vision enabled them to make the tough choices: Abraham Lincoln, Harry Truman, Dwight Eisenhower and Ronald Reagan. My vision, like theirs, is shaped by the aspirations of shopkeepers and farmers, workers and everyday Americans. Like them, I see the opportunities before us. Like them, I see the dangers. And like them, I'm willing to make the tough choices needed to preserve opportunities for generations to come.

On a sunny Washington afternoon one week before I announced for the presidency, I thought long and hard about the step I would be taking in Russell. I sat on a balcony of the Capitol Building overlooking Washington's inspiring panorama. Above me was the awesome Capitol dome—the symbol of our democracy. On the horizon, the monuments to Jefferson, Washington and Lincoln—people who really made a difference.

Across the Potomac River was Arlington National Cemetery. I paused to remember the courageous men and women buried there. They made a difference, too.

And I looked back on my career. Was I really ready, I asked myself? Was I strong enough? Could I really make a difference?

Then I thought about America, and what the giants of America's history—our past presidents and our people—have been able to achieve over the past two hundred years. And I realized that a president gets his strength from the people.

And then I thought about Russell, and the American people. And the fact that people have always been my strength. Together we *are* strong enough. Together, we can and will make a difference.

It's never easy, but I'll never stop trying. You see, I've always been inspired by my state's motto: "Ad astra, per aspera"—"To the stars, through difficulties."

CHAPTER ONE

The Doles
of Russell

Ad astra per aspera:
To the stars through difficulties.

—KANSAS STATE MOTTO

Shortly after my U.S. Senate colleagues elected me Majority Leader in November 1984, a banker friend from Wichita, Kansas, stopped by the Capitol to offer congratulations. The security people directed him to S-230, part of a handsome suite of rooms just off the Rotunda. As a fellow Midwesterner, he had no trouble recognizing earlier Republican Majority Leaders whose pictures lined the walls. He admired the portraits of Lincoln and Eisenhower, heroes of mine I had added as a personal touch.

Something about the place touched a common nerve. We fell silent before a marble fireplace, where we gazed at each other for a moment. Then a smile crossed my visitor's face.

"Imagine a kid from Russell, Kansas, having an office like this."

Imagine indeed. Such ambitions would never have occurred to me as a child, the son of a volunteer fireman, who lived during Dust Bowl days at the corner of Maple and Tenth; who along with my family looked on helplessly as the prairie blew away; and who later, in my own time of trial, would be rescued from despair by generous neighbors. I don't get back to my hometown as often as I would like, but when I do I find it crowded with ghosts. So many people I knew as a boy are gone. In their place is a community struggling to adapt to changed conditions on the farm and in the oil fields.

It is often remarked that in politics twenty-four hours can be a lifetime. In the turmoil of Washington, it's good to have some things that don't change. Elizabeth's love and that of my family provide a special kind of strength. The same is true of the memories and values I associate with Russell, Kansas.

Places shape people, Kansas more distinctively than most. The name conjures up a gallery of pictures. Sunflowers and cottonwood trees. Farmland flat as a tabletop. The Old West of Boot Hill and the Pony Express. And, of course, Dorothy Gayle forsaking her black-and-white surroundings for a more colorful neighborhood over the rainbow.

What people tend to forget is that Dorothy spent the rest of the movie trying to get *back* to Kansas.

Like most Kansans, I understand how she felt. It would take someone with a more poetic gift than I possess to convey the lonely majesty of the prairie, broken only by an occasional farmhouse or grain elevator. Few sights can match the reflected gold of a Kansas wheat field. Overhead, hawks swoop low over barns and over windmills drawing water for thirsty cattle. At night a blanket of stars covers the land, casting a glow unknown to city dwellers. With a little imagination, you can see a herd of Texas longhorns bound for Abilene, or a wagon train lumbering along the Oregon Trail.

The sounds of Kansas stir just as many memories for me. In the countryside around Russell, you can catch the hum of an oil rig, and the chime of cottonwood leaves tossed about by a restless wind. Nearby Dodge City lays claim to being the windiest place in America, with a constant speed of fourteen miles per hour. Somewhere between the breezes of Dodge City and Dorothy's tornado, the winds of Kansas have done a great deal to define the American landscape.

"When anything is going to happen in this country, it happens first in Kansas," vowed William Allen White, the homespun editor from Emporia, who combined the better qualities of Ben Franklin, Horace Greeley and Teddy Roosevelt. White wasn't indulging in Chamber of Commerce puffery. Kansas voters chose the first female mayor in America (Argonnia, 1887) and the first woman elected to the U.S. Senate in her own right (my colleague Nancy Landon Kassebaum). From the ground-breaking work of Topeka's Menninger Clinic to the record-shattering achievements of runner Jim Ryun and pilot Amelia Earhart and the works of playwright William Inge, Kansans have pushed out the boundaries of individual creativity and social conscience.

We're in the middle of things, geographically. And over the years a picture has been painted of us as a triumph of the ordinary. You know, Lake Wobegone on a grand scale. But there's more to Kansas than white picket fences and porch swings.

Kansas is two states. The first stretches from the Missouri border to the one hundredth meridian. Much of the land is buried under blue stem grass and a rich alluvial soil that is reminiscent of the Mississippi Valley. Here you'll find university towns like Lawrence, and newspaper readers who reach for the *New York Times* as well as the *Kansas City Star*. In the state's southeastern corner, a region whose ethnic diversity won it the nickname "the Balkans," men burrow into the earth for mineral wealth as their grandfathers did at the turn of the century.

Back then, oil siphoned out of eastern fields was used to grease wagon wheels carrying pioneers to the Pacific Coast. To get there, they had to cross western Kansas, once home to nomadic tribes like the Osage and horse-riding Arapahoes. As white men flooded the plains, they drove out the buffalo the red men relied on. Early explorers dubbed the area the Great American Desert, and some Kansans still call everything west of Salina "out there."

Life in the west was never easy. As a boy, I heard stories of hardship and the stoicism it bred, of men who lived on potato pie and women who covered the walls of sod houses with newspapers. The history of those times reads like a catalog of natural disasters. Fires leapfrogged the tinder-dry prairie, and droughts rendered the earth infertile. Tornados appeared out of nowhere, to do a dance of destruction. In the summer of 1877, grasshoppers came on the wind, so thick they blotted out the sun. From Texas to the Dakotas, they devoured clothes off people's backs. They also changed the shape of Kansas agriculture, by leading farmers to plant less of the vulnerable corn and more wheat.

The same plague inspired Kansas' distinctive brand of humor, part tall tale, part poker-faced witticism. The hoppers ate pigs' noses, it was claimed. This was no more an exaggeration than the boast that cabbage leaves are used for circus tents or that cornstalks are suitable for bridge building. If the Kansas wind steals your hat, it's said, don't bother running after it. The next gust is sure to bring a replacement.

I used to tell out-of-town visitors that on a clear day you can see all the way to Kansas City, 250 miles away. Kansas may be flat, but it isn't *that* flat.

Along with a hint of the absurd, Kansas humor is irreverent. If you can joke about natural disasters, you are not likely to take people too seriously, or to think that those who are put into office are any better or worse than those who put them there. We tolerate anything but snobs. John J. Ingalls found this out for himself during the Populist uprising of the 1890s. For eighteen years, the classically educated Ingalls had represented Kansas in the U.S. Senate, where he made no attempt to conceal his favorable view of himself. When the farmers lost their land, Ingalls lost his seat. As one wag put it:

> *Up was he stuck*
> *And in the upness of his stucktitude*
> *He fell.*

Anyone who wants to understand present-day Kansas, or its politics, needs to know a little bit about the Populists. In January 1886 the state was paralyzed by its worst blizzard ever. The windchill hit minus 100 degrees. Next came a severe drought. Crops failed. Land prices fell. Before long, westward immigration reversed itself, with wagons headed east proclaiming their own version of a state motto: "In God We Trusted, In

Kansas We Busted." In the state's Seventh District, a candidate for Congress who had lost a fortune in the Blizzard of '86 accused his Republican opponent of wearing silk stockings and was swept into office. Thus the legend of "Sockless Jerry" Simpson was born. Simpson joined with the Farmers' Alliance, a forerunner of the People's, or Populist, Party, and demanded the nationalization of railroads and a graduated income tax.

When the price of wheat went up, Populist fortunes plummeted. But Simpson and his allies left an insurgent virus in the state's bloodstream. Periodically activated by troubles on the farm, the Populists forced Republicans across the spectrum to soften their hostility to government action. Accustomed as we are to being the state's dominant party of government, the GOP in Kansas must appeal to the widest range of voters to earn its majority status. Perhaps this, along with the compromising spirit required in a state whose eastern and western halves are so different, explains my own brand of conservatism.

Another thing about Kansas: women have always played a significant role in its political dramas. In the late nineteenth century, rural audiences were spellbound by Mrs. Mary Elizabeth Lease, "Lady Orator of the West." When she wasn't warning against government "of Wall Street, by Wall Street, and for Wall Street," Mrs. Lease urged destitute farmers to raise less corn and more hell.

Another woman on the hustings, of even greater influence, was the wife of a Medicine Lodge minister. After her first husband succumbed to alcohol, Carrie Nation launched a one-woman crusade against the stuff in 1873. Members of the Women's Christian Temperance Union, which she founded, prayed in saloons before taking an ax to the bar. Within five years they had persuaded the voters of Kansas to impose prohibition. In 1905 the battleship *Kansas* was christened with spring water instead of champagne. I have a soft spot in my heart for Mrs. Nation. For years, the WCTU was the only union that had anything nice to say about me.

Joseph Talbott of Rising Sun, Indiana, and his wife, Elva, were part of a wide river of humanity which flowed westward in the years after the Civil War and was joined by tributaries from other already settled regions in the old Northwest Territory. Out of Ohio and upstate New York came fresh currents, bearing travelers like Robert and Margaret Dole. The two streams converged around a little crossroads settlement in north-central Kansas. Originally called Fossil Station, in 1871 it changed its name to Russell, in honor of a minor Union Army hero who never visited his namesake.

Others came in his place. German-Russian families from the Ukraine, escaping Czar Alexander II's universal conscription, built rock houses in open range country along the Smoky Hill River and harnessed oxen to plow up the ground. The last of the cattle drives wound through the area, led by cowboys who spent sixteen hours a day in the saddle and relaxed at night to guitar music. But their days were numbered by the spread of another kind of horse, this one made of iron.

By 1870 the Union Pacific had arrived to encourage the civic planners of tiny Fossil Station. A schoolhouse was built. A hotel opened its doors. After an intense dispute with neighboring Bunker Hill which stopped just short of bloodshed, Russell won designation as county seat. When a sizable number of Russian immigrants settled in the area, they imported the methods of cultivation first perfected on the steppes of their homeland. They brought something else as well, a foreign strain of wheat called Turkey Red. Slumbering in the earth during the long winter, ready for harvesting by late June, the new wheat crop ensured that agriculture would reign supreme in this part of the state.

Wheat, milo and alfalfa flourished in the black earth of Russell County. Trees were another story, and wood was so scarce that Russell merchants paid three dollars per cord for post rock, a honey-colored stone left behind by ancient oceans. Soft enough to quarry by hand or cut with a saw, it went into countless rail and fence posts which still dot the countryside around the town.

Before barbed wire, post rock divided one farm from another. Joseph Talbott, my grandfather, lived on such a farm ten miles south of town. He worked the land for what it would yield and also custom-butchered steers and hogs for delivery to local grocers. It was a hard, bloody way to feed his family.

Several miles to the east, Robert and Margaret Dole scratched a living from land they occupied as tenant farmers. Doles and Talbotts shared a common ethic in which work was instinct, idleness a sin. Affection was more often implied than stated. Likewise with praise for work done well.

Yet feelings ran deep and loyalties were for life. Among the latter was an old-fashioned patriotism. It led the Doles' seventeen-year-old son, Doran, to drop out of Russell High School in November 1917. Along with a friend who repaired shoes on the side, Doran Dole lied about his age, hoping to get into uniform and to go Over There. He got only half his wish, spending the last year of World War I at army posts in Texas and Illinois.

Doran returned in 1919 to a thriving village of two thousand people, the sort of place Sinclair Lewis would have recognized, even if he might not appreciate its virtues. An old dream of making Russell a commercial rival to Denver and Kansas City was gone. Still, town fathers were not short of promotable assets. There was a new $40,000 high school, an enlarged flour mill and what the *Russell Record* called "a real live Chamber of Commerce." Summers were enlivened by the tent-show lectures and popular entertainments of Chautauqua. Other times, people created their own diversions. They went to bridge parties, dropped in on friends, attended ice-cream socials and high-school athletic contests.

Home from the service, Doran opened the White Front Café on Main Street. It was there, according to local legend, that the cook prepared a wedding supper for Doran and Bina Talbott in February 1921. Two months short of her eighteenth birthday, Bina was the oldest daughter in a family of twelve. She was a pretty girl, with a gift for homemaking and an inexhaustible supply of energy.

Bina had even more reason than the average bride to rejoice on her wedding day. A freak accident had nearly deprived her of her groom. Doran had agreed to play Santa Claus for children in the nearby Pioneer neighborhood. Reaching behind a tree decorated with burning candles, Santa ignited the sleeve of his red coat. Fortunately, the ground outside was snow covered. The next day, those around the dinner table noticed that young Doran Dole had blisters on his ears. The resulting damage to the youngsters' faith in Saint Nicholas was far worse than any temporary burns sustained by my father. It wasn't the last time a Republican has been accused of killing Santa Claus.

The summer of 1923 was a busy one in Russell. President Warren G. Harding's train passed nearby twice. The first time was on the harried Chief Executive's way to Alaska, where he hoped to get a respite from the mounting scandals in his Administration. Two weeks later, a black-draped engine retraced the route, carrying a dead President past grieving crowds back to Washington. Russell closed its shops and held a memorial service in the hall usually reserved for Odd Fellows meetings.

Also that summer, an outbreak of pink eye was reported in local herds. Two blocks of Main Street were paved over for the first time, with red bricks produced in the county. People were singing a hit song by a University of Kansas student, "Daddy Stole Our Last Clean Sheet and Joined the KKK." Before William Allen White drove the Wizards out of the state, mostly by laughing at them, Klan activity briefly threatened both major political parties. A large crowd attended a Klan picnic south of Russell in 1923. Afterward, hometown papers noted that the main address of the day, a three-hour harangue delivered by a Salina preacher, alienated nearly everyone it didn't put to sleep.

By far the most excitement that summer was generated by the prospect of an oil boom. Attention was focused on Fairport, eighteen miles from Russell, where a group of investors jointly dubbed the Lucky Seven were surveying lime formations and preparing to drill at what they called the Carrie Oswald well. The rumors mounted for months. Oil leases and real-estate speculation replaced Kansas City cattle markets in conversations along Main Street.

Doran and Bina Dole paid little attention to all the talk of oil and impending wealth. Doran by then was busy running the

Fairmont Creamery Company and urging readers of the *Russell Record* to buy cows. That way, he insisted, they could produce one cash crop that wouldn't rob the soil.

On July 22 Doran went to work as usual. Before the day was out, he was called home. Home was a three-room house located a stone's throw from the Union Pacific tracks in the town's less fashionable North Side. It had a living room, a bedroom and a lean-to kitchen. Even by the day's standards, it was a modest address.

It was also crowded. A year before, Bina had presented her husband with their first child, a daughter they named Gloria. Now Gloria had a brother. The latest addition to the family was named for his two grandfathers, Robert and Joseph.

Writing about another small Kansas town, Dwight D. Eisenhower said of his boyhood home of Abilene that "it provided both a healthy outdoor existence and a need to work. The same conditions were responsible for . . . a society which, more nearly than any other I have encountered, eliminated prejudices based upon wealth, race or creed . . . any youngster who has the opportunity to spend his early youth in an enlightened rural area has been favored by fortune."

Russell was like that. It shared Abilene's devotion to self-sufficiency, but also thought of itself as an extended family. It had its social distinctions, humorously summed up in the handsome neighborhood south of Wisconsin Street dubbed Quality Hill. It also had a surprising degree of ethnic variety. In the southeast corner of town, German-Russian families clung to their old ways. In the winter they soaked a cloth in oil and applied it to the chest to ward off colds. First-generation immigrants munched on what we called Russian peanuts, or sunflower seeds. They used their teeth to crack open the shell, extract the seed inside and spit out the husk.

Today, as when I was a boy, few of Russell's people think that bloodlines or bank accounts are valid tests of character. The sudden wealth that followed the Thanksgiving Day 1923 discovery of oil at the Carrie Oswald site changed many things in town, but it didn't change Russell's fundamental beliefs.

There was no landed gentry to call the shots, there were few big houses or flashy cars. Banks still lent money to wildcatters or farmers with a handshake for collateral.

Of course, some things were different. Strange faces crowded the porch of the Driscoll Hotel. Aspiring tycoons unable to rent a room were forced to live in tents. And an influx of Democrats from Texas and Oklahoma reduced Republican margins on election day from crushing to merely huge.

Oil meant money and lots of it. It lured outsiders, many of them lonely men with cash in their pockets and time on their hands. Along Highway 40, just outside Russell, the oil boom spawned nightclubs and dance halls. Casinos like the Big Apple or the Wagon Wheel led some residents to fear that their community was becoming a regular little Chicago.

My folks passed up floor shows and slot machines for homelier pleasures. After the brutal heat of the day, a young couple might climb into the family car and drive out to the countryside, where temperatures were cooler than in town. Or they joined in the horseshoe contests at the Happy Hollow, a workingman's retreat on the banks of the Saline River. At the Hollow they could dance in the open air, under strings of electric lights. In between sets of music there was croquet. Some patrons indulged in homemade ice cream. Others preferred illicit 3.2 beer.

More than one Russellite padded his income by selling bootleg whiskey. Like many of his best customers, my father occasionally felt the urge to quench the public's thirst. But it wasn't the refreshments he served that attracted business to his Main Street creamery station or to the grain elevator he managed in later years. It was the fair prices he paid for locally produced milk, cream and eggs and for the cans of sour cream I helped him load onto an eastbound car of the Union Pacific.

But most of those clustering around "Doley's" each morning, talking politics, forecasting the weather or playing the Kansas City futures market, were there because of the proprietor himself. My father was the sort of man who never forgot a name, never went to a doctor and never felt as comfortable in a J. C. Penney suit as in his well-worn, immaculate overalls. He wore Old Spice and called women Sis. He cracked jokes and kept his dignity.

He rarely repeated himself. He didn't have to, because he spoke with such authority the first time that you would never question him. When the alarm clock went off by mistake at three o'clock one morning and he groggily sent me for some milk at the grocery store, I went. I waited outside the closed door for a couple of hours, until Dad realized what had happened and came to get me.

One thing he didn't do much of was relax. My father's proudest boast was having missed just one day of work in forty years. Since his workdays customarily began at six in the morning and rarely ended before sundown, he had little time for self-improvement in the modern sense. He never went to the scrubby pasture on one side of town fixed up as a golf course. To him, golf was a game for loafers. Dad found his recreation in the town ball team, a pitch game or the volunteer fire company he belonged to for fifty-five years. A shopping trip to Kansas City was a cosmopolitan adventure.

My father shared the Kansan's love of the outdoors. He liked to fish and hunt. My brother Kenny and I used to walk behind him on frosty autumn mornings as he tracked down jackrabbits. He sometimes let me try my hand at the wheel of our boxy old Whippet, a car that seemed to have more power backing up a hill than going forward.

Dad shared everything with his family except his own troubles. Emotionally self-contained, he could be a man of eloquent silence. All you had to see was his face as he approached the hospital door to know what he thought about what went on behind it, yet when his friends were sick he spent hours at their bedside. Sometimes he stayed at the hospital all night. Friends kept a watch over one another in those days. When a life ended, they put on Sunday suits and with sunburnt hands carried a friend to his grave.

Students of Freud might find repression in Dad's habit of greeting a loved one with a handshake rather than a hug. Not I. Around the Dole house, we were taught that gestures, like words, have an emotional currency, that compliments can be devalued by overuse. So if you mowed the lawn to perfection, on time and with every blade of grass in place, you treasured Dad's "Pretty good."

My father divided the world into two camps. As he put it, "There are doers and there are stewers." If you were on a sinking ship, some people would sit around stewing about the impending disaster, others would get up and do something about it. He didn't have to add that if the doer succeeded in radioing for help, he needn't expect a ticker-tape parade when he returned to port. Why make a fuss over doing your duty?

Yet if my father was sparing with his praise, he gave generously from a storehouse of wit. He couldn't even take a family argument too seriously. When tempers flared up, as they do sooner or later in most households, he would slip out the front door, a half-smile on his face. An hour later he'd be back, having put the time to good use by raking the lawn or clearing the sidewalk.

I'm not certain any boy can do justice to his mother. My own had a phrase she used to repeat. "Can't never could do anything," she told us. Obviously, my father had married a doer, not a stewer. If Dad laughed at the world, Mom set out to conquer it. Formal discipline was left to her. In fact, her whole life was an exercise in self-discipline. She was a perfectionist when it came to appearance and almost everything else. She even insisted on waxing the little wooden porch at Eleventh and Maple, the house I was born in and where I lived until I was nine, when we moved just down the street.

By then, Gloria and I had not only a brother, Kenny, but a sister, Norma Jean. We all shared one room, a bike, a pair of roller skates. Our home was humble, but it was always spic-and-span. Mom saw to that. Gloria still has the set of dining-room chairs we sat on as kids, hitching our legs up so they wouldn't touch the floor Mom had just washed and waxed. It was a long wait for that floor to dry. It was also a lesson in self-control.

Some people around town suspected Mom of washing Dad's overalls when he went home for lunch every day. I know that every night she washed the corduroy outfits Kenny and I wore to school. My mother made most of our clothes. And since she seemed able to make almost anything on a sewing machine, it wasn't long before she began a career as a saleswoman and a sewing instructor. During the week she sold Singer products door to door, and on Saturday mornings she conducted sewing classes for the women of Russell in a little shop downtown. I can still see her lugging those bulky old sewing machines and vacuum cleaners. In the afternoon we'd come home from school to find food she had left out for us. We didn't know it then, but we were latchkey children. Long before the term became fashionable, the Doles were a two-career family. We had no choice.

My mother's strength nurtured us through the same hard times experienced throughout America's Farm Belt in those days. But in her eyes it wasn't enough just to get by. She wanted us to get ahead. Never having finished high school, she was determined that we would do better. I'm sure that I owe much of whatever success I've achieved to her example.

I don't want to leave the impression that she was a taskmaster. She adored her family, doted later on her grandchildren, and delighted in decorating our house weeks in advance of Christmas. When a neighbor died, she was the one who knocked on doors to collect money for flowers. During the war, she invited servicemen from a nearby airbase into her home for weekends, capped by a Sunday chicken dinner she cooked herself.

Sacrificing her own comfort for others was a habit she never lost. For my sixtieth birthday, I flew out to Kansas to spend the day in Russell. Mom was up at five o'clock that morning, laying out the ingredients for my favorite meal, fried chicken and gravy. Over the years, I've probably eaten more chicken than Colonel Sanders—the fate of anyone who spends time on the political-dinner circuit—but none ever tasted better to me than the chickens prepared in the little kitchen at 1035 Maple.

Neither of my parents was politically active. Both were Republicans until an American Legion buddy of Dad's named Cliff Holland ran for Congress as a Democrat. Not until my own race for county attorney did they change their voter registration back to Republican. Mom always got mad when people wrote letters to the editor criticizing her son's performance. She was particularly outraged when the county Democratic chairman plastered a Main Street storefront with signs reading "Vote for Bob Dole and Twenty-five Cent Wheat."

It was all politics, I told her. Nothing more.

No matter how great her pride in my accomplishments, she was always one of my closest, and most helpful, critics. Following my vice-presidential nomination in August 1976, I delivered an acceptance speech before the convention in Kansas City in which I thanked delegates for their support and unleashed a few one-liners at the opposition's expense. Afterward I returned to the holding room just off the speakers' platform.

"How did I do?" I asked my mother.

"You usually do better."

His own family may have been poor, said President Eisenhower, "but the glory of America is that we didn't know it." In Russell as elsewhere, the depression that gripped agricultural America throughout the 1930s exerted its own leveling influence. Thanks to the chickens my father brought home and the cream my mother made into butter, we lived comparatively well. Other families traded chickens for groceries. A dozen eggs paid the doctor for the removal of a child's tonsils.

On Saturday mornings, I watched as farmers hauled sour cream into my father's store. The few dollars they were paid was a week's spending money. As usual in a farm economy, products in the greatest supply earned the smallest return. Wheat sold for a pittance, oil for a quarter a barrel.

Merchants borrowed money to pay their taxes. Housewives made rag rugs. Yet, even with their own hardships, people still paid attention to the plight of others. If you had your field plowed ahead of schedule, you helped your neighbor prepare his land for planting. When hoboes came through town, on rail or by foot, rarely were they turned away without something to eat. They too were seen as victims of forces beyond their control or understanding.

Even the weather turned hostile. Back in the days of the First World War, Washington had persuaded farmers to plow up their pastures and plant wheat. Food would win the war. At the time no one anticipated a drought. But that's exactly what happened after 1933. When the rains failed to come, the earth became powder dry. Soon there was nothing to prevent the wind from carrying off once rich topsoil.

Anyone who lived through those times remembers the first sighting of an ominous cloud, leading to hopes of rain. The clouds were real, but they contained dirt instead of water. Dust storms blotted out the noonday sun and made the air taste of grit. Kids raced home from school to stuff wet towels and rags under doors and windowsills. Some people lost their way, and there were stories of trains being derailed in the black blizzards. Standing on Main Street in Russell, unable to see the marquee of the Dream Theater fifty feet away, I wondered whether whole towns might disappear under the grimy film left by the storm. No wonder we called the Dust Bowl decade the Dirty Thirties.

During one of these storms, I got pretty dirty myself delivering copies of the *Salina Journal*. It wasn't my first job. My brother and I had been washing cars and delivering handbills since grade school. At the age of twelve I went to work at Dawson's Drugstore, a few steps down Main Street from my father's business. For a dollar a day I whipped up chocolate malteds behind the soda fountain, and gave curb service on weekends. I picked up the comic style of the Dawson brothers, who enjoyed a local renown for their tart one-liners. I also developed an appetite for ice cream that would horrify nutritionists. In my first two weeks on the job, I put on nine pounds.

Dawson's was the most popular watering hole in town. Sports figured heavily in the conversations that went on there. In later years, one side of the place was decorated in the purple and white colors of Kansas State University, the other in the red and blue of rival University of Kansas. Farmers would stop by after dumping their grain at the nearby elevator. On Saturday night, cars parked out front as families came into town to do their weekly grocery shopping. Stores along Main Street stayed open late then, and the drugstore itself rarely closed before eleven. The one exception was Sunday evening, when Chet Dawson hurried home in time to catch that week's broadcast of *Amos 'n' Andy.*

For me, Dawson's was a place to make friends, a marvelous listening post and a source of income, all rolled into one. Men who dropped by for coffee stayed to talk politics. In between their Bromo-Seltzer and cigars, they compared notes on Franklin D. Roosevelt's latest fireside chat. They debated Henry Wallace's controversial policies to limit agricultural production and thereby drive up prices. They calculated our Governor Alfred M. Landon's chances of unseating FDR in the 1936 presidential contest.

Spending so much time around the drugstore, I was bound to come into contact with medical men. A frequent visitor was Dr. Koerber, our family doctor, whose office was over the pool hall on Main Street. Another physician for whom I developed enormous respect was Fagin White. I can't think of anyone who contributed more to the life of the community than Koerber and White. It was a short step from admiring doctors to wanting to be one myself.

The hard times of the Depression were fertile breeding grounds for political extremists, some of them richly entertaining. As regular listeners to radio station KFKB ("Kansas First, Kansas Best"), my family heard the spoutings of a quack doctor (and would-be governor) named John R. Brinkley. "Goat Gland" Brinkley had earned his nickname promoting what he claimed was a restorative for male virility. By the early thirties he was a mainstay of Midwest airwaves, dispensing advice worth what it cost on his program, *The Medical Question Box of the Air.* Doc Brinkley was an early media star.

For less ephemeral values I visited my grandparents' farms outside Russell. Grandpa Talbott made regular delivery trips into town in a Model T with side curtains and lap robes. My brother Kenny and I often went along. If we were lucky, the grocer to whom we were delivering freshly butchered meat might generously hand us a nickel sack of candy. Grandpa Talbott sometimes came out with a stick of bologna and a loaf of store-bought bread. Then we were content to sit on the front step and watch the world pass in review as the old man completed his business inside.

My grandfather had little, materially speaking. But he shared whatever he had. The same was true of my Dole grandparents, whom we often visited after Sunday school and church. Grandmother Dole could make a chicken that had been scratching in the yard an hour before taste like ambrosia. Meat was a rarity in that house, refrigerators unheard of. The Doles had big crocks in which they covered fried-down sausage in warm grease for preservation. For Kenny and me, no visit was complete until we fished out a piece of sausage. After that we went outside to feed the chickens, gather eggs and help milk cows.

My Dole grandparents enforced a strict code of courtesy, honesty and personal integrity. Any youngster who slipped into slang or called an elder by his first name instead of Mister was sure to be reprimanded. And, like the Talbotts, like virtually everyone I knew in Russell and the surrounding countryside, Robert and Margaret Dole believed in self-reliance.

Farmers live out a paradox. Their way of making a living by working the soil often borders on the heroic, yet their survival largely depends on factors beyond their control, including, but not limited to, climate and government action. With so much riding on chance, it hardly seems fair to brand them personal failures when things don't go their way. Yet it happens.

In my experience, people can stand the loss of a house, however shattering, better than the loss of their self-respect. So while the residents of Russell believed in the individual work ethic, they were also reluctant to define personal worth with a dollar sign. Over the years, much of the town's economy has been based on agriculture and oil. The volatility of each is seen in how many may have been down on their luck at one time or another, only to scramble back at the next turn of the economic cycle.

Not everyone was so fortunate. When I was county attorney in the 1950s, it was part of the job each month to sign papers approving welfare benefits for my Dole grandparents, among others. Things were rough on farm people back then, roughest of all on their pride. For my grandparents, a lifetime of toil and sacrifice hadn't been enough to gain financial security for their final years. They weren't alone in their plight.

To the casual observer, Russell probably looks just like a hundred other Kansas towns. It is laid out on a familiar geometric grid, around a red-brick business block. Its streets have numbers for names. It's a product of the railroad, which comes by less frequently now than when I was a boy.

Once a year there was the Russell County Fair. On Memorial Day, which we then called Decoration Day, an ancient Civil War colonel named F. S. Ames led a parade down Main Street. When it was over, half the town crowded into Dawson's for banana splits. Five weeks later came the Fourth of July, one of those days when it would have been 105 degrees in the shade had there been any. That evening, when it had cooled off enough to raise the window shutters, Dad would bring home a big chunk of ice and a case of soda pop. The ice was placed in front of an electric fan while my father and his friends shot off fireworks.

The Doles were not globetrotters. In my first twenty years I went no farther east than Kansas City. One week when I was twelve or so, Kenny and I went with Dad to a friend's cabin in Estes Park, a couple hundred miles west of the Colorado line. We fished in mountain streams and reenacted Indian raids among piles of boulders.

Such exposure as we had to the larger world came mostly from the silver screen. Once a week, Russell's Dream Theater staged the Owl Show, a late-night performance which cost a dime. And children with good school attendance records received a free pass for a Saturday matinee of Hoot Gibson. At home, we gathered around a big old Philco radio placed outside on the porch so that neighbors could also hear Fibber McGee and Fred Allen. Sometimes at night I crept close to the set, turned the sound down low to avoid detection and listened to postbedtime treats like *The Shadow*.

Education came in many forms. Aunt Mildred Dole offered

twenty-five cents for a perfectly spelled paper. I accepted the bribe, and remain a stickler on the subject to this day. My schoolteachers did their best to draw out a rather bashful boy. I was more interested in history than in math, and the study of Latin verbs seemed pretty pale stuff beside the shoot-'em-up heroics of Bleeding Kansas and the farm revolt of Populist days. But my teachers persevered. Spurred on by my teachers' faith and my mother's encouragement, I was selected for the National Honor Society. As a regular at the local Methodist church, I was also elected president of a young Christian organization called Hi-Y.

I didn't go out for debating, being preoccupied with physical contests rather than verbal ones. I lifted homemade barbells made from concrete blocks and lead pipe. In those parts and in those days, if you breathed and walked and weighed eighty pounds you were a candidate for the football squad. And if you lived in our part of town, it was only a question of time before you joined the North Side Gang for some vigorous sandlot contests.

I played alongside friends like Phil Ruppenthal, the son of a local judge. Phil was the backyard genius who read every book in the town library before going off to Harvard. Maybe my closest friend was Bud Smith, a teammate on the Russell High School football team, the Broncos. Bud was killed when his plane went down in the South Pacific in the spring of 1945. News of his death reached Russell while I was on an Italian battlefield half a world away.

As a competitor in the 440 and the 880, I gave Glenn Cunningham no cause to worry about his place in the record books. Whatever I lacked in natural athletic gifts, I tried to compensate for with willpower. When that failed, my teammates and I invented unorthodox ways to psych ourselves for a big game. We played Glenn Miller's "In the Mood" before taking to the basketball court and drank a sugary liquid called Glyco Elixir before positioning ourselves in the starting blocks.

Most of the time, the only formula for victory was that old, unglamorous one of work. After two hours of football practice I would run a mile around the track in uniform, often with my friend Warren Cooksey. As a powerful middle-distance runner, Warren was a mainstay of the Russell track squad that won the Class A regional competition during my senior year.

He was also black, a fact which ensured second-class treatment in some towns on the track circuit. I was impressed by Warren's quiet dignity in the face of affronts. I was also angered at what seemed a blatant contradiction. If a man could be accepted on the running track for his talent alone, how could he be denied equal treatment in the race of life? I've never understood how anyone could cheer for a black man on the basketball court but feel uncomfortable sitting beside him at a lunch counter.

In June 1941, graduating seniors of Russell High School heard a Lutheran minister preach the Biblical injunction "Narrow is the gate and strait the way that leads into life."

I seemed pointed in the direction of Lawrence, on the other side of the state, and the hilly, shaded campus of the University of Kansas. Without a college degree I knew my ambition for a medical career was only a daydream. All that stood in my way was family finances. At that time, all six Doles were living in the basement of our small house. Continuing hard times had forced my father to rent the upstairs to an oil prospector.

A local banker came to my aid, lending me three hundred dollars and giving me some advice. Wear a hat, he told me. He even offered to buy me one. To him, I guess, it was a sign of maturity.

It would have taken more than a hat to instill seriousness into four thousand youngsters who gathered in Lawrence that fall. Much of the world was at war, but Europe's conflict occupied little space in the newspapers, still less in our thoughts. Like other communities in the American heartland, Russell was glad to be left alone. So were most university students. The siege of Leningrad was less important to us than getting through Rush Week or surviving a fraternity pledge court.

Most of us danced our way blindly through those last pre–Pearl Harbor months. As more of an athlete than a ladies' man, I was drawn to the basketball court before the dance floor.

Although I was enrolled in pre-med courses, the instructor who made the biggest impression on me was the legendary coach "Phog" Allen. Regarded by many as the father of modern basketball, Coach Allen trained such legends of the game as Dean Smith, Adolph Rupp and Wilt Chamberlain. Needless to say, I wasn't in their league. I was only on Allen's freshman team, so I definitely didn't spend all of my time practicing jump shots. With the war edging closer, farewell parties were frequent occurrences. And I didn't want to appear unsociable.

To a generation raised on *Animal House,* the Kappa Sigma fraternity to which I belonged would seem awfully tame. We suffered our share of paddling. But instead of toga parties we had lessons in dinner-table etiquette, conducted by dignified house mothers. Waiting on tables in the fraternity house, I received $12.50 a month and all I could eat. I was too busy to sow wild oats even if I had been so inclined. Besides waiting on tables, I had a milk route that had me out on the streets of Lawrence at five every Saturday morning.

By mixing me in with all sorts of people, living in a frat house was good preparation for what lay ahead. That's where I was on December 7, 1941. My brothers and I knew almost nothing about Pacific geography. We didn't have to, to grasp the enormity of the day's events and their implications for our futures. After December 7 we began to pay more attention to our studies and to the radio reports from exotic locations I had never seen on the Dream Theater's screen. However, this new-found seriousness didn't show up in my grades, which hovered stubbornly around the gentleman's C.

In the months following Pearl Harbor, the military draft reached into millions of Midwestern homes. Few males of athletic build and conventional patriotism were likely to escape its clutches. In December 1942, twenty-five years after my father joined the Army in hopes of seeing the world, I signed up for the Army's Enlisted Reserve Corps. I was nineteen years old, and eager to look life in the face.

CHAPTER TWO

The Hanfords
of Salisbury

In the spring of 1986, as part of its centennial festivities, the Charlotte, North Carolina, *Observer* held a public forum and invited me to speak.

For me, a native of nearby Salisbury, it was something of a homecoming. While I was growing up, the *Observer* had been a morning ritual in the Hanford household, like breakfast ham and grits. And in the summer of 1958, fresh out of Duke University, I had my first job interview at the paper. As the winner of Salisbury's annual fire-prevention essay contest and a silver loving cup handed out by the United Daughters of the Confederacy, I thought my journalistic credentials were self-evident. The editors thought otherwise.

Since then I've held many jobs, few of which were thought of as suitable for women back in the starchy fifties. This includes my most recent position as Secretary of Transportation. Selling railroads, pressing Congress for trucking deregulation, tackling drug and alcohol abuse in transportation and pursuing the commercialization of outer space—here was the stuff of a dozen speeches.

But they hadn't asked me to give a public-policy speech. I hoped instead to keep things on a personal level, to describe some of the experiences and people that had helped to shape my values. In preparing my remarks, I came across some words written half a century earlier by North Carolina's literary favorite son, Thomas Wolfe:

The unity that binds us all together, that makes this earth a family, and men brothers and the sons of God, is love. That love can take many forms. There is the love of one human being for another, the love which cements our attachment to a place of memory, the love of work and the sense of mission which must of necessity replace purely individual ambition if that work is to be truly fulfilling.

To love, to remember, and to work with a higher purpose in mind: Wolfe's words reflected the ways of Salisbury. And they brought back a host of memories of the state whose motto is: "To be, rather than to seem."

The first white settlers of Rowan County, in the hilly Piedmont region of North Carolina, were greeted with many demands and few promises. Their original plan was for a settlement of continental proportions, extending west to the South Seas. Salisbury, established as the county seat in 1753, was laid out on a more modest scale. It has always been called a "main-line" town, a distinction originally earned as an outpost on the fringe of a pathway known to colonials as the Great Wagon Road, a former Indian trail. A century later, Salisbury became a genuine hub of transport with the arrival of the Western Carolina Railroad en route to Asheville. As a girl, my mother rode the twenty-six miles from Salisbury to Statesville in a horse and buggy. The round-trip journey took most of a day.

Transport aside, Salisbury boasts a rich history. Twenty years before the Revolution the courthouse on the town square was the westernmost in America. Daniel Boone used Salisbury as a jumping-off point to explore the wilds of Kentucky. Another kind of trail-blazing pitted area residents against the British crown in a direct challenge. The people of Rowan County and neighboring Mecklenburg County were the first colonists to boycott British goods in protest of British tyranny. By passing the Rowan Resolves calling for "an indissoluble union" of the thirteen colonies in the spring of 1775, they anticipated by over a year the men of Philadelphia and their more formal Declaration of Independence. Aides accompanying the British commander Lord Cornwallis in his 1780 invasion of the Piedmont pronounced Rowan and Mecklenburg the most rebellious counties in America.

Nine miles south of Salisbury stands an old Presbyterian church once called Cathey Meetinghouse. As a girl, I learned its history from my Cathey grandmother. We kids were always told that pirates were buried in the adjoining churchyard. President James K. Polk's ancestors lie there. So do those of my distant relation, former Vice President Alben W. Barkley. A personal favorite is George Cathey, who as a signer of the Rowan Resolves was one of the first of my forebears to make a habit out of challenging the status quo. I also have a special affinity for Francis Locke, who, elected United States senator in 1814, turned back before ever reaching Washington, complaining that the roads to the capital were inadequate.

After the Revolution, a fresh wave of settlers passed through the area. Most were like the Catheys, of Scotch-Irish descent. Clannishness and frugality set the local tone, along with fierce independence and deep religious conviction. The latter were combined in a prayer attributed to early settlers of the Piedmont: "Lord, grant that I may always be right, for Thou knowest that I am hard to turn."

Salisbury needed such qualities, for it suffered badly in the Civil War and its aftermath. In her girlhood my mother was told stories of postwar hardship that followed in the wake of retreating soldiers, of cotton crops that failed, of grain substituted for coffee and honey used in place of sugar. My own generation would pay less attention to such tales and to the Confederate monument in front of the Lutheran church.

After Appomattox, Salisbury evolved a diversified economy. Less dependent than other Carolina towns on textiles or tobacco, it played host instead to shopkeepers and small farmers. In 1879, Livingstone College opened its doors as a coeducational school designed to prepare black youths for a place in what its founders hoped would be a racially enlightened South. Later, Catawba College was established as a church-sponsored institution of higher learning.

Local residents nurtured a distinctly Southern ambience. The pace of life was a little slower here, the greeting extended to a stranger a little warmer, than in Northern cities. Salisbury is still the kind of place where people on the street tip their hat in welcome, and where conversations start with a friendly "Hey." You don't need a holiday as an excuse to fly the flag. And families mean a lot, in part for their own camaraderie, but also for the foundation they lay for other relationships.

Religion exerts a powerful hold. In a world where so little seems permanent, we draw strength from eternal truths, expressed in customs handed on like fine family silver from one generation to the next.

All this may seem provincial to some. But to me such values show a pride of place and a perspective that transcends conventional wisdom. Instead of narrowing one's range of vision, they expand it and point up what is truly important. In an age when roots are shallow and purposes confused, they provide a distinct sense of who you are and why you are here.

Washington is full of excitement and professional challenges. But Salisbury is home. It is my personal Rock of Gibraltar.

The twentieth century was still young when Doles and Hanfords crossed paths for the first time. At almost the same time Robert and Margaret Dole decided to leave Ohio for Kansas, my grandfather John Wilbur Hanford headed east from Colorado.

As a young man Hanford had run a mercantile store in Carbondale, Illinois, where neighbors drafted him to serve on the local board of aldermen; newspapers still on file there show his contributions to the business and civic life of the city. He had next bought a Colorado fruit ranch, but his greatest pleasure came from the roses and other flowers he raised as a hobby. In 1905, a green thumb inspired him to change his address and his career. Because of his wife's delicate health, he sought out a new home at a lower altitude.

Both Hanfords loved music. On reading an article in a musical journal about North Carolina, "land of the sky," my grandfather was seized with an enthusiasm that never left him. Since Charlotte and Greensboro already had floral businesses, he split the difference and settled on Salisbury. After his wife and their only child, also named John, joined him, they helped him in the business. Young John, my dad, emulated his father's interest in music. He organized the Salisbury municipal band and for many years served as its conductor. In his handsome uniform with gold braid and buttons to match, he cut a distinguished figure.

Certainly my mother thought so. Mary Cathey first caught sight of her future husband on one of the electric trolleys that plied the streets of Salisbury in the early decades of the twentieth century. They shared a musical bond. Mary's mother wanted her to become a professional music instructor. Mary devoted herself to practice and performance, spending much of her youth at the keyboard of a pipe organ in the Second Presbyterian Church. To lighten the church's somewhat gloomy atmosphere, she often opened a stained-glass window. One day when she did so, she spotted a familiar face below. It was young John Hanford, working in a carnation bed. She called down to him and he responded, beginning a conversation that turned into a lifelong romance.

Some time later, Mary's parents proposed the next step in her musical training. The elder Catheys planned a trip north, including a stop in New York City to look at the famous Juilliard School. But John knew enough to fear the outcome of a prolonged separation.

"If you go," he told Mary, "someone else will come along and that will be the end of us."

He must have been a persuasive suitor, because Mary Cathey dropped her career plans and became John Hanford's bride. After their wedding, they moved into a house on South Fulton Street with John's parents. The elder Hanfords lived on the first floor, the newlyweds upstairs in what they called the love nest. This arrangement worked fine until the birth of a baby boy, also named John.

Thirteen years passed before John had a sister. A new medical facility, Rowan County Memorial Hospital, was due to open at the start of August 1936. My mother hoped to be among its first patients. I had my own schedule, however, and was born instead in a sprawling sanitarium called Whitehead-Stokes. We weren't there long. Three days later I was loaded into an ambulance for a ride to Rowan Memorial. Mother went along. So did Mrs. Snowdie Bean, a doting nurse who conducted us across town to the strains of a gift music box.

Selecting a name for the newest Hanford raised unforeseen complications. The morning after my birth, my father sent flowers to Whitehead-Stokes. Attached was a card: "With love from Big John to Big Mary." It was his whimsical way of lobbying for another Mary in the family. Mother liked the flowers more than the idea. In fact, she had already settled on Elizabeth Alexander, in honor of her grandmother. Besides, "Big Mary" reminded her of an elephant by that name, part of a circus that wintered in Salisbury. But when she saw how much it meant to her menfolk, Mother yielded. On Easter Sunday, 1937, I was christened Mary Elizabeth Alexander. A year later, I upset everyone's plans by giving myself the name Liddy. It stuck; Mary didn't.

I had my first accident at the age of three months. At the time, Mother was so engrossed in the just-published *Gone With the Wind* that she didn't notice the squirming infant headed for the edge of her bed. That little tumble stands out as the only recorded instance of neglect in the Hanford household.

Truth be told, I can't imagine a more loving environment in which to raise a child than the one at 712 South Fulton Street. There is the house itself, where Mother still resides, built of brick and stucco in the English manner. Inside is a formal entrance hall, with a spiral staircase connecting the floors. An attic room nestled under the eaves of the roof was a perfect rainy-day retreat for us youngsters. Off the living room is a side terrace, which was easily converted into a stage for childhood productions. A lovely old magnolia tree shades a yard spacious enough to have served as a pet cemetery for numerous small creatures, none of whom went to their Maker without such funeral rites as a small child could devise.

My brother John was too old to be a partner in such activities, but he was a major influence nonetheless. He combined the patience of Job with the deadpan humor of Jack Benny.

When not jogging around the house on his shoulders, I found other ways to get in his hair. I was all of three when he had some schoolfriends over for dinner one evening. I insisted on serving the rolls, with more enthusiasm than efficiency. "Most families have skeletons in the closet," Johnny told his guests, "but we can't keep ours *in* the closet."

In a household filled with role models, my brother stood out. He was a gifted musician and presided over the National Honor Society. At Duke he was president of his fraternity, Kappa Alpha, and a mainstay in the group of highly regarded campus leaders called Red Friars. In later years John added his personal creativity to the family business, helping it grow to worldwide scope. I put him on a pedestal as a child. As far as I'm concerned, he's still there. And John's wife, Bunny, his able business partner, is like a sister, always there physically and emotionally.

I used to kid my father by telling him he looked like Harry Truman. He had the same build, the same spectacles, the same Midwestern precision in his voice. He also had a similar gift for directing people with the fewest words possible. I discovered this for myself after covering the walls of my nursery with thirteen comic Valentines. Dad's approach was typically direct.

"Who put these up?" he asked me.

I blamed it on my imaginary playmate, Denaw.

"No," he said, "he hasn't been here today."

"Johnny did it."

"No, Johnny would have put them way up high."

This went on until I had to say, "Liddy did it." After each admission I was given a few pats with a broomstraw switch. They hurt much less than the thought of having disappointed this man whom I loved so much.

My dad liked work and plenty of it. Buddies who tried and failed to lure him on a fishing or hunting expedition finally persuaded him to try his hand at golf. Mother was delighted by the news. After he was gone most of an afternoon, she thought that at last her husband had found himself a hobby. She ought to have known better.

"I played two games," Dad informed her when he returned

from the links. "My first and my last. Mary," he went on, "if
you ever see me hitting a little white ball around and running
after it, I want you to make a reservation for me at Morganton."

Morganton was the state mental hospital.

One thing Dad didn't share with Mr. Truman was voting
habits. He had visited Weimar Germany during the peak of
hyperinflation there, and the sight of desperate people transporting their money in wheelbarrows was seared into his memory. My father was characteristically outspoken on the subject
of Franklin D. Roosevelt and inflationary spending. For years a
nominal Democrat, he kept his party registration so that he
could vote in the primary, which, in those days, settled elections
in North Carolina. When Dwight Eisenhower came along, Dad
switched his affiliation to reflect his true beliefs. Meanwhile, I
was twelve years old before I learned there *were* two political
parties.

My dad was an exemplary manager of any and all affairs
in which he was involved, including, of course, his business. His
judgment almost always proved to be right. He was a man of
integrity, analytical skills, thoroughness and industriousness.
This combination earned for him true respect from his employees, some of whom worked with him more than fifty years.
After his death in 1981, I had to visit a number of apartment
buildings he owned, whose construction he had supervised. In
talking with their occupants, I discovered that their rents had
been kept extraordinarily low. I also learned why. Some of the
residents were widowed and most of them would have to move
if rents were raised. At least that's what my father feared. So
that their lives wouldn't be disrupted, he simply carried them
on his books. It was Dad's expression of a practical faith that
regarded every man as his brother's keeper.

My mother is my best friend. She combines traditional
graciousness with a genuine interest in everyone who crosses
her path. Having abandoned her own career pursuit early on,
she poured all the more love and energy into the lives of her
children.

During the busy days leading up to Easter, Mother often lent a hand in the family business. She also chaperoned student-government trips to Myrtle Beach, South Carolina, and drove young Methodists to a camp at Lake Junaluska, in the mountains of western North Carolina. And when some of my church friends and I went on a hayride, Mary Hanford, with other mothers, was right behind in a car with the headlights turned up to discourage what Southerners of her generation called bundling.

Faith ranks beside family on her list of devotions. When I was a girl, she told me proudly of Francis Asbury, yet another blood relation, who helped John Wesley spread the Methodist gospel through frontier America. Like many women of her generation, Mother has never received a paycheck, but she has worked tirelessly with church committees, the P.T.A. and such organizations as the Colonial Dames.

Anticipating the historic-preservation movement, Mother joined with other local women to establish a museum and to rescue Salisbury's gaslights and grillwork. Each year for over three decades, they have staged a big antique show, the proceeds of which contribute to the restoration of Colonial and Victorian-era structures in and around Salisbury.

Whether she's reclaiming a neighborhood or whipping up a batch of persimmon pudding, Mother has never tackled anything without giving it her all. It was a quality she transmitted to those around her.

No less important to me were my mother's parents, who lived just two doors down South Fulton Street. I attribute Mother's affability to Grandfather Cathey. He was a large man with an equally big heart that made him a soft touch for any salesman and a friend to nearly everyone he met. As proprietor of the Cathey Buggy Company, he sold surreys, wagons and harnesses. He was an old Southern gentleman in the truest sense, valuing kindliness far more than worldly things.

Pop Cathey was the first to introduce Guernsey cows to the area around Salisbury, bringing them in from Pennsylvania Dutch country, where his natural warmth quickly thawed the suspicion most members of that reclusive community felt toward strangers. Pop never stayed a stranger to anyone for long.

As a true son of the South, he formed his political loyalties early. "Pop," my mother once said to him, "I think you would check the Democratic ticket and let them put the names in later."

"Yes, daughter," he replied, "you know, I believe I would."

My grandmother was more than a role model. Through her example, I was encouraged to have a vital, living faith. Mom Cathey, as we called her, was a continuous reader of the Bible. Next to her bed was a radio that was always tuned to religious broadcasts. In her eyes, we were each pilgrims on the road to grace. Yet it was a joyous faith she practiced. It had none of the smug or solemn piety that can sometimes frighten a child. Laughter came as naturally to her lips as prayer.

On Sunday afternoons, I sat with my cousin Anita Cathey and other children in my grandmother's living room, munching on cookies and drinking lemonade as she told us stories from Scripture. In middle age she lost a son, just out of college, to a drunk driver on a rain-slicked highway. Before he died, he had asked, "Lord, be with those I leave behind and guide me safe across the great divide." My grandmother was not a wealthy woman, but because she was concerned that Vernon never had the chance to make his contribution in life, she took the money from his life insurance and built a new wing for a mission hospital in far-off Pakistan.

Mom Cathey lived to within two weeks of her hundredth birthday. I can't remember an unkind word escaping her lips or an ungracious deed marring her path. When it became necessary for her to enter a nursing home, she thought only of what she could do for others.

"There might be some people there who don't know the Lord," she told us. "And I can read the Bible to them."

The Depression of the 1930s affected Salisbury less dramatically than it did the Kansas Dust Bowl. Or maybe it just seemed that way to a child whose family, thanks to Dad's business, was largely insulated from the economic shocks that hit so many. Still, a share-and-share-alike philosophy was imparted by Mom Cathey and others.

I once billed twelve dollars' worth of dime comic books to my parents' account at a local drugstore. When had I found the time to read so many funnybooks? they asked incredulously.

"I didn't read them all," I said. "Each day on the way home from school, I stopped in to get one and got some for all the friends with me. And you don't even have to pay for them. All you do is say 'Charge it.' "

Time was considered a precious commodity on South Fulton Street. If I had any to spare, Mom Cathey or my mother would suggest something. Once Mom said I should write an essay about my sixth-grade teacher. The result was a gold key and a certificate from a Chicago radio program called *Quiz Kids*.

Another teacher, Helen Jenkins, inspired me to write another paper. Each year, the United Daughters of the Confederacy sponsored a literary contest among Salisbury schoolchildren. First prize was a silver loving cup. For two years running, the cup had been won by the Wiley School, which I attended. I set out to retire the trophy by making it three in a row. An uncle told me about the General, a wood-burning locomotive that plied the tracks between Atlanta and Chattanooga during antebellum days. The train had a rich history, culminating in a daring wartime raid carried out by blue-coated guerrillas in the spring of 1862. For weeks, I corresponded with Chicago rail officials who opened their files and typed responses to my scrawled inquiries. In the end, Wiley extended its winning streak, and I was asked to read my essay on radio station WSTP.

I was a serious child, and eager to please. When my second-grade teacher sent me home to fetch a forgotten book, I considered myself such a total failure that I cried all the way down South Fulton Street. Books played a large part in my youth, both for the joy they brought and as a way of getting straight A's. Animals were another source of pleasure, from an old alley cat named Beauty to Penny the Chihuahua, whose death unleashed another flood of tears.

Mom Cathey liked to point out bluejays and cardinals in our backyard, and I guess you could say that even then I was interested in things that flew. The first political office I was elected to was the presidency of the third-grade bird club. A few years later, I resorted to less democratic methods when selecting the slate of officers for a junior-high book club I started. I simply declared myself president. It seemed a fair reward after a summer spent reading forty books.

I learned a strong work ethic on South Fulton Street. Self-improvement was a measure of personal growth. It was also a way to satisfy my goal-oriented parents. Piano lessons stretched into ten years of spring recitals and accompaniment for the men's Bible class of the Methodist church. My dance career was comparatively short-lived. As the curtain fell on one performance, Dad turned to Mother and said, "Mary, why in the world did you encourage her to take ballet? She doesn't have a single curve!"

As ringleader of neighborhood children, I was a precocious organizer. During the somber days following the Japanese attack on Pearl Harbor, I had little understanding of the war, even less of the battlefronts on which it was fought. This didn't keep me from joining forces with Miss Fanny Funderburke of the Girl Scouts in supervising what the *Salisbury Post* called the town's youngest defense group. We collected used postage stamps, tinfoil, wastepaper. Mother pitched in on wartime drives and greeted boys in uniform when they passed through town on their way to Fort Bragg. Everyone made do with rationed sugar and shoes.

However ignorant I was of the war's larger implications, I found it a continuing lesson in sensitivity to the feelings of others. It was one thing, for example, to adjust to three gallons of gasoline per week; it was something else entirely to go to bed each night uncertain whether your son was alive. With Johnny off in the Pacific somewhere, assigned to the carrier U.S.S. *Saratoga,* Mother wore a path to the mailbox. Thinking she simply wanted more mail, I wrote home at least once a day from the camp on the Outer Banks where I spent the summer of 1944. Her trial was made painfully vivid for me on Johnny's twenty-first birthday. That day florist trucks that had been repainted to read "J. Van Hanford and Son" appeared on the streets of

Salisbury. When Mother first saw one, she pulled her car over to the side of the road and wept. Dad, without telling anyone, had used the occasion to make the family business a partnership. Mother just wanted to make sure her son lived to see it.

Anticipation of Johnny's return overshadowed another news bulletin, delivered on a warm afternoon in April 1945. I was riding my bicycle that day through Salisbury streets that seemed more than usually quiet. The stillness was broken by a voice telling me of the death of President Roosevelt. Months later, Johnny came home for good.

Postwar turbulence did little to disturb the peace of Rowan County. The Cold War found its way into the *Salisbury Post*. So did Chambers and Hiss, Korea, Joe McCarthy and the first, tentative stirrings of the civil-rights revolution. But townspeople generally went about their business as usual. The daily patterns of small-town life gave most people the reassurance they were denied in the headlines.

The Hanfords were no different. On our farm outside town we had a cabin, with a grove of tall pines that sang a gentle lullaby in the night breezes. We had our cabin parties and Fourth of July fireworks. We also took to the American road. Throughout the 1950s I accompanied my parents on rail journeys to the walls of old Quebec and the falls at Niagara. We climbed the Rockies and gazed out over Puget Sound. Somewhere in those years, I developed a wanderlust that has never left me.

When I ran for Boyden High School president, a job pretty much off limits to girls, my campaign manager linked my candidacy to another Elizabeth, Britain's newly crowned monarch. "More and more," she contended, "the modern world is giving women a big part to play. Boyden must keep pace in this world."

Boyden turned down the invitation. Instead I was given a lesson in how to lose, something no one likes but from which most of us can benefit.

That same year, the high-school drama society at Boyden presented a one-act comedy, "If Women Worked as Men Do."

Few women in those days expected to work. We were taught the traditional patterns at school. Shop class was required of all boys, home economics for young women. Indeed, it was alleged that no girl could hope to graduate from Boyden unless she could sew a button or attach a zipper.

Whether such rumors were true or not, they were enough to strike fear in me and my classmates. When I was having trouble putting a zipper in a green cotton skirt—after seven tries—I took it to my friend Virginia Bibb's house, where her mother guided me through a final successful attempt. Wyndham Robertson, another close friend, was struggling to master cheese croquettes, and worried that her diploma would be withheld if the mayonnaise in a beet salad turned pink. Wyndham went on to become a distinguished journalist and later a vice president of the University of North Carolina.

Although my mother is an excellent cook, the kitchen was not my natural habitat. Neither was the playing field. In those days, women's athletics were relatively neglected, denying many like me the opportunity to test ourselves. Wearing glasses was no help on the baseball diamond, and my disdain for the American Game (perhaps brought on by embarrassment over line drives dropped) prompted me to stay home from school once or twice.

One thing that was definitely expected of both sexes was a driver's license, which in my case almost didn't happen. On one trial run in the family car, I stepped on the accelerator instead of the brake and ran over a neighbor's dogwood tree. My profuse apologies did nothing to ease the pained expression on the owner's face. Of course I told her that I would gladly replace the tree if it died.

"Oh, I'm sorry," she informed me, "but you couldn't replace it. My poor dead husband planted that tree."

At that moment, the mangled dogwood looked more robust than Mother, slinking down in the seat beside me.

In the spring of 1954, we held our senior prom. "Around the World or Bust" was probably suggested by a creative classmate named Betty Dan Nicholas. Everyone was supposed to come dressed as their fantasy persona. There wasn't a Southern belle in the place. Editors of the class yearbook predicted that I would spend my life as "a French interpreter in an airport."

A more immediate concern was college. I applied to only one school, Duke, for the simple reason that my brother had gone there. That fall I checked into Room 304 of Alspaugh House, on Duke's East Campus. In my first letter home I told my parents I was "crazy" about the place. I also told them I was thinking of majoring in political science, adding, "I think it would be fascinating to learn about American government, history in the making."

At 712 South Fulton, my announcement caused a ripple of concern. Mother's secret wish was that I study home economics. She thought this would be a natural prelude to marriage and life next door. Armed with my letter, she sought counsel from a professor at the University of North Carolina.

"Let her take political science," said the professor. "We need women in government. And anyway," he added, "they all get married eventually."

CHAPTER THREE

Hills and Valleys

Learn to make the most use of what you have.
Don't worry about what you've lost.

—Dr. Hampar Kelikian

On December 14, 1942, I joined the Army's Enlisted Reserve Corps. Up until then, my primary concerns in life were catching a football and outrunning competitors in the quarter-mile dash. Whatever leadership skills I possessed had never been tested off the playing field. At the University of Kansas I contributed more to the social life of my frat house than to the intellectual life on campus.

Before enlisting that December, I had never flown in an airplane or ridden in a bus. Of course I had never been shot at either. Except for the last part, I liked just about everything military life offered. There was a camaraderie in uniform that reminded me of what I'd known on the football fields and basketball courts of Russell and Lawrence. On the battlefield, men shared everything as if their lives depended on it. Often they did.

Any military organization is a structural pyramid. What could be more hierarchical than the Army? Yet it was also a family, and highly democratic at that. The only privilege given to rank was proximity to the front line, where survival involved

37

split-second timing and character was forged in the heat of battle. It was the work ethic raised to the highest degree.

In June 1943 I was stationed at Camp Barkley, a few miles outside Abilene, Texas. For the next few months I trained to be part of the Army Medical Corps. After a brief reunion with my brother Kenny, who had joined up also and would go on from Texas to the South Pacific, I was shifted to an engineering class at New York's Brooklyn College.

Brooklyn itself was an education. Back in Russell I had known only a sprinkling of black or Jewish families. Now every time I rode the subway or walked the streets around the college I was exposed to the world in miniature. Surrounded by such a mix of cultures and accents, I thought to myself, This is the real glamor. Flatbush Avenue held more fascination than Park Avenue.

In the spring of 1944 I left Brooklyn for Camp Polk, Louisiana, and then for training as an antitank gunner at Camp Breckenridge, in Kentucky's bluegrass country. Two months after applying for officer candidate school, I enrolled in Class 360 at Georgia's Fort Benning. The Benning School for Boys, as it was popularly known, was mass-producing officers for an Army that was rapidly losing its leadership stocks.

I arrived at Benning a corporal and left a second lieutenant. In between, I experienced the Army's version of Southern hospitality. This meant strenuous days packed with marches and combat practices, classroom lectures on the use of mortars and machine guns, field instruction on how to hurl a hand grenade and how to operate an antiaircraft gun.

After every exercise there was an intensive round of questioning.

"What did you learn from the march you just completed?"

You learned to adjust the backpack you carried on your shoulder, for one thing, since even a slight change could make a big difference over twenty miles. You also learned how to shift your weight while covering the red-clay roads of southern Georgia in a half-trot.

Field operations came under the same scrutiny.

"What did you experience?"

"What do you think?"

"What do you know?"

At the end of the OCS assembly line was a class of ninety-day wonders, with a question of their own: What next?

My answer came in December 1944, when I was put on board a troopship headed for Italy. The next two weeks convinced me that Kansans are born without sea legs; they also gave the words "green soldier" a whole new meaning. I arrived in Naples Harbor a few days before Christmas and was assigned to the 24th Replacement Depot, stationed near Rome.

The battle for Italy, the long campaign that started in Sicily and dragged on for nearly six hundred days before coming to its victorious conclusion, was already a year and a half old by the time I joined it. It had originated in the fertile imagination of Winston Churchill, whose gift for strategic thinking usually matched his penchant for memorable phrases—but the great statesman's love of vivid language betrayed him on the subject of Italy. As early as the Casablanca Conference of November 1942, Churchill had set out to persuade his reluctant allies that here was the Axis' "soft underbelly." Putting aside their own doubts, Roosevelt and Stalin went along with an Italian offensive, just so long as it did not divert forces from a cross-Channel invasion of Hitler's European bastion.

In July 1943, separate contingents from the U.S. Fifth and British Eighth Armies had stormed the beaches of Sicily. Their occupation of the big island paved the way for Mussolini's downfall. Allied flags were flying over Naples by October 1. Thereafter, the resistance stiffened as Hitler annexed his former ally. Berlin ordered that Italian soil should be defended with the last drop of German blood. The "soft underbelly" proved anything but.

Little of the war's grand strategies filtered down to the average GI. We knew only what we read in *Stars and Stripes* and what we heard from the scuttlebutt of rumor common to any army in the field. In the third week of February 1945 my perspective changed abruptly when I was sent to the front lines to plug a vacancy in Company I, Third Battalion, 85th Mountain Regiment.

The 85th was part of a larger unit, the Tenth Mountain

Division, whose origins lay in an earlier conflict, the 1939–40 border war between Soviet Russia and tiny Finland. Impressed with the gallant resistance put up by Finnish troops on skis, Charles Minot "Minnie" Dole (no relation) and others in the National Ski Patrol urged the War Department in Washington to create a similar force. In the fall of 1941 the National Ski Association began recruiting applicants, who were required to submit letters testifying to their athletic ability. The result was a division with a highly unusual profile. Side by side with forest rangers and cowboys, over half its members were men with doctorates, many from the Ivy League. The youthful captain of Dartmouth's ski team, Charles McLane, belonged to the Tenth. So did Torger Tokle, the world's premier ski jumper, and American Olympic coach Friedl Pfeiffer.

The Tenth had a crack commander. He was Major General George P. Hays, a polo-playing hero whose exploits during the Second Battle of the Marne in the First World War had earned him the Congressional Medal of Honor. Hays and his men were offered first to General Eisenhower for use in his sweep across Fortress Europe. But Ike declined, and the division wound up spearheading an assault against the Germans' heavily fortified Gothic Line, a 120-mile barrier stretching across the lofty Apennine Mountains north of Florence and guarding the entrance to Italy's Po Valley. The key that would unlock the valley was Bologna, an ancient university town nestled in the shadow of 3500-foot Monte Belvedere.

On a map of Italy, you can see that it is only fifty-six miles from Florence to Bologna. Yet the fighting along this largely forgotten front was so savage that it took Allied armies a full six months to cover the distance. Like a stopper in a bottle, the hills around Belvedere prevented entry into the valley beyond.

On the night of February 18, members of the Tenth moved to break the logjam. In sheer daring, their assault on 1500-foot Riva Ridge compares with the Union Army's sweep up Lookout Mountain and far surpasses Teddy Roosevelt's attack on San Juan Hill. Within twenty-four hours, they had dislodged the entrenched Germans from the mountain itself and then held their ground against seven furious counterattacks.

By the morning of February 25, when I arrived to take up my new assignment, Monte Belvedere was securely in Allied hands. At first I felt a little out of place in the Tenth. This had nothing to do with the fact that Kansans don't get much practice on the ski slopes; the division had long since dropped its stringent requirements on that score. But it was still a top-drawer outfit, proud of its record and emotionally bonded with the blood of fallen comrades. My own company's commander, an All-American from Nebraska named Butch Luther, had been killed just days before my arrival. And now here I was, a second lieutenant straight out of Fort Benning, dropping in on everyone else's party.

As a platoon leader, I was responsible for three rifle squads and a machine gun unit, nearly fifty men in all. My chief task was finding ways to keep everyone busy: cleaning weapons, doing calisthenics, going on patrol. Most of our patrolling came after dark, and on one such foray, the night of March 18, I had my first taste of battle.

We were sent out against German snipers holed up in a nearby farmhouse. As we approached the enemy, there was a brief exchange of gunfire. I took a grenade in hand, pulled the pin, and tossed it in the direction of the farmhouse. It wasn't a very good pitch (remember, I was used to catching passes, not throwing them). In the darkness, the grenade must have struck a tree and bounced off. It exploded nearby, sending a sliver of metal into my leg—the sort of injury the Army patched up with Mercurochrome and a Purple Heart.

For the next few weeks, the Tenth Mountain Division tried to pick the lock barring entrance to the Po Valley. We didn't get very far. Roads in the area were more easily covered on mule than by a modern, mechanized army. A single dynamite blast to an exposed bridge or roadway could halt traffic for miles. And with the winter now on us, even a dusting of snow was enough to hide enemy minefields from view.

March can be pretty cold in the Apennine Range of northern Italy. Digging trenches was one way to stay warm. Dodging sniper bullets was another. Like soldiers everywhere, we killed more time than anything else. We waited for mail from home.

We sweated out news from the front. Men lay flat on their bellies for hours, peering through a twenty-power scope at enemy soldiers on a nearby ridge.

In the face of pervasive boredom and uncertainty, nerves frayed easily. Artillery fire punctured an uneasy calm, making sleep all but impossible and keeping men emotionally off balance. I learned this for myself one morning when I talked with a young private who had been wounded in the assault on Monte Belvedere. The kid had left the platoon for ten days, receiving treatment for his injuries. Now he was back, with a leg healing faster than his psyche. While he was away, memories of earlier combat and premonitions of future fighting had combined to weaken his confidence. In fact, he told me, he thought he was a coward. He was anything but. Like the rest of us, he was tired, far from home, and nervous about rumors of an impending breakout for Bologna. What he needed most was a receptive ear.

After that morning, he no longer talked of cowardice, real or imagined. Small as it was, the incident taught me that listening can be a form of leadership.

By the first week of April 1945, it was obvious that Hitler's thousand-year Reich was on the brink of collapse. How much longer could it hold out? The question had life-and-death importance to me and my buddies. While we wagered over the date of Germany's surrender, our commanders were formulating battle plans to bring the war to a quick end.

Operation Craftsman was one. Beginning in the rugged hills around the village of Castel d'Aiano, forces spearheaded by the Tenth Mountain Division would leapfrog the mountainous spine of central Italy. If all went well, Bologna would be snared and the Po Valley secured, clearing the way for Mark Clark's Fifth Army to chase the retreating Germans to—and perhaps beyond—the Brenner Pass.

Enemy soldiers were well dug in around Castel d'Aiano. No one thought they would be easily dislodged. To help tip the scales, planners of Operation Craftsman enlisted unprecedented outside firepower. On the morning of the attack, tentatively scheduled for April 12, waves of fighter bombers would leave their fields around Pisa to soften up German defenses in the hills to our north. In addition there would be hundreds of artillery pieces shelling from the ground.

With so much riding on air support, the attack was held hostage to the weather. On April 12, due to fog and low overcast, it was put off for twenty-four hours. Similar conditions the next day led to a second postponement. In the meantime, soldiers in the field were jolted by news of Franklin Roosevelt's death at Warm Springs.

Like most of my buddies, I shed tears over the loss of our Commander in Chief. The fighting in Europe would end soon, maybe in days. For FDR, time had run out. Few men on the eve of battle cared to ponder the implications of such a cruel fate. No one wanted to be the last casualty of World War II.

I'm often asked to describe what happened to me on April 14, 1945. To be honest, I've always thought that telling old war stories is like showing slides of the family vacation. You had to be there. Other than that, I'm not the first person to avoid unpleasant memories. Most of us who have left something of ourselves on a foreign battlefield are reluctant to talk about it. Fewer still use stock expressions like "the glory of war."

Certainly there is heroism in the line of fire. And there is courage in the soldier's willingness to risk his life for the sake of others. When men who have been pushed to the brink of endurance discover hidden emotional reserves, there's inspiration in that. But when all is said and done, war is infinitely more wasteful than glorious.

Pins stuck in a field map hardly do justice to the organized chaos of battle. Vision is blocked and distance distorted, until, for the average foot soldier, the whole war shrinks to a few hundred yards of unfamiliar terrain. Survival takes precedence over grand strategy. If you can find your way into a protective shellhole, the fifteen miles to Bologna will take care of itself. When it's over, you carry away only pieces of a memory puzzle. Old soldiers hold reunions to try to put them together.

April 14 was a long day for me, but a short battle. At its

start, the 85th Regiment occupied the left flank of a two-mile front along the slope of Monte della Spe. Directly opposite was a ridge of hills held by enemy gunners. Separating Company I's staging area from the flat-topped summit of Hill 913 were a thousand yards and a shallow valley called Pra del Bianco. Dotting the sides of Hill 913 was an intricate system of bunkers and gun emplacements manned by German defenders. Minefields added to their security and our danger.

Early that morning air attacks were launched against the entire enemy line. Smoke filled the air, and our ears were still ringing when, shortly after ten o'clock, I Company started down into the green basin of Pra del Bianco. We were headed in the direction of a stone wall and some hedgerows, beyond which lay a clearing and the gradual incline of 913. A sweeping flank movement brought us into an exposed position, where my platoon was pinned down by sniper and small arms fire.

At that, we were comparatively lucky. Others made it over the wall, only to step on land mines called "Bouncing Betties." Such an innocent name for so lethal a weapon. Adding to the carnage were a couple of machine guns off to our left, raking the field and cutting down attack forces near the foot of the hill. Pulling my men back to such cover as I could find, I chose a small squad to help find a less deadly passage up the slope. According to Technical Sergeant Frank Carafa, I altered the original orders, which called for him to lead a party into the clearing while I remained behind.

I don't remember the exact sequence myself. Everything happened so fast. All around me, men were being hit. A combination of raw anger and protective instinct for my buddies took over. We resumed our flanking movement, this time approaching the farmhouse from which German machine gun fire was coming. I tossed a grenade at the target and hastily took cover as our little squad was detected and a fresh barrage opened up. The field was pitted with holes as a result of the morning's aerial bombardment; I dived into one of them. From where I crouched, I could see my platoon's radio man go down. I crawled out to retrieve him, but it was too late to do much.

After pulling his lifeless form into the foxhole, I scrambled back out again. As I did, I felt a sharp sting in my upper right back. Exactly what caused it remains a matter of guesswork. Most likely, an exploding shell had ripped into my body, smashing the right shoulder and scattering metal fragments along its path. Whatever it was, it crushed my collarbone, punctured a lung and damaged vertebrae, leaving me paralyzed from the neck down.

I lay face down in the dirt. Unable to see or to move my arms, I thought they were missing. In fact they were stretched out above my head, until Frank Carafa made his way across forty yards of scarred earth to drag me to safety and cross them over my chest.

Other men disobeyed orders to leave the wounded to medics. Not many medics were going to survive this battle. My second in command, Platoon Sergeant Stan Kuschik, gave me a shot of morphine. Kuschik then dipped his finger into blood and made a cross on my forehead. It was an old battlefield precaution, used to alert any medics who happened by and keep them from administering a second, fatal dose of the powerful drug.

The rest of the day was a fever dream of pain and confusion. Nine hours passed from the time I was hit to my arrival at the Fifteenth Evacuation Hospital. During those hours I wondered about my injuries, and wandered back in time. It was like watching a movie of my life. I saw Russell and kids I had played with, and my parents at the dinner table. I remembered Spitzy, a little white dog we had when I was a child. Maybe it was the morphine, or the strange sense of release that attends utter helplessness. All I know is that I knew almost nothing. That is, I had no idea where I was or where anyone else might be. So I went home.

From the field hospital I was transferred to a larger facility in Pistola, near Naples. For weeks I couldn't move my legs. Feeling was slower still returning to my arms. The letters I wrote home at the time—or, rather, that the Red Cross wrote for me—spoke of restlessness and "a little trouble with my right arm."

I was getting better every day, I informed my parents at the end of April, "and there isn't any reason why I shouldn't be as good as new before long." I believed it, because I wanted to. I went on believing it when I was loaded onto a hospital plane, like furniture in a crate, bound for Miami by way of Casablanca. Under the circumstances, Miami seemed like the Promised Land. I was back on American soil; nothing before or since has ever felt quite so good. The first thing I did was call my folks back in Russell. Someone held the receiver for me as I assured them that I would soon be home. And home meant recovery.

By the twelfth of June, when I checked into Topeka's Winter General Army Hospital, it was harder to deny what had happened. I arrived in a plaster cast that went from my ears to my hips, and with a persistent fever that doctors couldn't figure out.

Meanwhile, my wounds were hardly more terrifying than telling my mother I had taken up smoking—a habit I have long since abandoned, but in those days a godsend for me. I couldn't light my own cigarette, so someone else would have to come and light it for me. That meant a chance to talk, maybe to laugh, and a break from the monotony of hospital life. My mother detested cigarettes, but, sitting there at Winter General by my bedside, she held them for me and pretended the smoke didn't bother her.

Mom moved to Topeka to be with me around the clock. She was there early in July when my temperature reached 108.7 (axillary) and Dad was summoned from Russell. They looked on as doctors wrapped me in a rubber sheet and packed me in ice. It was touch and go for a while, but I survived the night, and on July 11, my right kidney was removed.

The immediate crisis past, my thoughts turned to the future. I was going to live; I never doubted that for a moment. But what kind of life would it be? In moments of self-pity, I saw myself going through life unmarried, selling pencils on street corners and living off a disability pension. My dream of being a star athlete and perhaps a doctor was shattered along with my body.

For nearly a year I couldn't feed myself. It took longer still to reach the point where I could get dressed unassisted. Six months went by before I was back on my feet. Even this modest accomplishment was overshadowed when the attendants helped me out of bed and I saw myself in the bathroom mirror. It was the first good look I'd had at myself since April 14. Back then I had weighed a strapping 194 pounds. Now I was down to 122. The shock of recognition made me go weak in the knees.

I didn't walk that day, nor for a long time after that. Forty years later, I still have trouble looking in the mirror.

In November 1945 I left Topeka. My home for most of the next two and a half years was Percy Jones Army Medical Center in Battle Creek, Michigan. Opened the summer after Pearl Harbor, by V-J Day it had over eleven thousand patients. The hospital specialized in orthopedics, neurosurgery and X-ray therapy. It was also the Army's leading amputee center.

I arrived in my by now familiar suit of plaster, with my right hand strapped to a device that looked like a tennis racket and was intended to stretch splayed fingers back into shape. As it happened, a deformed hand was soon the least of my concerns. A few days before Christmas, I woke with pains in my chest. Doctors traced the problem to a "pulmonary infarct" and prescribed dicumarol to dissolve blood clots.

This latest crisis interrupted my family's holiday plans. In Topeka my mother had practically lived at my bedside. Now Dad took the train from Russell, standing up most of the way in a car crowded with servicemen, so that he could spend Christmas with me.

At Percy Jones I had my second brush with death since returning from Italy. To guard against possible blood clotting, doctors prescribed total inactivity. They came by constantly to stick needles into my veins and monitor the dosage of the blood-thinning drug. Seven weeks after it was started, the dicumarol was stopped. My temperature soared again, this time to 106 degrees. Despite massive doses of penicillin, the infection persisted. As a last resort, doctors suggested an experimental drug originally developed in the fight against tuberculosis. It was called streptomycin.

Still in the early stages of testing, the drug could not be

administered without a consent form signed by a patient's next of kin. My parents gave their consent, and I became one of a handful of patients in the country cleared to receive the medication.

The wonder drug lived up to its name. By early March 1946, I was even out of bed for short periods of time. Thereafter, my physical health improved steadily.

What still had to be fought was a quiet battle against the emotional ravages of war. Much of it was played out in a brightly lit ward on the fourth floor of the main hospital building, in a whitewashed room, maybe twenty by forty feet, that housed a dozen other young men. Most of them had spinal injuries of one sort or another. Philip A. Hart, whose name today graces the building in which I have my Senate office, was in that same ward with me. In another ward at Percy Jones was Daniel K. Inouye, now a Senate colleague from Hawaii.

One day a young Air Force captain named Bill Fitz arrived in our ward. He had been seriously injured in a plane crash, and his spirits seemed more broken than his body. As the days passed and Billy received no visitors or mail, the rest of us took him on as a special project. We tried to get him to talk, to laugh, to show some interest in anything.

When someone heard a song on the radio called "Nancy with the Laughing Face," we immediately adopted it as our standard. It was fresh and positive, qualities sorely needed on the fourth floor. Any infantry officer worth his salt is a natural-born scrounger. It's part of his unofficial job description. I managed to scrounge up the record, and a big old Stromberg-Carlson set on which to play it. From then on you couldn't walk past our ward without hearing the honey-on-toast baritone of Frank Sinatra, singing about his good-natured Nancy.

It did us all a lot of good, all but Billy Fitz, who remained mute and immobile. Late one night we heard a noise from his corner of the ward, a sort of quick, shallow gasp. Men surrounded his bed across from me. We summoned a nurse, but it was too late. The next few days were pretty grim on the fourth floor.

As doctors in our area of the hospital tried to ward off

osteopathic deterioration, patients battled decay of another kind, one that destroys the spirit before it takes the body. Fighting back, we took emotional inventory of whatever spiritual and mental resources we could find. If you were in pain, the doctors would give you morphine and Demerol. I didn't want that forever. Yet thinking about how much you hurt makes you hurt more. So you tried not to think about it. There was a choice: spend your time complaining about needles and bedsores or open your eyes to the suffering around you and decide to become useful.

I said a lot of silent prayers in those days, at least some of them tinged with initial bitterness. Why me, I demanded—why hadn't someone been watching out for me? In time, I came to realize that someone *was* watching out for me, and had been from the morning of April 14. Maybe it was all part of a plan, a test of endurance and strength and, above all, of faith.

There were still times when I became angry at a body that was my enemy. In order to restore the feeling and the strength to my lifeless hands, I was given muscle-relaxing baths and hot-wax treatments by therapists who pulled clawlike fingers apart. Some days I spent hours trying to close two fingers of my right hand.

It was like starting life over again, in a second childhood of unknown length and without one's original physical attributes. But when I saw men around me who had lost their arms or legs or sight, it had a way of putting my own condition into perspective.

One late-winter morning when I sat out in a hospital parking lot, waiting to be shuttled between sections of the medical complex, I struck up a conversation with a patient beside me.

"Don't your feet get cold out here?" I asked.

He pointed down and tapped his artificial legs with his cane. After that I stopped asking "Why me?"

I began to look beyond external appearances in judging a person. At first glance, the guy in the next bed or the room down the hall might seem fine. Physically whole, not a scratch or a scar on him. But then you saw doctors making regular visits, and you knew he was suffering from something much worse than not being able to move his fingers or walk on two legs. My only phobia from the years when I lay flat on my back is a fear of fire. When staying in hotels, I prefer the ground floor. I'd have a pretty tough time letting myself down from a burning building on a bedsheet.

Meanwhile, I learned to hide my feelings behind a wisecrack. Laughter really was a medicine. At least, that's what hospital officials seemed to believe. They started wheeling me around to wards where morale was low.

I spent my early months at Percy Jones in traction. Later I was able to sit in a wheelchair. Unable to roll it myself, I relied on others to push me around. Physical helplessness changes the way you see yourself. It demolishes conventional views of time and distance. Like everything else at Percy Jones, regaining the use of my legs was an exercise in patience. From wiggling a toe to bending a knee, the slightest sign of movement was a cause for celebration. With a right arm in a cast and a left of not much greater use, crutches were out of the question. So I took slow, wobbly steps, baby steps at first. I got up and walked around my bed, then around the ward. I rested awhile, read awhile, and started the process all over again. Unless leg tremors set in.

Sometimes I fell. When that happened, I tried to pick myself up without assistance. I didn't want to depend on others for more than essential help. Even today, I don't like to ask Elizabeth to help me put on formal evening wear, except for the tie and those little tux shirt buttons that drive most men crazy.

All this was like athletic training on a field no longer than a hospital corridor. But at least I began to see progress, more so than in the agonizingly slow attempt to regain the use of my hands. After several months, I could reach the second-floor dayroom on my own and join in bridge games by the hour. Someone else shuffled and dealt the cards.

I began experimenting with Velcro jackets and shirts with snaps or zippers, anything to get around the buttons that were my nemesis. I wore clip-on ties and laceless shoes. A couple of times each day I had therapy to strengthen my arms and legs and speed the laborious process of becoming mobile. To help their patients pass the time, the nurses organized birthday parties, with favorite dishes supplied by the hospital dietitian. We watched movies, played chess, ransacked the local libraries.

I conducted a little business on the side. Auto production was just starting to crank up again after the restrictions of wartime, and disabled veterans were given priority. I sold cars to fellow patients—at 6 percent commission—until the authorities put a stop to it. Subsequently, thanks to a generous government, I got a specially designed model that I could drive with my left hand.

I also used much of my hospital time to go back to school, figuratively speaking. Fellow patient George Radulescu and I began a personal survey course of sorts, rooted in our wartime experiences. Conceding to the Germans good field command and armaments capacities, we decided that our own victory must have resulted from the individual character of Allied soldiers. Working back from this premise, we traced the history of warfare and the organization of armies. From Alexander the Great to Lee and Grant, we analyzed tactics and pursued the essentials of leadership. We studied societies as well as individuals. We read Plato (I thought his ideal society much too regimented) and subjected the Ten Commandments to our relentless quest for positive thinking.

Reading on through the Renaissance and English common law, we eventually came to the foundations of the American republic. I liked George Washington better than Benjamin Franklin. Washington appealed to my interest in practical organization. Franklin, by contrast, seemed just a tinkerer. Lincoln was my hero, the voice and symbol of American democracy. His humble origins inspired me. So did the way personal tragedy only deepened his sensitivity.

In a different context, I admired Dwight Eisenhower, himself a product of small-town Kansas who had gone on to forge history's greatest alliance. This was no small undertaking. Anyone who could work harmoniously with Bernard Law Montgomery, George Patton and Charles de Gaulle had to be some kind of genius.

At about ten o'clock most nights, the nurse came around

to announce, "School's out, Lieutenant." That was the signal to go across the street to the Hart Hotel, a brick hostelry with a coffee shop that served grilled-cheese sandwiches until two in the morning. Since the elevator near our ward was an unpredictable relic, getting to the Hart called for a certain resourcefulness. More than once, George and I slipped out disguised in an outlandish costume of oversized trench coats scrounged from the supply closet. Safely across the street, we could rehash our theories until closing time. Then we retraced our steps, whispering all the way to avoid detection by the powers that be.

Eventually, I was well enough to escape the hospital walls for longer periods. I got leave to visit Russell, where I moved into my parents' old room and worked out in a little exercise area my dad set up in the backyard. I squeezed a rubber ball to build up the strength in my left hand. It was already good enough to hold a hand of playing cards for hours, as friends dropped by and my family rearranged their schedules to spend time with me. Mom would come back late from selling sewing machines and sometimes do a load of wash at midnight while the card games went on around her.

On one of those visits, I went to see my old friends at Dawson's Drugstore. Walking down Main Street that first time was the hardest thing in the world. Thinking the eyes of the entire town were on me, I felt that my disability was an embarrassment. My mood in those days was summed up in the tunes I played over and over on Dawson's jukebox. "Laughing on the Outside, Crying on the Inside" was one. "You'll Never Walk Alone" was another. One day, someone called me a hero to my face. I disagreed. I had come home; the real heroes hadn't.

By now I had made as much progress as seemed possible at Percy Jones. When I went back in early 1947, it no longer seemed a premier orthopedic center, much less a miracle factory. Miracles were in short supply just then, but that didn't keep me from wanting one.

That's when I ran into Hampar Kelikian.

His friends called him Dr. K. He was a short man, but a giant in the operating room. As a boy Kelikian had escaped the blood-spattered landscape of his native Armenia. Three of his sisters were less fortunate; a fourth sibling, a brother, was killed in Italy during World War II. Hampar arrived in Chicago in 1920 with two dollars in his pocket and a rug from his homeland under one arm. He got a job on a farm, where he impressed his employer into paying his way through college. The young immigrant went on to medical school and an apprenticeship at Cook County Hospital.

When war broke out again in Europe in 1939, Dr. K shared his talent with his adopted country. He was a pioneer in the surgical restoration of otherwise useless limbs. For his contributions to military medicine, Harry Truman gave him a medal. Those whom he rescued gave him their love.

I first heard about Kelikian from Lamont Jahn, an uncle of mine who had served in the Medical Corps with the Armenian-born physician whose special interest was wounded GI's. When I went to see Dr. K in Chicago early in 1947, I was still looking for a miracle.

My definition of recovery was simple. It meant being put back the way I was before April 14. Any good surgeon should be able to restore my ability to shoot baskets and catch passes. In my search for such guarantees, I had already consulted doctors in Wichita, Kansas City and Denver. They talked about nerve damage and impaired functions, but none of them did anything to discourage my search for a magical scalpel.

Now Dr. K sat me down and administered the verbal equivalent of a slap in the face. There would be no miracles, he told me. He would do all he could to give me back as much use of my arm and hands as possible, but after that it was up to me to make the most of what I had. What he was really saying was, accept the situation and get on with the business of life.

Kelikian reserved an operating room for June 1947. For this first procedure, and for a half dozen that followed, he refused to take a penny. But there were still hospital bills to pay. So Chet Dawson and my high-school buddy Phil Ruppenthal joined with VFW Chapter 6240 and started the Bob Dole Fund.

It began with a few paper bills tossed into an old cigar box

—a box I still have in my Senate desk. Local banks volunteered to handle contributions. Free publicity was given by the *Russell Record*. From thirty cents to a hundred dollars, dozens of my neighbors dug into their pockets to give whatever they could. One man brought in a live duck. In the end, the contributions added up to around eighteen hundred dollars. I can never repay the people of Russell. When I needed them, they were there. Their gifts were not limited to money. A friend named Adolph Reissig spent hours designing and building a special lead weight, covered in felt, to help me straighten my arm.

Dr. Kelikian strained his own ingenuity to the limit, first removing the head of the humerus bone, then replacing the damaged ball and socket by drilling a hole in the humerus. Taking a piece of muscle sheathing from my left leg, he re-attached the arm as if threading a needle. When Kelikian was through, my right arm was two and a half inches shorter than my left. The arm couldn't be rotated, and Dr. K's efforts to implant tendons in the right hand were largely unsuccessful.

Today I am unable to grasp objects with my right hand or carry anything heavier than a pen. Limited sensation in the fingers of my left hand makes it impossible for me to tell the difference between a quarter and a dime with my eyes closed. Getting dressed each morning is a time-consuming process, and I rarely loosen my tie in public, given the effort it requires to knot it back again.

Yet none of this detracts from Dr. Kelikian's medical achievement or personal influence. Even if he couldn't restore my right arm, he gave me something much more important: an example to live by, and a philosophy of making the most of what you have.

"The mechanical part of surgery," he once explained, "is like carpentry. Anyone can learn that. The important thing is to be able to suffer with the patient, to see if they are in pain."

Whether economic or physical, suffering can do one of two things to someone. It can toughen him or it can harden him. It can make him more, or less, sensitive to the needs of those around him. He can say to himself, "I overcame this, the toughest challenge of my life. And if I did, then everyone else ought to be able to do the same thing."

Or he can develop a special bond with other sufferers, seeing the world through their eyes and combating the smug belief that physical wholeness is an accurate gauge of a person's abilities. I've known victims of physical disability who, in their emotional and mental depth, go far beyond people with conventional appearance and mobility. Today this sounds so obvious as to barely require stating. But it was a different story in 1947, when disabilities were still kept in the closet.

When Dr. K died, in the summer of 1983, I took the unusual step of quoting poetry on the floor of the Senate. The words came from Robert Frost:

> *Nature's first green is gold,*
> *Her hardest hue to hold.*
> *Her early leaf's a flower,*
> *But only so an hour.*
> *Then leaf subsides to leaf,*
> *So Eden sank to grief.*
> *So dawn goes down to day,*
> *Nothing gold can stay.*

Hampar Kelikian was pure gold.

In November 1947, I returned to Percy Jones for extensive therapy on my rebuilt arm. Within a few months I gained another kind of right arm, one that would be invaluable in the painstaking process of emotional and professional reentry. Phyllis Holden was a pretty brunette, originally from New Hampshire, where her parents were active in conservative Republican politics. She was working as an occupational therapist at Percy Jones. As she tells it, she was having coffee with a couple of other nurses one day when I walked by.

"There goes that poor Bob Dole," declared one of her companions. "He's not supposed to live."

Actually, by the fall of 1947 I was well on the way to recovery. Expressions like "poor Bob Dole" were exactly the opposite of what I wished to hear. Phyllis understood this, and behaved accordingly. I think maybe that was what first made me think she was special. We met formally at a dance for patients. She was in charge of decorating around the theme of heaven (the dance floor) and hell (the bar). I arrived with a friend who had originally been admitted to the hospital with two broken legs. Before the evening was over, he was jitterbugging. And Phyllis and I were dancing close. That was the only way we *could* dance, since I couldn't extend my right arm.

Three months after I asked her for a date at the hospital coffee shop, we were married in St. Paul's Cathedral in Concord, New Hampshire. Among the notes of congratulation we received was a wire from Dr. Kelikian. He said he hoped I would make loving use of the arm he had gone to such length to restore.

Up to this time, I hadn't expected to walk down the aisle with any woman. As I explained to my family, I didn't think I had a right to impose on a wife the burdens that would accompany marriage to someone in my physical condition. Phyllis made me forget my injuries. She helped me think, not in terms of disability, but of ability. She treated me like everyone else.

As my nervous system came back to life, I experienced occasional tremors in my arms and legs. They made me shakier than usual, and more self-conscious than ever. One hot summer day in Russell we were all sitting around the dinner table. I was holding a glass of iced tea somewhat unsteadily in one hand and suddenly it slipped out of my grasp and shattered on the floor.

"Can't you hold anything?" Phyllis said in a jocular voice. She was thinking only that the glass was moist, and was determined to laugh the accident off. The rest of my family was a little shocked. They were used to treating me as a fragile object, like the glass on the floor. But Phyllis was right.

By the time we were married, in June 1948, I was out of Percy Jones for good. Thanks to the GI Bill, I was about to pick up on the college education so rudely interrupted by the war. The doctors in Battle Creek urged me to go to Arizona for its warm winters and dry climate, so I enrolled at the University of Arizona for a year. In between classes, I ran in the hills around Tucson. Except for a brief recurrence of lung problems which put me back in the hospital for a week, my recovery was uneventful.

Phyllis went with me to my classes, taking notes and writing exam papers from my dictation. Later on, I got a tape recorder, a primitive machine the size of a breadbox that I hooked up beside the professor. Nights were given over to transcribing the lectures in my left-handed scrawl. It was pretty slow going.

In the fall of 1949 I began lugging my tape recorder to class at Topeka's Washburn University, where I enrolled in a joint program for an undergraduate degree in history and a graduate degree in law. Phyllis meanwhile worked at the Topeka State Hospital and at the State Rehabilitation Center for the Blind. We lived in a small complex called the Senate Apartments, where I wore a hole in the living-room carpet pacing around with a book in my hand, reciting the day's lessons. Phyllis told me I didn't have to work so hard. Not every grade had to be an A.

"I don't know how to study for a C or B's worth," I told her. That's what I had done in my prewar days at the University of Kansas. A lot had changed since then, including my study habits. From now on, the only way I could study a subject was to master it.

The classrooms of Washburn were filled with older students, many of them beneficiaries of the GI Bill. Some were married, with small children. Not only had the war consumed their youth, it had also burned away frivolous notions. Remaining were a seriousness and an almost desperate wish to find meaning in the recent past. It was a class taught by some first-rate professors who challenged us to live up to all our noble-sounding precepts.

Perhaps the most influential politically was Beth Bowers, the law librarian, who was only a couple years older than I, and a registered Democrat to boot. Miss Bowers encouraged my classmates and me to take an active interest in politics. Having just fought a war for the survival of democracy, she explained, we might presume to hold a franchise on the democratic process. When Bowers suggested I run for the Kansas state legislature in the fall of 1950, I cocked an attentive ear.

It was a time for taking stock. I was never going to play football or wear a surgeon's gown. New ambitions sprang up in their place. It might take extra effort to achieve them, but that was no excuse to go home, rock on a porch and collect disability checks for the rest of my life.

Politics was a natural substitute for athletics. Knocking on a stranger's door, looking him in the eye and asking for his vote was a way to overcome my disability without denying it. Public service was also a way for me to give back a little of what had been showered on me by a generous community.

I had a more optimistic view of the human race than those who had stamped the GOP with a sour face and a country-club image. Having benefited from an extraordinary outpouring of affection and support, how could I feel otherwise?

It wasn't just my neighbors in Russell. In Topeka, Roy and Inez Finney, parents of a Kappa Sigma brother of mine who had been killed in the war, became virtually a second set of parents, inviting me into their home and taking me around to spend time with their friends. There was M. C. Shell, who ran a Phillips gas station near our apartment. One of his employees was a guy named Shorty who would do anything for me, from fixing my car to getting it started on cold winter mornings. And, of course, there was Dr. K, who helped me begin again, with a fresh outlook, seeing possibilities where others saw only problems.

I've said many times how much I regret losing four years out of my life, and being determined to make up the loss by living each day as if it were my last. Actually, my years of hospitalization gave me more than they took away. Before the war I'm not sure what kind of career I had in store. Being injured narrowed my options, but it broadened my outlook.

Beginning the morning of April 14, 1945, I learned the value of adversity. A handicap can become an asset, I've since discovered, if it increases your sensitivity to others and gives you the resolve to tap whatever inner resources you have.

Something else I learned, surrounded by so many survivors. Courage is mental as well as physical. It is the resistance to fear rather than the absence of fear.

Much of my life since April 1945 has been an exercise in compensation. Doors have been closed but windows opened. Maybe I couldn't use my hand, I told myself, but I could develop my mind. If unable to greet voters with my right hand, I could always reach out with my left.

Physical limitations teach perseverance and humility. Since I have trouble enough lining up shirt buttons with the proper holes, breaking a fingernail can be a minor crisis. That's when a buttonhook comes in handy. I've long since gotten over my early feelings of embarrassment. Often these days I write to youngsters who are themselves disabled. Every time I sign my name I'm reminded of my mother's old maxim, "Can't never could do anything."

CHAPTER FOUR

Against the Grain

In the fall of 1954 I entered Duke University, a great research institution that at times resembled a finishing school. A freshman handbook set forth the prevailing criteria for academic success: "A Duchess should have the tact and good judgment to know when the occasion requires her to be serious and when to be gay, when to dress up and when to be casual. Everything she does is in good taste and up to the highest standards."

Incoming students were given a long list of the established dos and don'ts. Eat breakfast every day. Wear hats and hosiery to church. Go down receiving lines at dances. Write thank-you notes to your date and your hostess. Avoid blue jeans.

Early in its history, Duke separated the sexes, first with screens dividing the classroom, later by painting over dorm windows so that young women couldn't look out at passing boys. In the 1950s the university continued to play the role of surrogate parent, requiring every freshman to take religious studies, and prohibiting young ladies from staying out later than ten-thirty at night. Alcohol was off limits to both sexes. To enforce the Eighteenth Amendment at Duke there was a semiofficial watchdog, the Delta Patrol in undergraduate parlance.

Contrary to later portrayals of a Silent Generation, my classmates were neither frivolous nor irresponsible. A more accurate reading of the class of '58 was that its values were fixed in a simpler time, when a college degree meant different things for men and women.

There might have been a moat surrounding the Duke Forest, so insulated was our world. Back then students found relief from their studies at Harvey's Cafeteria and the Blue Light. We drank Coke at the Devil's Den. If you wanted dancing with dinner, there was the Saddle Club over at Chapel Hill, fifteen minutes away if you kept a heavy foot on the pedal. More than one Saturday night, my date rounded the corner leading into the Duke campus on two wheels to beat curfew.

Student customs dictated student calendars. In November 1954 I joined Delta Delta Delta, which since its formation at Boston University nearly seventy years earlier had emphasized service projects like raising scholarship funds to aid needy young women. Later that fall the Blue Devil football squad generated excitement on its way to a nationally televised game in Miami's Orange Bowl.

At Christmastime, Duchesses were reminded to leave gifts for the maids and to attend parties for the underprivileged children of Durham. A winter cotillion featured name performers like Louis Armstrong and Perry Como. In the spring we had Joe College Weekend, highlighted by a parade, Les Brown's dance band, and a dramatic performance from the Hoof 'n Horn Club. Glossy boxwood scented the air around Carr Gymnasium, where classmates liked to sunbathe. As the days lengthened, so did the lines to get to nearby Grandma's Lake. Religious Emphasis Week preceded Easter. Mother-Daughter Weekend followed close behind.

It was social convention that got me to a debutante ball in Raleigh, an evening I vaguely remember as a haze of satin and chiffon. As an international-affairs major, I was more interested in writing a paper examining the decision-making process leading up to America's use of the first atomic bomb.

I plunged into student government, and found it almost as instructive as my textbooks. In the fall of my freshman year I ran for class representative. Encouraging classmates to take a more active interest in campus politics, I did the unpolitic thing of comparing them to Rip Van Winkle.

"Then let us show that we're alive," I declared in somewhat overwrought language, "and strain and strive, that we may say at set of sun, 'So much to do, but something done.' "

Rip Van Winkle woke up long enough to defeat my candidacy.

There weren't many feminine-support systems in those days. I was tapped for White Duchy, a semisecretive honor society which paralleled my brother John's Red Friars and served as a primitive sort of old girls' network. At the time of my appointment as Secretary of Transportation in 1983, I received many messages of support and encouragement, but none meant more than six white carnations from the other women who had been selected for membership in White Duchy that spring of 1957.

Among the most influential figures in Durham was the dean of East Campus, a professor of English literature named Florence Brinkley. Miss Brinkley was a tall, stately woman whose surface reserve masked an almost maternal warmth. She taught her students to think for themselves, and to think hard. It is not going too far to describe the Women's College at Duke as her lengthened shadow.

One of the regular events on our calendar was Sunday-afternoon tea at Dean Brinkley's home, located behind Giles House. It was close enough to Giles for her to hear the sounds of undergraduate partying the night before, but the dean never called to complain. She always looked the other way when walking through the Giles parking lot at night. As a token of sisterhood, undergraduate admirers once gave her a pair of red tennis shoes.

I had a number of opportunities to work with this remarkable woman after my March 1957 election as student government president. (This time around I had avoided Rip Van Winkle in my campaign speeches.) With Dean Brinkley's permission, I shuffled my academic schedule, dropping a couple of courses to accommodate my new responsibilities, and making them up by attending summer school at the University of Colorado.

The mountains of Colorado only whetted my appetite for exotic scenery and experiences. One by-product of that Western summer was the discovery that I wasn't a total athletic klutz. Members of the Pacific Coast championship team, led by a very handsome blond, had me water-skiing on one ski by the end of an afternoon.

That's not all I learned. At the end of my junior year I had been criticized by Fred Sheheen, editor of the campus paper, *The Chronicle,* who said that my command of parliamentary procedure was a little shaky. Spurred on by his comments, I pored over *Robert's Rules of Order.* Come September and the start of a new school year, I could have held my own with the legislature at Raleigh. Meanwhile, a series of student town meetings furnished their own training in mediating, presiding and public speaking.

Returning to Durham in the fall of 1957, we launched a series of raids against campus tradition. Heading the list of reforms was establishment of a university-wide honor code. East and West Campuses had different views on the subject, however, and the idea died aborning. Not so with dorm hours: by the time we were through, Saturday-night curfew was pushed back to one o'clock Sunday morning.

With help from Duke administrators, including Dean Brinkley, a leadership-training program for women was established and a variety of speakers were imported from around the country. We set up a permanent foreign-student fund and raised money to bring a Danish girl to Durham. One evening, E. E. Cummings read his modernistic verses before an only slightly puzzled East Campus audience. More traditional rites led up to the selection of a May Queen. On a Friday night in May 1958, Duke president A. Hollis Edens put a crown on my head, a few weeks before he placed a diploma in my hand.

A diploma is not a compass, and the end of my college days found me groping for direction. My brother John offered to tailor a job in the family business to fit my interests. As he explained it, I would be free to write a newsletter or become a buyer, traveling to the Orient and other corners of the globe where the Hanford name was a familiar one among floral suppliers. A typically thoughtful gesture, John's proposal fell victim to my own restlessness and uncertainty.

That summer after graduation was spent pounding local pavements in search of I didn't really know what. During an interview at the *Charlotte Observer,* I learned something that had nothing to do with journalism. I went in assuming that if you wore the right dress and nodded at appropriate moments your credentials would speak for you. But I soon discovered the hard way that if you couldn't, or wouldn't, make the case for why you should get the job, you could hardly expect a prospective boss to make it for you. It was a mistake I would not repeat.

In my imagination I caught the rhythm of a different drummer. It beat a cadence familiar since childhood. Life was more than a spectator sport, and I couldn't settle for observer status. For the moment, however, I was like that old standard "I'm Just an In-Between." So were a lot of other women in the transitional 1950s.

Around East Campus it had been said, somewhat cynically, that there were girls with dates and girls with data. My own priorities were less restrictive. I was pinned to a young man from nearby Davidson College, and though I cared for him very much, I simply was not ready for marriage. Not yet anyway.

It wasn't as if I had a carefully drawn blueprint for the future. Women in that era rarely had one; you might take a job, almost by accident, only to discover ten years out that it had turned into a career. Meanwhile there were so many things I wanted to do, like attending graduate school and sampling the broad, eventful world that lay beyond Salisbury and Durham.

My first steps toward a career grew out of my old curiosity about remote places and lifestyles. According to the mapmakers, less than seven hundred miles separate Salisbury's courthouse square from Harvard Yard in Cambridge, Massachusetts. However, the two are in many ways worlds apart.

In the fall of 1958 I took a job in the Harvard Law School library, and all of New England became a classroom without walls. For a girl from Salisbury, there was something almost magical in the salt air of Marblehead and the icy perfume of a winter's morning in Vermont. I took to the ski slopes like a duck to water. When friends or family came north, I delighted in showing them around Harvard or pointing out the historic sites of Boston, Lexington and Concord.

The next summer was another course of study-in-travel, undertaken at the suggestion of Dean Brinkley. My old friend advised me to sample the glories of Oxford University, where many years earlier she had fallen under the spell of Milton and other giants of seventeenth-century literature. I had first been to Europe two years earlier, visiting châteaus and art museums with a group that included my best friend from Salisbury, Jean Stanback. More memorable than Versailles or the Swiss Alps was the day in Rome when Jean and I escaped from our group long enough to be driven around the Eternal City by a couple of Italian boys on motorcycles.

I approached Oxford in similarly adventurous spirit. Ostensibly there to study English history and government from 1870 to the present, I had no intention of limiting my education to the classroom. C. S. Lewis had just left Magdalen for Cambridge, but his departure had done nothing to lessen the majesty of Evensong under the vaulted roof of Christ Church. At other times, I rode my bicycle out to the Trout, or went to the Mitre Hotel for tea and crumpets. On weekends I rambled through Welsh coal-mining valleys and attended the Edinburgh Arts Festival.

If rules are meant to be broken, then walls are perfect for hurdling. Such was the reasoning of a twenty-three-year-old eager to experience everything possible in that city of dreaming spires. One night I deliberately stayed out late, until the gates of Exeter College were closed. Then I climbed a ladder to the top of the wall, jumped over and landed in the don's garden. I had barely enough time to scamper to my room without the housemaster identifying the intruder in his yard.

My Oxford sojourn was a brief one. From the land of Milton to the false utopia of Marx: I suddenly got a hankering to visit the Soviet Union. Maybe it was all those newspaper stories about Sputnik and spy planes that sparked my curiosity. Certainly it had nothing to do with any political illusions about the men in Moscow. To me, it was one more challenge, a chance to go where few Americans had been.

My father had built one of Salisbury's more elaborate bomb shelters, which showed how he felt about the Iron Curtain and the leaders operating behind it. Mother shared his feelings. I had tipped them off by letter about my planned trip, so when the long-distance operator alerted them one night to a call from Oxford they were both ready. They shook hands at the bottom of the staircase before taking up battle stations at separate phones.

It was tempting fate, Dad told me, to be in the USSR at the same time Soviet leader Nikita Khrushchev was touring America. What if someone took a shot at Khrushchev in New York? The Russians would lock up every American they could get their hands on. Fortunately, I was prepared. Before placing my call I had covered a legal pad with arguments to convince my folks that the trip's dangers were far outweighed by its educational benefits.

Besides the family debate preceding it, what stands out about the journey isn't Red Square, the vast GUM department store or the artistic treasures stuffed inside Leningrad's Hermitage. Instead, I remember a badly infected foot that was swollen to twice its normal size, and which landed me in a People's Clinic for a night I'll never forget. In the ambulance on the way there I used sign language to have a conversation of sorts with the first average Russians I had encountered on the trip.

I didn't want to go home having seen no more than the sanitized version of Soviet life you get through the Intourist guides. When a Russian emigrant stepped out of the hotel crowd that surrounded me as I was placed in the ambulance, I saw my chance. He identified himself as a member of my tour group and said I shouldn't be afraid. He was in Moscow for a short time to visit his mother. With typical audacity, I asked if later I could tag along with him.

My new friend hesitated, but I persisted, and he agreed to ask his mother. The next night we went to one of the cold gray apartment complexes that give the Soviet capital such an impersonal character. If his mother was at all reluctant to host such an unusual gathering, she didn't show it. After a few minutes of spirited conversation, I noticed that she kept her radio on, its volume turned up to frustrate would-be eavesdroppers. That simple gesture taught me a lot about a claustrophobic society. It made my homecoming especially joyous.

Back in Cambridge, I hedged my bets. In September 1959 I enrolled in a joint-degree program that combined the study of government with the occupation of teaching. The first was my emerging passion, the second a vocational insurance policy.

As far as instructional techniques were concerned, I was green as Boston Common. No matter; Harvard believed that the best way to learn the art of teaching was to teach. It was sink or swim, with the students of suburban Melrose conducting the swimming lessons. I remembered from my own schooldays the difference between a creative teacher and one who taught literally by the book. The one might fan a spark of student curiosity; the other could just as easily smother the fire before it was ever lighted.

My assignment was to teach history to a class of eleventh graders. Determined to avoid the dull, numbing recital of kings and battles and treaties that can drain life from the past, I hoped to show how front-page events had affected earlier generations —how it felt to be making history before the historians made it over.

At first glance, the Boston police strike of 1919 seemed as distant as the Punic Wars. Then I spent an afternoon in the Police Department archives, combing through records buried in forty years of dust. In the process, I unearthed a surviving member of the striking force, and after tracking him down, recorded his memories on tape. He was such a hit with my class that they insisted he come in person and tell his dramatic account of the labor dispute that had paralyzed post–World War I Boston and, coincidentally, elevated Calvin Coolidge to national prominence.

Next we turned to the Prohibition era of flappers and speakeasies and the rise of organized crime. How could one make so remote an age come alive to a class of seventeen-year-olds? I went back to the library and researched the national commission appointed by President Hoover to investigate and pass judgment on the dry decade. Sifting through contemporary accounts of its work, I kept stumbling over the same name.

Roscoe Pound.

But I *know* Roscoe Pound, I thought, confusing the occasional glimpse I'd had around Harvard of this legendary scholar and law school dean with a firsthand acquaintance. I figured that all it would take to close the gap was a little initiative, or a lot of nerve. Lacking neither, I tapped on Dean Pound's office door in the law school's Langdell Hall one afternoon. Inside I found an elderly man with a green eyeshade, alone in a room full of books and a life's worth of memories, both of which he willingly shared. As a matter of fact, Pound told me, he had the complete minutes from the commission meetings. Would I like to look at them? Perhaps take them to school with me?

At that moment, I couldn't have been happier had I discovered DNA.

Not all my efforts were aimed at transporting students to a distant past. One day I met a Buddhist monk in Harvard Square. He became part of a curriculum designed to open kids' eyes to a culture far removed from the manicured comforts of suburban Boston. Such experiences showed me what a noble profession teaching is. When professors at the School of Education urged me to pursue it as a career, I was flattered, but the lure of government outstripped the satisfactions of the classroom.

It was a time of awakening for America's youth. Public policy was being made in Southern streets and department stores. Early in 1960, four black college freshmen refused to accept Jim Crow treatment at a Greensboro, North Carolina, lunch counter. They joined a lengthening procession that had begun with a Birmingham housewife named Rosa Parks. They insisted that promises of legal and social justice which had been delayed for a hundred years could no longer be put off. In Salisbury, the civil-rights revolution was peaceful. Thanks to moderating influences on both sides, no one afterward could recall precisely when racial barriers came down in the balcony of the local movie theater or the bus station waiting room.

During the summer of 1960, I worked on Capitol Hill as a secretary in the office of North Carolina's B. Everett Jordan. Jordan was a senator from the old school, a courtly figure who was unfailingly kind to staff and youngsters like myself. Although I had known his niece Elizabeth at Duke, I got the job by appearing in the doorway one day and announcing that I wanted to work there. For the next few weeks I did exactly that, all the while envying Suzanne Rodgers, a receptionist who was later a housemate of mine. Suzanne had a front-row seat at the legislative parade, while I was lucky to sit in the bleachers.

Before 1960, my most vivid memory of Washington was a childhood stay at the old Willard Hotel on Pennsylvania Avenue. My friend Jean Stanback and I said our nightly prayers in a room overlooking the floodlit Washington Monument. Now it was as if those prayers had been answered. When not staring at senators, gaping at Statuary Hall or climbing to the top of the Capitol Dome, I sought out prominent women in government for professional guidance.

Topping my list was Margaret Chase Smith, a Maine Republican who was one of only two women in the upper chamber. Known affectionately as "the lady from Skowhegan," the feisty, thoroughly independent Mrs. Smith was regarded by many as the conscience of the Senate.

When I walked into her private office, Senator Smith was wearing her trademark rose. She spoke briskly, with the clipped Yankee accent of Down East. Mrs. Smith recommended that I bolster my education with a law degree. That way, I would bring more to a public-policy job than aptitude or an M.A.

I don't know how many busy legislators would share an hour with a total stranger seeking advice. The incident impressed me deeply, so much so that whenever a young woman calls my office with a similar request, I make time to see her. It's my way of repaying a debt to the lady from Skowhegan.

Nineteen sixty was a presidential-campaign year. It was also my introduction to national politics. Suzanne Rodgers revealed plans for an old-fashioned whistle-stop tour of the South by Democratic vice-presidential nominee Lyndon B. Johnson. Senator Jordan's administrative assistant, Bill Cochran, offered to help me get on board. Added to all that, there was a handsome advance man on the train. With him, Suzanne and a prospective Vice President of the United States along for the ride, how could I resist?

As a dedicated Republican, my father didn't think much of

his daughter riding Lyndon Johnson's campaign train through the heart of downtown Salisbury. Deep down, he was probably drawing a line through all my activities of recent years and extending it to the logical conclusion—a full-time career in government.

"Now, Dad," I said, "it will be perfectly all right. It's just a learning experience. It doesn't mean anything."

Secretly, I think, he was rather proud to have me riding on the Johnson train. The next few days were a blur of cheering crowds, rear-platform speechmaking and trackside renditions of "The Eyes of Texas Are Upon You." As befitted a candidate from the Lone Star State, there were enough yellow roses handed up from the throngs to impress even a florist's daughter.

Through her warmth and vivacity, Lady Bird Johnson endeared herself to everyone on the LBJ Express. But if she had a calming presence, her husband swept through the train like a Texas tornado. At the first sight of Lyndon Johnson's towering figure, staffers made themselves scarce. From engine room to caboose, doors could be heard slamming as orders were barked out.

I returned to Cambridge in September 1960 and resumed work at Harvard Law. During each of the next two summers, I forsook the library of Langdell Hall for New York, drawn to the Big Apple for the sheer challenge of living there and in hopes of getting a job at the United Nations. Admittedly, I had been told that UN employment required a two-year commitment and the ability to speak five languages. But whenever anyone says, "It can't be done," I have a way of double-checking, just to be sure.

I made my way to the UN placement office overlooking the East River and told them I had a yen to work for the international organization; I couldn't stay for more than three months; I'd have to return to Cambridge in the fall. A few days later I was taking tour groups through the UN complex as a $162-a-week employee of the Public Information Section.

The next summer I lived with other UN interns at Riverside House in the Morningside Heights section of Manhattan. Being assigned to the General Secretariat provided a worm's-eye view of international diplomacy. I also stumbled onto some cloak-and-dagger stuff. I had casually gotten to know some of the members of the Russian delegation. Because he knew I'd been to Russia, it seemed perfectly natural for one of the Soviet diplomats to invite me to dinner. Before saying yes, I checked with my superior, who assured me there was nothing improper about dining out with a Russian envoy. She came along anyway.

The next thing I knew, the FBI asked me to meet some agents in a nearby parking lot. The upshot was a request to let federal investigators know should my Russian friend call me for another dinner date. I was willing. Apparently he wasn't. At least, I never heard from him again.

Meanwhile, there was no shortage of other social opportunities in that exuberant city. My chief interest at the time centered around a fellow North Carolinian, a young doctor whose friendship dated back to my Oxford summer. He was probably the most brilliant person I've ever known. He was also the most intense, with a pale, nearly ghostlike complexion, the result of too much studying and not enough sunshine. Because of his grueling schedule, he had suggested we get better acquainted by taking the train home together the previous Christmas.

I probably should have been flattered that he broke away from Harvard Medical School long enough to visit me in New York that summer. Instead, we quarreled, leading up to a scene worthy of a Woody Allen movie. We were at Grant's Tomb, and I was rambling on about the UN and all the fascinating people I had met there. My friend was less impressed by the global village than I was. Loving music and philosophy, in his cerebral way he wished always to be surrounded by the very best. But the best as defined by his narrow code.

"You are totally out of touch with the common man," I told him.

"I have no desire to be in touch with the common man." It was an honest answer; but one can be honestly wrong.

"You just go live in your test tube," I said, "because that's not the life for me."

"You're a political animal," he replied, "and that's not my cup of tea."

Inscribed over the portal of Grant's Tomb is the Civil War hero's famous admonition "Let us have peace." There and then, we decided to take his advice and go our separate ways.

The future began to press in on me. In May 1962, as queen of the First Naval District's "Space Age Frolics," I was photographed with the Red Sox pitching staff. Baseball players have short careers, but so do women who wear cardboard crowns. I was getting a little old for this sort of thing. But was the space age ready for women with more substantive ambitions?

My Langdell Hall mentors, librarians Earl Borgeson and Vaclav Mostecky, thought it was. They urged me to apply to the law school. So did others.

"Submit the application," one said. "There's no harm in submitting an application."

My brother thought I was making a mistake.

"Here you are, in the golden years of youth," he reminded me. "Do you really want to bury yourself in a monastery for three years?"

But it wasn't going to be like that at all, I assured John. Since I had no intention of going on to Wall Street, I was under no pressure to make A's. I would apply myself as usual, but not at the cost of enjoying the experience. This time out, I would lead a more balanced life. Rationalizing law school as an experiment, I concluded that even a year at Harvard Law would be excellent training and background. So I told myself. So I told John.

Neither one of us really believed I would be there only one year.

And why should I? Listening to my dates from the law and business schools discuss their cases and papers, I had a strong sense of being able to hold my own academically. My grades were as good as or better than many, and I already had an M.A. from Harvard's Graduate School of Education. Why not go forward like all the men around me? Why did I have to take a backseat?

My parents saw it a little differently. I broke the news to them at the end of a long day of sightseeing in New Hampshire. Mother's reaction was less one of opposition than of puzzlement.

"Don't you want to be a wife, and a mother, and a hostess for your husband?" she asked.

I told them I wanted to be all those things. In time. But just then I had other aspirations. As usual, Mother and Dad understood. Even though law school wasn't something they would have chosen for me, they would stand behind me. After all, it was my life, my little red wagon.

Later that night I was awakened by sounds of distress coming from the adjoining bathroom. Mother had lost her dinner. No doubt she thought she was losing her daughter.

I was embarked on another pioneer experience. There were 550 members of the class of '65 at Harvard Law School, only two dozen of them women. (Today, by contrast, the female contingent at HLS is almost 35 percent.)

On the first day of classes a male student approached me in Langdell Hall Library. "Elizabeth, what are you doing here?" he demanded, in tones of moral outrage. "Don't you realize that there are *men* who would give their right arm to be in this law school, men who would *use* their legal education?"

Such insensitivity thrived on both sides of the lecture podium. That first year I took a course in property, taught by an august personage named Leach. Among the class's 150 members were five women, none of whom was ever called upon. We did our reading and analyzed our cases, we held up our end of the Socratic bargain, but it wasn't enough. As far as Professor Leach was concerned, we simply didn't exist. The only exception was an annual display known as Professor Leach's Ladies' Day, when the women in property were summoned to the front of the room to read a poem of their own composition. Once this ritual was over, Professor Leach, seated with the male students, would pelt us with questions. Charles W. Kingsfield at his most perverse could not have devised a more public humiliation.

All this added up to the academic equivalent of boot camp. Friends turned a deaf ear to the inevitable complaints. As one put it, "You *worked* at Harvard. You saw for yourself the agony of first year. But you went into it anyway. How could you?"

In fact, I was less prepared for my first year of law school than I thought. There was nothing at Duke or the School of Education that compared with the impossible hours or beady-eyed competition of Harvard Law. None of my prior classmates had ever torn pages out of a textbook in order to deny them to rivals, as was sometimes done at HLS.

Studying fifteen hours at a stretch during exams, pausing only for a can of soup eaten directly from the saucepan: this was a far cry from the Devil's Den and Durham's tobacco-mulched lawns. First-year students had the added insecurity of not knowing whether they were candidates for law review or in danger of flunking out, because there was no full-scale exam until June. Then we filed into a stifling hot room for a four-hour test. The first question alone filled twelve pages.

Outside the classroom, student–teacher interaction was sporadic and perfunctory. A few years after graduation, I happened to sit next to the school's former dean, Erwin Griswold, at a Washington dinner party. By that time he was Lyndon Johnson's Solicitor General. (His old job at the law school had been filled by a youthful reformer named Derek Bok, who a few years later would become Harvard's president.) I greatly admired Dean Griswold and his wife, but I couldn't resist pouring out three years' worth of pent-up frustrations. Did law school have to be so thoroughly unpleasant? I asked. Did students (among them some of my own classmates) have to come close to nervous breakdowns trying to cope with Harvard? Why couldn't there have been a sense of community as well as classroom excellence? Although Dean Griswold accepted my assault in good humor, he stood his ground. No minds were changed that evening.

Bob likes to say I'm never content to ask what time it is. I want to know how the clock was made. While I've always had a healthy appetite for information and a disciplined approach to work of any kind, Harvard reinforced these traits. At the same time, it has taken me years to see that you don't *have* to always strive for perfection, that "perfection" itself can become a kind of social tyranny, and that there is most definitely a point of diminishing returns.

Author and critic Marya Mannes has summed this up, memorably, in describing the different set of expectations governing male and female conduct: "Nobody objects to a woman being a good writer or sculptor or geneticist if, at the same time, she manages to be a good wife, a good mother, good-looking, good-tempered, well-dressed, well-groomed, and unaggressive."

In the legal fraternity of 1962, perfection, as defined by Miss Mannes, was not so appealing on the social front. Jean Eberhart, later a justice of the Colorado Supreme Court, was a roommate of mine. We sat on our beds one afternoon convincing ourselves we were on the fringe of spinsterhood. Finally I put into words the question plaguing us both: "Do you think that *anyone* will take us out, once they learn we're Harvard Law students?"

Most of my dates were with men from the Business School on the other side of the Charles River. Not only were they closer to my age, but they also didn't discuss cases over candlelight and wine, nor were they so blinded by torts and contracts that they lost sight of the real world.

On the afternoon of November 22, 1963, I was studying in the international-law library when someone blurted out the news that shots had been fired at President Kennedy's motorcade in Dallas. Harvard suspended classes and grieved with special poignance over its most famous alumnus. For the next few days the young man I was dating and I sat glued to the television screen, mesmerized like the rest of America by the public rituals of farewell.

It was no accident that I was in the international-law library that tragic afternoon. As a break from my corporate law classes, I liked nothing better than courses in Russian and Chinese law, international codes, diplomatic statutes. In the fall of 1963, like-minded classmates elected me president of the international-law club named for John Marshall. (I also con-sented to run for class secretary, thinking that it was only a five-year term. More than twenty years later, I am still sending out those gossipy class newsletters.)

The women of HLS have made the most of their legal educations. Today Patricia Schroeder is a well-known congress-woman from Colorado. A generation ago she was a fellow law student, first encountered one morning when my unoccupied car rolled down the driveway and slammed into hers. In the course of clearing it all up, we became friends. It still helps to have that common point of reference these days, when we often find ourselves on opposite sides of the political street.

Pat and I were not the only ones to disprove the chauvin-istic view that only men could properly utilize a legal education. Jane Roth, wife of Delaware Senator William V. Roth, Jr., is another former member of our class. She sits on the bench in Delaware. Elizabeth Holtzman, former member of Congress, is district attorney of Kings County (Brooklyn), New York. Other women from the class of '65 are law school instructors, judges, and influential members of the bar.

Like legal students everywhere, I spent my final year sifting options. Wall Street held no allure, and Washington law firms were nearly as reluctant as their New York counterparts to recruit women to their ranks. Teaching belonged to my past; marriage was part of a still dim future. One thing held imme-diate and continuing appeal: the governing process.

Under John F. Kennedy, Harvard had come to be known, only half in jest, as the fourth branch of American government. While there, I had gotten caught up in the enthusiasm for public service that flavored the early sixties. One summer it had led me to a personnel job in the Peace Corps's Washington head-quarters. The agency reflected a missionary impulse as old as America and as youthful as the operatives who were sent in her name to sixty countries. They were the best of the best and brightest.

Twenty years later, I would accompany UN Ambassador Jeane J. Kirkpatrick on a visit to the African nations of Senegal, Togo, Rwanda and Burundi. Wherever we went, we met tribesmen whose lives had materially improved thanks to the Peace Corps and its seat-of-the-pants diplomacy. The trip confirmed my respect for a generation whose desire to serve made its members our most valuable export.

In 1965 the White House Fellows program was created as an apprenticeship matching would-be public servants with Cabinet officers and high-ranking members of the White House staff. Three thousand candidates applied for fifteen slots. Among the final panel of judges were David Rockefeller, John B. Oakes of the *New York Times* and John W. Macy, Jr., chairman of the old Civil Service Commission that was precursor to the Office of Personnel Management.

Several months of essay writing and preliminary interviews led up to a regional competition in Atlanta. After making that cut, I found myself competing with two other women and forty-two men at Virginia's Airlie House. While the other finalists were enjoying themselves around a swimming pool, I indulged my tendency to overprepare. It did me in. Staying inside, reviewing notes for the next round of interviews, I missed out on a critical piece of information. One of the judges happened by the pool and dropped the hint that he and his colleagues were looking for people who would apply what they would learn in Washington to their own backyard.

I could honestly have told the judges, "I love North Carolina, and may go back and run for office there someday." Or I could have said that Washington looked irresistible. I chose the second. More rankling than not winning the fellowship was the realization that I'd blown an opportunity that was unlikely to come again.

The game of "If only" is a form of torture invented by and for second-guessers, control seekers, and perfectionists of every stripe. As a disease of ego, it is something that can take a lifetime to overcome. In the meantime, the best medicine is the ability to laugh at yourself—something Bob prescribes in large doses.

Opening the 1965 Harvard commencement where I received my law degree, university president Nathan M. Pusey delivered the traditional greeting to graduating seniors, welcoming them into "the fellowship of educated men." As usual, words trailed behind deeds. Even then, Harvard's sexual caste system was crumbling. Take it from an old hand at leaping walls.

Robert Joseph Dole, age four, against a treeless terrain so flat that people joke about being able to see from Russell to Kansas City on a clear day—a distance of 250 miles.

Two-year-old Mary Elizabeth Alexander Hanford makes her debut on the front page of the Salisbury (North Carolina) *Post* in time for Christmas 1938.

The house where I was born, on July 22, 1923, during the dustbowl Depression days that hit families hard all across Kansas. Photo taken in 1975.

In the fall of 1941, I entered Kansas State University at Lawrence. With a little talent and a lot of perseverance, I was able to break the tape at a quarter mile.

After Pearl Harbor, millions of American boys were drawn into the armed forces. By the end of 1942, I was one of them.

New York City was an education in itself. A world in miniature. I spent more time on Flatbush Avenue than Park Avenue, but who could pass up the Empire State Building?

TWO PHOTOS: U.S. SENATE

Life changed forever on April 14, 1945. In the months that followed my wounding on an Italian battlefield, my weight dropped from 194 to 122. I nearly died from an infection until doctors administered a new miracle drug called streptomycin.

Here my Dad and grandfather help me out of the house on a leave from the hospital.

One way or another, I've spent most of my life looking up to my brother, John. Here's an early instance of our seeing eye to eye when I was mascot at John's high school graduation.

When I applied to college in the spring of 1954, only one school would do. I went to Duke because John had gone there.

A decade after leaving Duke, I was part of the consumer movement, working in the Nixon White House with Virginia Knauer, who would become my mentor and cherished friend.

In December 1973, I was sworn in as a Federal Trade Commissioner at Georgetown University Hospital, following a New Jersey auto accident involving a drunk driver who rear-ended my car. After the swearing in, we celebrated with quiche and champagne cooled in a bedpan. So much for the glamour of government!

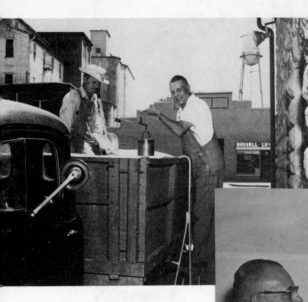

Here's my dad, Doran Dole, shown outside his Main Street cream-and-egg station. He never missed a day's work, never felt as comfortable in a J. C. Penney suit as in his well-worn overalls and never failed to see the humor in some otherwise bleak surroundings.

Dad used to divide the world into two camps: doers and stewers. The woman he married was first, last and always a doer. Mom's favorite saying was: "Can't never could do anything." Not a bad philosophy.

The man who played a role in my early life that was second only to my family's was Hampar Kelikian, an Armenian-born surgeon who performed numerous operations on my arms and helped restore a sense of purpose to my postwar years.

The neophyte candidate for Congress, circa 1960, flanked by a pair of Kansas political legends: incumbent Congressman Wint Smith (left) and U.S. Senator Frank Carlson. I learned a lot from those two.

My first race for Congress was a homegrown affair, washed down with plenty of Dole pineapple juice. This bevy of "Dolls for Dole" was literally priceless.

ELIZABETH: Bob and I married on December 6, 1975, in Washington Cathedral. Bob said life would never be dull. Little did I know that barely eight months later, I'd be plunged into a crash course in American politics when Gerald Ford tapped Bob to be his 1976 running mate. One of the campaign's emotional highs came early, when the President accompanied Bob and me to a Russell homecoming.

WIDE WORLD PHOTOS

BOB: In October 1976, millions of Americans tuned in for the first ever vice-presidential debate. When it was over, Jerry Ford called. "You hit hard but fair," he told me. I thought so too—until I read the next day's papers.

Election day in Russell, with my daughter, Robin (to my right). Before voting, I was assured by a Secret Service agent that after November 6, I'd never have to drive my own car again. I was less confident of victory, an assessment confirmed early when the Southern states lined up behind Carter.

Here Elizabeth and I campaign for Nancy Landon Kassebaum, my Senate colleague who has added luster to the most distinguished name in Kansas.

Fifty years ago, I worked as a soda jerk at Dawson's Drugstore in Russell. I go back as often as possible. The day you forget where you come from is the day you should leave public service.

ELIZABETH: At my confirmation hearings, Bob likened himself to Nathan Hale, and expressed regret that he had but one wife to give to his country's infrastructure.

On February 7, 1983, I was sworn in as Secretary of Transportation. My mother, Mary Hanford, is shown here with President Reagan.

In between highways and airline safety, deregulation and ridding transport of illicit drugs, I often met other women in the traditionally male-dominated field of transportation.

BOB: In 1985, after some tough behind-the-scenes negotiations to salvage Social Security, it was all smiles as President Reagan exchanged quips with Tip O'Neill at a Rose Garden signing ceremony.

ELIZABETH: Not far from the Rose Garden, the President's Cabinet grapples with its own problems, in discussions lively and freewheeling.

It's not all affairs of state at 1600 Pennsylvania Avenue. No President brought more warmth or personal graciousness to the presidency than Ronald Reagan, shown here with Bob and me at the White House barbecue.

In November 1984, I presented Bob with a miniature schnauzer rescued by the Washington Humane Society. He was named Leader to commemorate the Senate Republicans' selection of Bob as their new Leader.

That same year, we left budget battles and the Conrail sale long enough to sample the majesty of China.

On November 9, 1987, we went back to Russell, Kansas. That day we were greeted by 5,000 well-wishers as Bob Dole became an official candidate for the presidency in 1988.

CHAPTER FIVE

Through the Ranks

Politics are almost as exciting as war, and quite as dangerous. In war you can only be killed once, but in politics many times.

—WINSTON CHURCHILL

War has many by-products. For the victorious side, there are peace treaties, ticker-tape parades and candidates for public office. An old soldier's political philosophy matters less to voters than the number of stars on his cap or ribbons on his jersey. If you've been shot up and lived to tell about it, odds are that some slate-maker will ask you to run for office.

That's exactly what Clifford Holland, Sr., an old family friend from Russell, did in the spring of 1950. Holland was a lawyer widely known in the state and a major figure in Kansas Democratic politics. Cliff hoped he could sign me up as a card-carrying Democrat.

More persuasive was John Woelk, a former Navy pilot and current Russell County attorney who thought I was a natural-born Republican. Woelk urged me to run that fall for the state legislature. The honor of legislative service in those days far exceeded the financial reward. Lawmakers received a daily wage of five dollars (to a maximum of $350) plus seven dollars expense money for each day of the biennial legislative session. Since many would-be legislators were reluctant to forgo a business or a law practice and drive two hundred miles to Topeka, my own proximity to the seat of government was of no small advantage.

Washburn's law school already served state departments as a kind of think tank and employment agency. Many of the Kansas Supreme Court's law clerks were Washburn trained, and the legislative galleries on the third floor of the Capitol building were regularly filled with my classmates. John Woelk laid out the reasons for my running in practical terms. "Just remember, Bob," he said, "there are hundreds more Republicans in this county than Democrats." A pretty persuasive argument.

Notwithstanding those registration figures, there was nothing assured about my first campaign.

To win a place on the floor of the House, I had to defeat an incumbent legislator from nearby Dorrance named Elmo J. Mahoney. Mahoney was a tough-talking self-styled populist, considerably older than myself. Name a problem, he had a solution—a verbal one, anyway. Discontented farmers were his natural constituency.

To be honest, there weren't many issues dividing the local electorate. Legislative candidates were graded on how many homes they visited, how many pairs of shoes they wore out. Campaign funds in that part of Kansas were scarce as sea gulls, so I served as my own ad agency, speechwriter and press agent, calling editors and hand-delivering newspaper ads.

I'm not sure who suffered more through my early speeches, the audience or me. Gradually, I got over my stage fright. I also began a habit that has stayed with me ever since, of leaving head tables and mingling with those out front. At first it was just a way of avoiding the embarrassment of asking someone next to me to cut whatever was on my dinner plate, but I soon found I preferred chatting with people in the crowd to staring down at them from a raised platform.

Nineteen fifty was a Republican year. Kansans chose 105 Republicans and 20 Democrats to serve in their lower house. And Russell County voters made me their youngest legislator ever. A few days after the election, a reporter for the *Topeka*

Capitol came by to do a human-interest story. He asked me whether I had a legislative agenda.

"I'm going to sit and watch for a couple of days," I told him, "and then I'll stand up for what I think is right."

Brave talk, coming from a twenty-seven-year-old back-bencher.

The legislature that took office in January 1951 had a new governor to work with, Edward F. Arn. As Kansas' attorney general, Ed Arn had carried out a series of raids under the state's prohibition laws. These forays showed how difficult it was to enforce a law so widely laughed at. They paved the way for a 1948 referendum repealing the ban on alcohol sales in the state, sixty years after an outraged Carrie Nation first wielded an ax against a Kansas saloon.

The 1951 legislative session was marked by evasion, confusion and occasional bursts of inspiration. A right-to-work law was bottled up in the state Senate. Plans to reorganize state government by creating a "little Hoover Commission" were sidetracked with the Governor's acquiescence. The House endorsed voting rights for eighteen-year-olds one day, but reversed itself the next.

Most of the time, lawmakers did what they always do— spend money. And in 1951 we ought to have been counting our change. Revenue windfalls derived from wartime taxes were all but exhausted. A new conflict in Korea promised a fresh round of inflation. The decade-long agricultural prosperity couldn't last forever.

But legislators are more predictable than the weather; and few things are more permanent than a temporary tax. So a provisional levy on gasoline was extended, and a sales tax originally earmarked for educational and welfare programs was stretched to finance hospital construction.

One argument that spring featured a proposed Fair Employment Practices Commission. The bill as introduced in the House was mild enough. It would establish a state FEPC whose mandate was to educate Kansas employers on the virtues of color-blind hiring. However meager its budget and staff, the FEPC would make an important statement, a declaration of intent consistent with Kansas history and Republican politics. I was part of the House majority that voted on March 16, 1951, to pass the bill. The Senate was another kettle of fish. There it took two years and the personal involvement of Lieutenant Governor Fred Hall to override the opposition of commercial interests and to force a public roll call. In the end, it was Hall who cast the deciding vote to create the commission.

The legislature did not meet in 1952. My only visit to the House chamber that year was in the spring, when I took my bar exams there. A few weeks later, when Dwight D. Eisenhower returned to Abilene to launch his late-blooming campaign for the Republican presidential nomination, I was in the crowd of rain-soaked admirers on hand to greet him. Kansans of both parties were intensely proud to see one of our own achieve international fame and the highest honors a nation could bestow.

My ambitions were humble by comparison. Eric "Doc" Smith, a young lawyer recently established in Russell County, reassured me that my physical disability needn't interfere with a legal career. Smith didn't stop there. As soon as I finished my legal studies and passed the bar, he told me, I could count on a place in his office. That same year I took him up on his offer. To formalize our partnership I moved a battered old desk into an empty room over L. Banker's mercantile establishment at the corner of Eighth and Main in Russell. In a fit of extravagance I went out and bought a handsome leather chair to go with the enormous desk. Someone said my new chair looked like a hundred-dollar saddle on a ten-dollar horse.

Like most small-town lawyers, Doc and I took just about any case that came through the door. This was oil country, so title matters were our bread and butter, a diet offset by the usual probate and family disputes. In June 1952, I announced my candidacy for Russell County attorney. Looking back, some have interpreted my race that year as a logical step on the road from Russell to Washington. At the time my sights were fixed on more immediate concerns. Like earning a living. With the legal contacts developed over a couple of terms as county attorney, I hoped to build a Russell law practice that would sustain my family for the rest of our lives.

Politics at the grass-roots level is almost always personal. The smaller the town, the fewer the secrets and the greater the importance placed on personal connections. To many voters, the chief function of the county attorney was springing their friends nabbed on traffic charges. On primary day I scored a narrow win over Dean Ostrum, a Yale-educated lawyer whose professional credentials probably counted less than the local voters' sympathy for a banged-up veteran. November was much easier, as Kansans trooped to the polls to ratify Dwight Eisenhower's candidacy and almost incidentally vote in the rest of the Republican slate.

My new position paid $248 a month, four dollars less than the salary of the custodian who swept the courthouse. Maintaining a private practice on the side, in what passed for spare time I sought out the classic unpaid advertising of small-town lawyers everywhere. There were meetings of the Elks and the Masons to attend, 4-H fairs to patronize, the county Red Cross to chair. I taught Sunday school at the Methodist church. After October 18, 1954, I had a fresh incentive to keep the courthouse lights burning late. That was when Phyllis presented me with a baby daughter, whom we named Robin. Life was full, and full of promise.

As county attorney I was forced, on a couple of occasions, to step in and take abused children away from their parents. Aside from this, my official duties were not burdensome. There was the usual run of traffic and liquor violations, some bad checks, an occasional burglary. The attempted bribery of a city commissioner enlivened front pages for a season. Probably my biggest day in court came when a majority of the Kansas Supreme Court agreed with me on technical grounds that a one percent severance tax on oil and gas production was unconstitutional.

By the late 1950s, I was all ears when my old hospital buddy Phil Hart, by then a United States senator from Michigan (and a Democrat, at that), urged me to take a look at a political career. The House seat in question was very much occupied by Wint Smith, a Republican who had spoken for Kansas' Sixth Congressional District since 1946. At six feet five inches and three hundred pounds, Wint cut a memorable figure whether in

Washington or Mankato. In style and philosophy he combined the country squire's love of tradition with the combative instincts of the brigadier general he'd been in World War II. Before that, as director of the Kansas Highway Patrol, Smith had fought his own private wars against rural bank robbers he liked to take off the hands of local law enforcement officials and transport back to Topeka in chains.

His approach to politics was just as blunt. The New Deal appalled Smith. But he was hardly less offended by so-called "modern Republicans" who had willingly accepted much of Franklin Roosevelt's emergency-generated safety net. In 1952, when Republicans nationally were choosing sides between Robert A. Taft and Dwight Eisenhower, Wint got himself a big button that said "MacArthur." His congressional newsletter was a forum for attacks on foreign aid in general and the Marshall Plan in particular. Sooner or later, he argued, Americans would pay dearly for making wartime enemies into industrial competitors.

As Smith readily acknowledged, he was frozen in opposition to trends he could neither halt nor compromise with.

"I was all right until we elected a Republican President," he remarked to a friend soon after Eisenhower's 1952 triumph, "but now there are things I can't go along with. Any man who can be elected President of the United States can't go along with some of my positions and I'm not about to change."

In 1958, the Congressman from Mankato had been challenged in the GOP primary by Keith G. Sebelius, a young state senator from Norton. Wint interpreted his 51-vote victory margin as handwriting on the wall. Not long after, he appeared in the Phillipsburg, Kansas, newspaper office of McDill "Huck" Boyd and told Huck that after a cold-blooded appraisal of his chances in a 1960 rematch he had decided to write his own political obituary.

The conversation turned to possible successors. Sebelius was one of a half-dozen people mentioned. I was another. Wint said he doubted he could "pick ships in a primary by endorsing one candidate over another." But the heat of a campaign can easily melt resolves made in the political off season. Privately,

Smith made it clear that he hadn't forgotten the help I'd given him in the 1958 contest and he expected his conservative supporters to repay the favor in 1960.

Smith's theory was quickly put to the test. I went to see Dane Hansen, a staunch Smith ally and a power broker in his own right, whose influence and connections stretched from the crossroads villages of northwest Kansas to the Governor's Mansion in Topeka. Hansen lived according to an unorthodox schedule. He began his workday around the supper hour. Then he held court with visiting politicos or businessmen, often until dawn broke over the boundless prairie.

It took only one postmidnight visit to Logan, Kansas, to convince Hansen that I was ideologically trustworthy. As Hansen put it later, "Hell, I knew he was a fiscal conservative. The tires on his car were threadbare."

No one in rock-ribbed Kansas seriously doubted that the state would go with Republican candidate Richard M. Nixon over John F. Kennedy in the 1960 presidential race. We were still a lot closer to Oz than to Camelot. But beneath the surface flowed currents of dissatisfaction, even within GOP circles. In the Sixth District, Keith Sebelius' strong showing against Wint Smith in the congressional primary two years earlier had served notice of a desire for change among the party rank and file.

For all the signs of restlessness, however, one ritual never varied. Each January on the anniversary of Kansas' statehood, Republicans flocked to Topeka's venerable Jayhawk Hotel. Few of those jammed into the Jayhawk's public rooms for Kansas Day, 1960, to trade gossip and float balloons had ever heard of Bob Dole. Fewer still were prepared for the hoopla designed to change that.

Ordinarily, such gatherings were pretty sedate affairs— county barons like Dane Hansen, J. Harm Voss and Harry Darby holed up in smoke-filled rooms. In the evening, everyone donned uncomfortable clothes and ate in the hotel ballroom, where an out-of-state luminary expounded the party gospel. The routine was as fixed, and the effect as predictable, as a Buckingham Palace garden party.

So when a rough-and-tumble caravan of Dole supporters from Russell County rolled into town on Friday, January 29, 1960, it bordered on the subversive. Out of nowhere appeared twenty pretty girls dressed in identical red felt skirts and matching handbags. They were accompanied by a quartet of "Bobolinks," led by a ukulele-playing songstress. In their wake trailed a football player riding a tricycle, a middle-aged farmer wearing an elephant's head, and a group of pallbearers transporting a mock coffin containing the Frankenstein monster, who held a placard reading: "You Have Nothing to Fear with Dole."

There was method to our madness. At the beginning of the campaign I faced a special problem of name identification. It wasn't only that Keith Sebelius was already a familiar figure throughout the district and I was not. What really complicated things was a third candidate on the ballot, a state senator named Phillip J. Doyle. I was less worried about Doyle's appeal to the farm vote than about the confusion that was sure to arise from the similarity of our names.

What I needed was a means of distinguishing between us, a gimmick that people would remember. The Kennedys were famous for their kaffeeklatsches. Why couldn't the Doles serve —pineapple juice?

"Roll with Dole" was my 1960 campaign slogan. Soon we had it emblazoned across a mock Conestoga wagon, which became a familiar sight on the streets of communities like Colby, Ellsworth and Hoxie. So did a bevy of "Dolls for Dole," adorned in campaign outfits designed and stitched by Phyllis and friends from Russell.

We developed an unvarying routine. The wagon team set up cardboard tables in the local square, its members began distributing cups of pineapple juice, and I went off to stalk voters in barbershops and five-and-dimes. Or I worked a parade crowd while a dozen campaign workers passed out enough pineapple juice to float a battleship.

Hungry campaigners said I refused to let them go to dinner until I'd met every single voter lingering on Main Street. Even six-year-old Robin became part of our road show. She wore a skirt announcing, "I'm for Robin's Daddy."

One morning, my daughter wished me luck in winning what she called the "collection." Given the state of our finances, I could only hope she was right. After Wint Smith changed his mind about a public endorsement and flooded the district with five thousand letters in my behalf, some editors printed letters of their own that linked me to "grain barons" and "millionaire oilmen." The allegations were quickly disposed of, since our largest contribution was under two hundred dollars.

The entire campaign cost less than $20,000. Even so, long before November we were forced to take out a mortgage on the family's five-room house. With the help of the mortgage money, we managed to patch together some primitive TV spots. Add to that the free media coverage, plenty of shoe leather and the ubiquitous cups of pineapple juice, and I got my message across.

I drove over forty thousand miles during that campaign. If I saw a farmhouse light burning I took it as an invitation to drop in and make my case. All the candidates agreed about the dangers of selling grain to the Russians and the need to keep America's military defenses up. Most of our time was spent on homelier concerns: repeal of an excise tax on phone calls; support for a third federal judgeship, to be located in Salina; money from Washington to help pay the cost of educating the children of military personnel on area bases.

For weeks, our basement served as a central command post, a place where friends could hand-letter placards or make phone calls to uncommitted voters. On primary night, it looked more like a bunker fortified against defeat. Early reports from Sebelius strongholds in Salina and Norton County were discouraging. But the race began narrowing as outlying communities weighed in. By dawn it was virtually a dead heat. It wasn't until early Wednesday afternoon, however, after UPI announced it had erred in transposing Russell County votes for Dole and Doyle, that the deadlock was broken.

By a scant one thousand votes, I was the Republican candidate in a district whose traditional party loyalties all but ensured victory in November. When it was over, a good-natured Keith Sebelius gave me his explanation of what had happened.

It was quite simple, he said. "You drowned me in pineapple juice."

As a very junior member of the Eighty-seventh Congress, I was invited to a White House reception and spent much of the evening gawking at famous faces in the East Room. As the Marine Band struck up "Hail to the Chief," Phyllis and I drew back for the ceremonial entrance of President and Mrs. Kennedy. Later we were introduced to the youthful President and his elegant First Lady. Although impressed by the surroundings, I wasn't swept off my feet. All glory is fleeting, as I reminded Rose Mary McVey, the wife of another freshman in the Kansas congressional delegation.

"Live it up while you can, Rose Mary," I told her. "Just remember, we're in a ten-minute parking zone."

I arrived in Washington a marked man. As a result of the 1960 census, Kansas was due to lose one of her six House seats. That meant there would likely be a merging of my district with neighboring territory represented by Democrat J. Floyd Breeding. Job insecurity cast a pall over my early years on Capitol Hill. It also placed strains on the Doles' family life.

Given the centrifugal forces of a political career, I sometimes think that anyone who would marry a politician should have his/her head examined. (If you're reading this, Elizabeth, I'm only kidding.) The hardest thing for a politician to do is say no. It becomes virtually impossible when he knows he's facing a strong challenge at the polls and the folks back home are counting on him to open a supermarket or address the local Rotary. Before you know it, you're on a plane bound west every Friday night, mending fences in the district, which often means neglecting your own family back in Washington. It's awfully tough to sustain a marriage when one partner is usually in the office fourteen hours a day and spends most weekends on the road.

I am happy to report that my daughter Robin grew up to be completely unaffected by the Washington limelight. (She has never held a federal job, for instance.) Her mother insisted on it, and it no doubt helped that Robin inherited the family sense of humor. When she was a teenager and wanted our permission to pierce her ears, she researched and wrote a decision memo similar to one a congressional staffer might prepare for his boss. At the bottom of the memo were two option boxes, one marked "Yes," the other "No." The next morning Robin woke to find the memo slipped under her door, with a third option scribbled in by her father: "Maybe."

One thing about teenagers: just being around them is a constant education in popular culture. I'm afraid I missed out on a few lessons. After hearing Robin go into raptures over a British rock band that was planning a visit to the U.S., I wrote to the British Embassy asking them whether they could get the band to surprise her and play at her high school. Unfortunately, embassy officials replied, the Beatles would be unable to accommodate Miss Dole and her classmates on their forthcoming American tour.

Meanwhile, I discovered that a congressman gets a lot of invitations on his own. Speaking on the mashed-potato circuit is a bit like KP in the Army—it's part of the job. At the same time, anything that keeps a politician humble is good for democracy. Certainly that was the case with a visit I made to a small town in Indiana. The name Bob Dole had little marquee value in 1961, so the GOP dinner committee had to hype the box office. When I arrived in town, I was whisked off to the local radio station, where the announcer was supposed to give people some incentives to boost attendance. He began with a more or less accurate rendition of my résumé.

"The guest at this evening's dinner," he said, "will be Congressman Bob Doyle [sic]. He will speak at the American Legion Hall. Tickets have been slashed from three dollars to one dollar. A color television set will be given away. You must be present to win, and we're not going to draw till Congressman Doyle gets through talking.

"Doyle was born in Kansas, raised in Kansas, educated at the University of Kansas. Prior to World War II, he was a premedical student. He fought in Italy, where he suffered a serious head injury. Then he went into politics."

As president of the GOP's freshman class in the House, I came to the attention of Gerald R. Ford, a genial six-term veteran from Grand Rapids. Jerry Ford's relaxed manner did nothing to conceal his competitive instincts or his fierce partisan loyalties. I also struck up close friendships with Robert P. Griffin and Donald Rumsfeld after they arrived on the scene—both fellow Midwesterners who later served in Ford's White House Cabinet and his informal Kitchen Cabinet. Perhaps my closest friend from those days is Bob Ellsworth, who was sent to the House from Lawrence the same year I was elected, and who would play a significant role in Richard Nixon's successful 1968 campaign for the presidency.

I was practically invisible to the Democratic side of the House. I'm not sure whether Speaker Sam Rayburn of Texas or John W. McCormack, his white-haired successor from South Boston, ever knew I was there. In the House of 1961, seniority was the password to power. Young men in a hurry, especially those who belonged to a seemingly permanent minority, were thought of as party crashers.

It's a popular lament that in this mediagenic age statesmanship often runs a poor second to showmanship. In fact there is nothing new about congressmen playing the role of watchdog to bring them attention. By presenting a 1962 resolution to investigate the dealings of Billy Sol Estes, I did a little barking of my own. Estes' manipulation of government-owned agricultural stockpiles was sufficiently scandalous to land him—and me—on the front page of the *New York Times*. Taking a jab at Estes' White House connections, I made up some acerbic buttons for the occasion: "S.O.B." they read, for Save Our Billy.

This illustrates the first and riskiest avenue to success in the House: playing to the outside audience. A second is accepting the institutional ethic, mastering a few subjects and allowing time and the seniority system to work their will. A third path, one heavily traveled by freshmen, is to forgo most larger issues in favor of diligent casework and constituent services.

But even this brand of micropolitics strained available resources. Office staffs were small in the sixties, which meant long hours and professional versatility. Administrative assistants mimeographed newsletters. Office managers doubled as case-workers. I read every letter that came in the mail, and dictated personal responses to most. I also played tour guide. More than once I went down to the White House to plead personally for tour passes for visiting constituents.

Visibility was pursued like the Holy Grail. I sent all graduating high-school seniors in the Sixth District a certificate to mark their commencement. No bride walked down the aisle without a copy of *The Congressional Cookbook*. I once mistakenly extended congratulations on the birth of a baby to a couple observing their golden wedding anniversary. So many pictures of myself with visiting Kansans appeared in local papers that I was accused of not having an office and conducting my business on the Capitol steps.

My voting record faithfully reflected district sentiments: in favor of rural electrification, soil conservation and economy in government; against foreign aid and most of Lyndon Johnson's Great Society programs. When the Supreme Court handed down its famous one-man, one-vote ruling, it was a body blow to western Kansas, whose population was less concentrated than in the more urbanized east. I proposed to take the sting out of the decision with a constitutional amendment allowing states to consider factors other than population in apportioning at least one house of their legislature.

On the subject of grain sales to the Soviet Union and Red China, my initial preference was to give the surplus wheat to America's friends rather than sell it to her enemies. Anything else, I thought, would put us in the position of fighting Communists with one hand while feeding them with the other.

But the world economy was changing. Global interdependence and our own abundant harvests harmonized in the Food for Peace program, which built upon an Eisenhower Administration initiative to distribute U.S. agricultural surpluses to underdeveloped nations. I supported the program (which had been revised by JFK to stress nutrition and to target specific foreign needs) after amending it to send U.S. farmers overseas as agricultural technicians and advisers. Though hunger was nonideological, it was often exploited for ideological purposes, especially by antidemocratic forces who would trade personal freedoms for a bowl of rice. Here was a chance for the United States to exert moral leadership rather than military might, to share her expertise as well as her surpluses.

I met up with Huck Boyd in the spring of 1960. Driving through Russell around ten o'clock one night, Boyd noticed lights on at the courthouse. They aroused his journalistic curiosity. He found me inside the county attorney's office poring over card files, spadework for that year's race to succeed Wint Smith in Congress.

My late hours impressed Huck more than my sense of humor. Early in my House career he informed me, "We don't need a Jack Benny in Washington."

I wasn't laughing in the spring of 1962, when I asked Huck to take the organizational reins of what was going to be a tough reelection campaign. I hired a campaign manager; I got a mentor. Huck Boyd's political experience dated to the summer of 1936, when he had sat spellbound at the feet of Alf Landon's presidential-campaign strategists. For twenty years, with the help of his wife, Marie, Huck represented Kansas on the Republican National Committee. Although his was a familiar face around Republican White Houses and on Capitol Hill, the publisher of the *Phillips County Review* never felt as happy on Pennsylvania Avenue as he did on the main street of Phillipsburg, Kansas.

From the start, Huck and I knew we had our work cut out for us. With fifty-eight counties sprawling over nearly half the state, Kansas' new First District—known locally as the Big First —was geographically the largest in America. My opponent was Democrat J. Floyd Breeding, a farmer who had stepped down from his tractor in 1958 to run for Congress in what had been a Democratic year. Breeding was better known than I and had been in Congress longer. And he already represented a majority of the new district's population.

To overcome these obstacles, I set out on a campaign to convince normally conservative voters of the basic differences between Breeding and myself. He was a strong supporter of John F. Kennedy's New Frontier. While I admired Kennedy personally, I disagreed with much of his program. Breeding believed in more federal control of agriculture. I preferred a voluntary approach which would let market forces operate to the greatest extent possible.

Like any contest, this one had its unexpected twists. *Time* magazine caused bipartisan laughter by running a picture of some of my opponent's campaign workers outside a storefront. Over their heads was a sign that read: "BREEDING HEADQUARTERS." Breeding himself was less amused when I dramatized the differences in our congressional attendance by sending him tongue-in-cheek reminders of all the votes he was missing— messages like "Dear Floyd: While you were in Ness City today, dedicating a new post office, I was in Washington, voting to help the wheat growers."

I was just as aggressive in challenging the *Hutchinson Daily News,* which, under the fire-breathing editorship of John McCormally, was openly pro-Breeding. When McCormally's preference spilled over from his editorial page to the paper's news columns, I began calling his paper "the prairie *Pravda*." It was the start of a long-running feud, since ended.

In November 1962 I defeated Breeding by 21,000 votes. Two years later I faced an even stiffer test. As one of forty-three House members who were charter supporters of Arizona Senator Barry Goldwater for the 1964 Republican presidential nomination, I spent most of that summer and fall defending our nominee against charges that he was a pistol-packing, bomb-dropping relic of the Old West. As Ronald Reagan's success would demonstrate, Goldwater was actually a man ahead of his time. Few politicians outlive their enemies, but Barry has had the much greater satisfaction of seeing his ideas vindicated.

For me, the fall of 1964 was notable in another respect. Richard Nixon swooped into Pratt, Kansas that October on a political rescue mission in my behalf. He stood on some hay bales and delivered one of the best speeches I've ever heard. Without a note. It was the first time I witnessed up close Nixon's mastery of issues. Neither then nor later did he ever find it necessary to halt in midsentence and look over his shoulder to have an "expert" brief him on his position.

From Pratt, the former Vice President flew east to attend

funeral services for Herbert Hoover. I rode with him partway. Politics dominated our conversation, as it would every time Nixon and I talked. He wanted to know how old I was, and the age of Kansas' senior Senator, Frank Carlson. What about the rest of the state's congressional delegation? Who excelled on the campaign trail? Who was most comfortable in a committee room? Before I had given it much thought, Nixon was sizing me up as a possible successor to Carlson in 1968.

I survived another close call that fall, despite the best—or worst—efforts of the *Hutchinson Daily News*. Back in Washington, the 1964 election had decimated Republican ranks on Capitol Hill. In Congress, as everywhere else, the party seemed dead in the water, a victim of internal divisions and intellectual malnutrition.

So when Jerry Ford, the forty-nine-year-old chairman of the House Republican Conference, announced he would challenge Minority Leader Charles A. Halleck, I quickly added my name to the Young Turks who were supporting him. We were part of a restless minority, tired of simply reacting to Democratic legislative proposals and eager for more aggressive leadership.

I watched Ford during my early years on the Hill and was impressed by his intelligence, industry and capacity for growth. Before the GOP caucus met on January 4, 1965, I had a talk with other members of the Kansas delegation, three of whom followed me into the Ford camp. We gave the new Minority Leader his margin of victory.

Ford more than lived up to my expectations. He never abandoned his essential conservatism, but he wanted to restrain government, not dismantle it. As anxious as LBJ to attack poverty in America, Ford was convinced that government alone would fail in the effort, and that only the private sector could create jobs with a future. Ford's commitment to civil rights reflected a Midwestern concern for fair play and the politics of inclusion.

In the 1964 Civil Rights Act, Congress struck down racial barriers in the workplace and public accommodations. With the 1965 Voting Rights Act, it moved to enfranchise millions of blacks. I supported both measures. I did so for sound conservative reasons. If American conservatism stands for anything, it is the protection of individuals in all their rights, the right to vote being the most basic in any democracy.

President Eisenhower once said that if the only thing the American people wanted was security, they could find plenty of that in jail. Conservatives believe in the economic and social benefits that come with competition. Life is a contest, with rewards in proportion to the risks taken. But to be valid, the contest must be open to all equally, and the same set of rules must be applied to everyone.

Conservatives abhor waste, whether it's measured in dollars or in human lives. But until 1964 the plain truth was that millions of Americans were prevented from developing God-given talents because of restrictions imposed by manmade laws. In denying our heritage, we were endangering our posterity.

Two years later, President Johnson requested that I visit India to see firsthand that country's chronic food shortage. Johnson was under heavy pressure to increase U.S. grain shipments to the subcontinent. He responded with a shrewd reading of domestic politics combined with a long-range vision for which he was rarely credited.

When he was a young man fresh out of college, Johnson's first job had been teaching students in what residents of sun-baked Cotulla, Texas, called "the Mexican school." At his best, LBJ retained the educator's passion for knowledge, along with his capacity for changing minds. Before long, he had taught himself everything there was to know about rain patterns in the Ganges Valley and the amount of wheat leaving Wichita granaries for Bombay. Armed with such details, he tried to enlist other countries' help in preventing mass starvation in India. At the same time Johnson hoped to prod the Indians themselves toward future self-reliance. Finally, he saw a chance to blunt congressional opposition to foreign aid by sending Farm Belt congressmen to witness India's agony for themselves.

In India, we went from official dinners in our honor to Calcutta slums teeming with homeless people, beggars and flies. Hunger stalked every city street. Outside the urban areas, bar-

ren fields showed the severity of a drought brought on by unusually light monsoon rains. I visited rural-electrification
projects, met with Prime Minister Indira Gandhi, and slept
under mosquito netting in a government guest house while liz-
ards crawled over the ceiling.

When we returned, the delegation advised President Johnson to send 1.8 million bushels of grain immediately to the
desperate country. Congress readily went along with the President's request. Ultimately, American farmers shipped one fifth
of their 1967 harvest to Indian ports. For me the experience
was a learning one. No doubt that's exactly what the old
teacher from Cotulla, Texas, had in mind.

Frank Carlson was an authentic Kansas institution. The
son of Swedish immigrants who settled in Cloud County in the
1880s, he was also that rarest breed of political animal, one
who by refusing to court power and popularity assures himself
of both.

Carlson began his career in public service in 1928, when
he was approached in a Concordia wheat field by four local
businessmen who were looking for a state legislative candidate.
Carlson turned them down. He would be too busy shucking
corn for cattle feed to spend the first three months of the year
in Topeka.

"Don't worry," one of the men told him. "You won't win
anyway."

Carlson's supporters wore buttons that fall with the slogan
"I'd Rather Be Farming." Voters disagreed. In November 1928
they launched Carlson on a trajectory that would take him from
the Topeka legislature to the governor's office and both houses
of Congress. As governor in the late 1940s, Carlson was a road-
builder and a ground-breaker. He instituted workmen's compensation and hatched initiatives in education and medicine. In
1950 Kansas sent him to the Senate, where he served on a
committee investigating the anti-Communist activities of Joseph R. McCarthy and later voted to censure the Senator from
Wisconsin. Carlson also played a leading role in drafting his
fellow Kansan Dwight Eisenhower in 1952.

Soon after taking office, Ike expressed a familiar presidential lament. "Frank," he said, "this is the loneliest house I've ever been in. What can I do?"

Carlson responded by inviting Eisenhower to meet with a small senatorial prayer group. In 1953 Eisenhower attended the National Prayer Breakfast which Carlson had helped initiate. And Presidents have been doing so ever since.

In the first week of January 1968, the man who forty years earlier declared his preference for farming bowed out gracefully from the Senate. Carlson had told me his decision in advance, and within twenty-four hours I jumped into the race to succeed him. For the next eleven months, I stumped Kansas in a '68 Oldsmobile driven by Bill Frazier, one of the best friends I ever had. We first met when Bill was a student in a Sunday school class I taught in Russell. He came from a family that loved politics, and in time he became what you might call my Bebe Rebozo—a delightful companion whom I could trust completely and who desired nothing for himself except mutual friendship. His death in 1982 at the age of forty-one was a heavy blow.

Running for a statewide office gave me a chance to discuss more than agriculture. I talked about law enforcement and drug prevention and an early proposal to repackage federal education money in the form of block grants that would be used as state and local officials saw fit.

Traveling across the state, I saw just how far the Republican Party had come in attracting fresh blood since we burst onto the scene at Kansas Day, 1960. There were plenty of volunteers to spread the word. The press was friendly. Kansas' largest paper, the *Wichita Eagle,* noted my "growing concern about the problems of the underprivileged at home and the underfed abroad." More surprising were some carefully measured words of praise from my old nemesis the *Hutchinson Daily News.*

In the August primary, I defeated my good friend former Governor William H. Avery. By carrying all but two of the state's 105 counties, I put to rest lingering doubts about whether I could expand my agricultural base into urban areas and the Kansas City suburbs.

That fall Republican candidates everywhere were bolstered

by disenchantment over Vietnam and the Johnson Administration. My Democratic opponent for Carlson's Senate seat was William Robinson, a highly regarded Wichita lawyer. On election day, just over 60 percent of Kansas' voters put a check beside my name.

Two months later, I sat down and wrote a very special message.

> Dear Robin:
>
> Today is a most important day in my life, and I trust in yours. The days and months ahead will be hectic, exciting ones, but my one hope is that I can share more time with you and your mother. In future years, as you look back, you might recall that my first letter after taking the oath as a United States Senator on January 3, 1969, was written to you.
>
> In the rush of today's activities, just remember that I always appreciate, more than you know or I can express, your patience, understanding, and devotion.
>
> Love,
> Dad

Politics has many rewards. But it can also make demands, on no one more than your loved ones.

In the spring of 1969, for the first time in eight years, there was a Republican President in the White House. Implicit in Richard Nixon's election was a popular rebuff to liberal dogmas that had been unchallenged since the early days of the New Deal. Americans were emotionally spent by Vietnam and the cultural strains of the 1960s, and they wanted a period of healing. The President-elect took note of this in his inaugural address.

"We have endured a long night of the American spirit," said Nixon, "but let us not curse the remaining dark. Let us gather the light."

Along with the new President's chance to "bring us together," his party was given a golden opportunity to pursue lasting political realignment through policies of conservative innovation. Whatever the history books may say about the

Nixon years, they shouldn't forget such domestic advances as revenue sharing, pension reform, clean air and water legislation, energy conservation, the first steps toward meaningful welfare reform—and the last balanced budget of the twentieth century.

While voters may have seen Nixon's election as a mandate for change, their message was all but lost in the partisan fog of Capitol Hill. Nixon was the first newly elected President to confront hostile majorities in both houses of Congress since Zachary Taylor in 1848. Democrats controlled the Senate 57 to 43. Their dominance was psychological as well as numerical. Only a handful of Republican senators could recall being in the majority, and few were Nixon loyalists. Their allegiance was to the Senate itself.

One of Washington's wisest observers likes to describe a particular senatorial pretension he calls the "I Have Been Chosen" Syndrome. Chance and not choice, he argues, is the biggest factor in getting to the Senate. An incumbent decides not to run again, or falls victim to a presidential landslide for the opposition party, or becomes tainted by questions about his finances or the company he keeps. If you are the beneficiary of his demise, you suddenly find yourself in a chamber whose illustrious ghosts include the likes of Webster, Clay and Calhoun. You grow to like the historical company. Reelection confirms your sense of personal destiny. You have been chosen, so the theory goes, and it's only a matter of time before you decide you should return the favor by offering your services to the voters in a much higher capacity, such as the presidency.

The early years of the Nixon Administration confirmed the theory. Democrats who regarded Nixon's election as a fluke turned the Senate into a launch pad for their own 1972 aspirations. It got to the point where I urged the presiding officer to set aside sixty minutes each day for the Senate Presidential Hour, during which senators who thought they were President, senators who thought they should have been President, senators who thought they wanted to be President and senators who were willing to settle for being Vice President could express themselves.

It was customary in those days to regard first-termers as

children to be seen and not heard. Three and a half months passed before I made my first floor speech, an appeal for experimental housing for the handicapped. Over time, I became closely identified with the disabled and their legislative agenda. I also supported a constitutional amendment giving eighteen-year-olds the vote, proposed legislation to help economically depressed rural America and opposed court-ordered busing and abortion.

The unexpected death that September of Senate Minority Leader Everett M. Dirksen deprived the Nixon Administration of a forceful and vastly experienced Capitol Hill advocate. There was much more to Ev Dirksen than the tousle-haired Wizard of Ooze depicted by cartoonists. He was a partisan who loved the Republican Party second only to his country, and whose loyalty to both country and party never came into conflict.

Similar qualities distinguished Howard Baker of Tennessee, who as Dirksen's son-in-law inherited both the old man's well-traveled De Soto and a gift for reconciling legislative differences. Howard came to the Senate two years before I did, as part of a large, unusually prominent freshman class that included Edward W. Brooke of Massachusetts, Michigan's Bob Griffin, and Mark O. Hatfield of Oregon. The fact that most of them were to my left philosophically didn't prevent us from working together for the day when Republicans would control the levers of congressional power as well as the White House.

So it was only logical that when Howard threw his hat into the ring for the Minority Leader's position, I supported him enthusiastically. Baker was narrowly defeated by Hugh Scott, a sixty-nine-year-old former congressman from Philadelphia's suburbs whose owlish appearance and ever present pipe complemented his scholarly interest in Chinese porcelains. Politically, Scott was a Rockefeller man, a fact sure to increase friction with White House staffers who were openly contemptuous of Congress and its untidy methods of operation.

Personally, I thought the Pennsylvanian was far more conservative than Nixon detractors like Clifford P. Case of New Jersey or New York's Charles E. Goodell. It's just that Scott liked the Senate well enough to want to stay in it. A reading of home-state politics may have influenced his opposition to Nixon's choice of South Carolina appeals judge Clement Haynesworth to fill the Supreme Court vacancy left by the resignation of Abe Fortas. On November 21, 1969, after a long campaign by labor and civil-rights groups to discredit Haynesworth's record, Scott and sixteen other Senate Republicans voted with the majority to reject the nomination. Even more humiliating for the White House was the subsequent defeat of Fifth District appeals judge G. Harrold Carswell, a Floridian named to replace the ill-fated Haynesworth.

I voted for both men. In retrospect, I was right on Haynesworth, wrong on Carswell. As I saw it, Haynesworth had been unfairly victimized by headlines over minor stock holdings and alleged conflicts of interest. (Carswell was another story, a man who probably would never have been nominated except in the heat of presidential anger at senators who had denied Nixon his Southerner on the Court.) "You've got guts," South Carolina's Ernest F. "Fritz" Hollings remarked to me at the height of the controversy. It was his way of thanking me for standing by an earlier commitment to support the judge from Greenville. Fritz and I have been friends ever since.

On the heels of the Carswell fiasco, Nixon faced more dissension from Senate Republicans over an antiballistic-missile system and production of a U.S. supersonic plane to compete with Europe's Concorde. His Administration struggled to unite GOP lawmakers behind Vietnamization, Nixon's attempt to extricate America from the Southeast Asian tar pit by turning battlefield responsibilities over to the South Vietnamese.

Politics, like nature, abhors a vacuum. Since freshmen had relatively little influence on committees, I began spending a lot of time on the floor reminding colleagues just who had won the 1968 election. I didn't have much company. Sometimes there were so few Republicans in the chamber that the Democrats could have stolen the furniture and no one would have complained. Barry Goldwater, at least, seemed appreciative. Barry was no more than his usual frank self when he described me as "the first fellow we've had around here in a long time who can grab 'em by the hair and haul 'em down the aisle."

There's nothing wrong with partisanship as long as it's

constructive and doesn't descend to the level of personalities. Adlai E. Stevenson, a Democrat noted for his bipartisan appeal, went so far as to label it "the lifeblood of democracy." By cloaking his loyalties in elegant phrases and self-mocking wit, Stevenson earned plaudits for civility. Take a less polished—or less orthodox—approach, you're liable to be called a gun-slinger.

In truth, as the Haynesworth nomination showed, there was a lot of political hardball played in the Senate back then. Most of it originated on the Democratic side of the aisle, as senators who had dutifully backed Lyndon Johnson's conduct of the Vietnam War turned on Nixon with all the fervor of converts. But Nixon had been elected to bring the conflict to the earliest honorable conclusion. "Honorable" was the key word. I couldn't see any honor in congressionally imposed deadlines for troop withdrawal or funding cutoffs for field op-erations.

In the first months of 1970, U.S. ground forces in Vietnam were reduced from 543,000 to 340,000. Nixon assured the country that another 60,000 boys would be coming home by May 1. But at the Paris peace talks, the North Vietnamese negotiators dug in their heels, confident that American war-weariness would give them what twenty years of combat had not.

On April 30, the President went on television to announce a military thrust into the Parrot's Beak area of neighboring Cambodia, thought to be a nerve center of Vietcong activities for the entire region. The action ignited a firestorm of protest on America's campuses and in the halls of Congress. Nixon said he intended to withdraw the invading force from Cambodian territory by June 30, and I plunged into a fight to stop Senate doves from pulling the plug before that date.

For seven weeks, the Senate was tied up in knots. By the time they were unsnarled, Nixon's self-imposed deadline was at hand. And I had stolen a march on one of the war's most outspoken critics, Foreign Relations Committee Chairman J. William Fulbright. My call for repeal of the 1964 Tonkin Gulf Resolution, the measure repeatedly cited by Lyndon Johnson in justifying his undeclared war in Southeast Asia, both astonished and angered Fulbright. He had wanted to present such a motion himself. What I had done, claimed Fulbright, was like stealing another man's cow. I didn't want to steal his cow, I replied. All I wanted to do was milk it a little.

The 1970 midterm elections fell far short of what political analyst Kevin Phillips called "the emerging Republican majority." The two seats gained in the Senate were more than offset by losses in the House and among state governorships. Strident rhetoric from Nixon, Vice President Spiro T. Agnew and others about law and order and student unrest failed to galvanize voters who were chiefly worried about the war, inflation and 6 percent unemployment.

Almost immediately, steps were taken to prevent a repeat performance in the presidential year of 1972. Agnew was effectively muzzled. President Nixon, whose standing in the polls suffered from a campaign that had him, in Attorney General John Mitchell's phrase, running for sheriff, was distanced from day-to-day political management. At the same time, Rogers C. B. Morton left his job as Republican National Committee chairman to become Nixon's Secretary of the Interior.

Washington was rife that fall with rumors of prospective replacements for Morton as chairman. Most of those mentioned were reluctant to take a job that had lost much of the prestige it had enjoyed in the days of strong party structures independent of the White House. Modern Presidents were less willing than their predecessors to entrust their political fortunes to a James A. Farley or a Leonard W. Hall. As a result, party chairmen have become media point men instead of back-room strategists.

I understood this, and was willing to accept the limitations that the job entailed in exchange for the opportunity to reach some groups previously neglected by the GOP. I was especially eager to expand Republican appeal among farmers, young people, veterans and minorities, and to take our case into neighborhoods where traditional liberalism had failed.

John Mitchell told me in the first days of January 1971

that the job was mine. Or it would be, following the National Committee's regular midwinter meeting a few days later in Washington, Mitchell said. No sooner had I passed along the good news about the offer to friends in Kansas and on Capitol Hill than it was withdrawn.

White House chief of staff H. R. Haldeman once said, "Every President needs an S.O.B. and I'm Nixon's." The night before the National Committee was to ratify my selection, Haldeman lived up to his own billing. He called me from the Western White House in San Clemente, California, to tell me that Nixon had changed his mind. He was sorry, said Haldeman, if the President's abrupt volte-face caused me any trouble back home. He said Nixon had concluded after thinking it over that the business of the Senate was too pressing for me to serve as a full-time chairman.

Haldeman didn't say so at the time, but later the same night I found out whom the palace guard preferred. Thomas B. Evans was a favorite of the party's money men. A Delaware native, he had distinguished himself as a Southern coordinator in Nixon's 1968 campaign. Tom was an impressive guy, and in time we became good friends. But just then I had no intention of quietly folding my tent. Bond lawyer or no bond lawyer, John Mitchell was enough of a politician to know that in this business your word is your bond. And I had Mitchell's word on the chairmanship.

There had to be some reason why, in just twenty-four hours, both Nixon and Mitchell had changed their minds. There was: they had been warned of the consequences of having a national chairman who might be too independent or irreverent for the White House's tastes. It wasn't hard to trace such reports to the Senate Minority Leader's office, and to Ohio's maverick Senator William Saxbe in particular. Bill Saxbe hadn't forgotten my earlier support of Howard Baker over Scott, as he demonstrated by telling reporters that as the so-called "Sheriff of the Senate" I'd have trouble selling beer on a troopship.

Hugh Scott, with his own sense of institutional protocol, could hardly have relished the thought of a Senate newcomer like myself being out front as a party spokesman. (Ironically, as a young congressman Scott himself had once held the chairmanship. In 1948 presidential nominee Thomas E. Dewey had relegated the Pennsylvanian to a sidelines role. Maybe Scott wanted to spare me a similar fate; in any event, we drew much closer in later years, swapping stories of all the hot coals tossed in the direction of any national chairman.)

The next few hours were a whirlwind of intense negotiation between Capitol Hill, the RNC and San Clemente. Around midnight, Rog Morton telephoned Bryce Harlow at home. Harlow headed the White House congressional-relations staff during Nixon's first two years in office. Until his death, in February 1987, he was one of Washington's most esteemed Wise Men. ("If judgment were oil" was the way columnist Mark Shields put it, "then all by himself, Bryce Harlow would be OPEC.")

Harlow's talent for damage control made him indispensable. Of course, had people listened to his advice in the first place, they probably wouldn't have had to call on him later to pull their chestnuts out of the fire. This was one scrimmage Bryce would just as soon stay out of. It was late at night, he had put a log on the fire, and the streets outside were glazed with the residue of a violent ice storm.

"You're out of your mind," he told Morton. "I couldn't get there from here if I wanted to. Which I don't."

Refusing to be put off, Morton sent a car to pick up Harlow and bring him to party headquarters at 310 First Street. Harlow arrived to find the mood grim. For months I had carried water by the bucket for the Administration. Yet it wasn't enough to get Haldeman or others in the West Wing Mafia to return my phone calls.

I remember saying to Harlow in the heat of the moment, "If this is the way you're treated as a loyal Republican senator, after all I've done for the President, all the battles I've fought on the floor, all the heat I've taken in the press—well, I'm not so sure I want to be a senator."

Harlow told me to dismiss any such thought. He didn't begrudge me my anger, however. Even with Bryce's ingrained loyalty to the party and the President, he could hardly contain his resentment of a White House staff that wanted only a chairman subservient to them.

The lights on First Street burned late that night. By three

in the morning, when Harlow finally escaped RNC headquarters, he had negotiated the outlines of an acceptable deal. I would become chairman, in fact was well as title. Tom Evans would become my deputy, in charge of administrative and financial oversight. (Subsequently I named Anne Armstrong of Texas as deputy chairman, the first time the title had been bestowed on a woman.)

A final hurdle remained. It took Huck Boyd's intervention as chairman of the official nominating committee to prevent a rules change that would have led to separate elections for myself and Evans. As Huck explained it later, the White House wanted this unprecedented step to show publicly that the new chairman's power was to be shared. Thanks to Huck, Nixon's men couldn't get anyone on the nominating committee to approve the scheme.

And I wasn't about to budge from my position.

"I'll be pleased to appoint Evans," I told Rog, "but there can be only one chairman."

On the morning of the vote, I was roused from a short night's sleep by another call, this time from Nixon himself. Whatever his true feelings, on the phone the President managed a more or less convincing note of satisfaction.

Our contacts thereafter were sporadic. Signals got mixed, as when I insisted in a San Diego press conference in August 1971 that the Nixon Administration would never accept wage and price controls. When I got back to my hotel room, White House staffers called to tell me that the President was about to make a speech that would knock my economic predictions into a cocked hat.

Occasionally, I was invited to sit in on a Cabinet meeting and give a short briefing on my political travels. Nixon didn't need anyone to give him a report. He knew more about politics than anyone in Washington. He also knew what he wanted. Though generally removed from RNC operations, Nixon took a hands-on approach when he personally ruled out a strong Republican challenge to Alabama Senator James B. Allen. Besides personal affection for Allen, Nixon felt gratitude for his pro-Administration voting record. Having concluded that an ideological majority was better than no majority, Nixon could easily be forgiven for wishing that his own party's leaders would support his programs as much as an unreconstructed Democrat from Dixie. In the meantime, he made clear to me that Allen was to have a free ride.

There's never a perfect package. In office, Richard Nixon combined visionary statecraft with a surprising grasp of detail. But he was a man haunted by the past, unable to escape the shadow of defeat at the hands of John F. Kennedy. Kennedy hovered over the Nixon entourage like Banquo's ghost. It was as if, ten years after the fact, Nixon couldn't forget the cavalier, even cruel judgment supposedly pronounced on him by JFK during their 1960 campaign: "No class."

I wish he could have. As far as I was concerned, Nixon had every reason to be proud of his origins and the determination that enabled him to overcome the hardships of his youth and a lack of social connections to reach the highest office in the land. Quite simply, he had worked harder than anyone else, studied longer, become more knowledgeable. He had taught himself the minutiae of precinct organization and the intricacies of super-power relations. In many ways Nixon's was a classic American success story. Out of his own will to succeed, he could identify with millions of people—the so-called Silent Majority—whose values were his values, but who for years had been taken for granted or laughed at by the sophisticates of Georgetown.

As part of our party-building activities at the RNC, we tried to capitalize on Nixon's appeal among voter groups not often receptive to Republicans, particularly ethnics and blue-collar workers. The door to the chairman's office was literally removed from its hinges. In a similar spirit of openness, we organized the Black Council and began other programs to reach Hispanics and voters of Eastern European descent. Under Secretary of Labor Arthur Fletcher, an old Kansas friend and the ranking black in Nixon's Administration, addressed an RNC meeting in Denver in May 1971. His success there spurred more invitations, including a major speech to a gathering of Southern Republicans in Memphis.

Working through communications director Lyn Nofziger

and others, we introduced state-of-the-art television and radio facilities. We conducted a series of field schools to help recruit strong candidates and train campaign managers. Tom Evans did a superb job of broadening our financial base, until it included thousands of small contributors giving ten, twenty-five or fifty dollars. The RNC itself channeled more money to more local candidates than ever before. And it was a rare night when I wasn't attending some party function which might be hundreds of miles from Washington.

All of this took a personal toll. For some time before we divorced in 1972, Phyllis and I had been drifting apart. I was caught up in one life, whose demands were escalating, she in another. While Robin was still young she helped keep us together, but it wasn't a happy time for either of us. I had been raised to believe that anyone who couldn't make his marriage work was a failure. It was a lesson my mother, among others, didn't hesitate to remind me of.

Before going ahead with the divorce, I went to see Nixon in the White House and offered to quit the chairmanship if it would spare him and the party any embarrassment. He turned the offer aside, later sending me a copy of Lord Blake's biography of Benjamin Disraeli to underline his message that public and private lives are to be judged separately.

Mine was not the first or, sadly, the last marriage to founder on the political rocks. Fortunately, Phyllis and I remained friends—if not always political soulmates. When President Ford asked me to be his running mate in 1976, Phyllis, by then remarried to a Kansas banker and rancher, expressed her relief at having escaped the intense media scrutiny and round-the-clock campaign duties inflicted on modern political wives. A strong Reagan backer, she reacted to the news of my selection with typical candor. As she put it, Ford had chosen the second-best conservative for the job.

The 1972 campaign was notable for the tensions it spawned between the Republican National Committee and the Committee to Re-Elect the President (CREEP). Privately I told John Mitchell and others at CREEP how unhappy I was over their failure to develop a strategy for translating Nixon's personal popularity into support for other GOP candidates. Their caution reached absurd proportions when campaign officials refused to allow a public presentation of a sweater with an elephant on it to Mrs. Nixon.

"We have to appeal to donkeys," one CREEP official informed me.

"I'll give her a donkey sweater next week," I said.

Sorry. Elephants were out of fashion.

CREEP's indifference was matched by an almost excessive interference in our work by some of Nixon's own staff. Special counsel Charles Colson's White House office sent us cartoons for *First Monday,* the RNC's monthly periodical. One showed Democratic hopeful George McGovern in a Vietcong uniform. A second, to be mailed out on plain stationery, suggested that former Vice President Hubert H. Humphrey, another Democratic contender, had a drinking problem. After Alabama Governor George Wallace was gunned down by a would-be assassin in May 1972, Colson dispatched a list of pre- and post-shooting comments by Senator Edward M. Kennedy and other leading Democrats. Underneath was the caption "What a Difference a Bullet Makes."

Tom Evans, who later described Colson's "bombshells" to me, made sure none of them saw the light of day. In the meantime, I had my own run-in with the human bottleneck surrounding the President. Nixon wanted the 1972 Republican convention to be held in San Diego. The selection of San Diego, a short helicopter ride from his San Clemente residence, would not only be a convenience to him but would also acknowledge California's growing clout in presidential politics. RNC legal counsel Fred Scribner discovered that among the convention's financial guarantors in San Diego was a host hotel owned by ITT, the conglomerate that had an antitrust dispute pending before the Justice Department. Scribner said he was concerned about the possible appearance of conflict of interest. When San Diego failed to come up with a replacement guarantor, the convention was shifted to Miami Beach. Such independence didn't go over well with the West Wing crowd. They had long memories.

On June 17, 1972, five middle-aged men looking for documents were arrested in the Watergate offices of the Democratic National Committee. Their captain was E. Howard Hunt, sometime spy novelist and CIA operative. Hunt's links to the White House were soon revealed. Prior to that, my own reaction had been to dismiss Hunt and his band of Cuban emigrés as the Gang That Couldn't Shoot Straight. Besides, the break-in at the DNC occurred on my night off.

More seriously, it made no sense to spy on an opposition that was headed over the cliff. At the time of the break-in, Nixon was far ahead of George McGovern, his probable Democratic rival, in the polls. McGovern was badly out of step with popular attitudes on practically every important issue. The antiwar movement that had made him its champion seemed openly contemptuous of millions of regular Democrats for whom a distant war was less threatening than a perceived assault on traditional values of work, faith and family. With all this going for us, why engage in acts of criminal stupidity to run up the score?

At a White House meeting a few days after the break-in, I raised the subject and, along with it, the eyebrows of everyone present.

"Out on the road I'm getting some questions about Watergate," I remarked. "Do you think we should clear the air, just to put people's minds at ease?"

Bryce Harlow predicted the story would have a short life, because, as he put it, it had "no legs." Nixon brushed the subject aside without comment.

That was the only time before the election I heard the word "Watergate" used around the Oval Office. Not that I was there that often. At public events I'd go up to the President and suggest that as national chairman I wanted to see him. Nixon would be perfectly agreeable, but it was often impossible to penetrate the little circle that was rapidly becoming a noose around the President's neck.

When I was asked embarrassing questions about this arm's-length treatment, I described an imaginary call to Haldeman:

"Bob, I'm the national chairman and I need to see the President."

"You want to see the President? Fine. Tune in Channel Nine tomorrow night at ten o'clock."

Less easily laughed off was the growing alienation of National Committee members and party activists who were also excluded from campaign involvement. Money is one measure of political status. The RNC's budget for 1972 was $4 million. CREEP, by spending ten times as much, showed what can happen when money floods the normal channels of political communication. No matter what Mae West said, too much of a good thing is *not* wonderful. An organization that can afford computer banks, tracking polls and other devices of modern, high-tech campaigning is often tempted to put its faith in flow charts and focus groups and overlook human emotions and intellectual substance. Telephone banks don't drive people to the polls; their convictions do. Anyone who forgets that fact is in danger of undermining the political process, whether or not he violates formal campaign law.

Nixon campaigned as if he were above the fray that fall, emphasizing his peacemaking journeys to Peking and Moscow and leaving a small army of surrogates in charge of answering opposition charges. For most of the campaign, I played the loyal soldier, assailing McGovern's platform for its isolationist strain and calling the Democratic candidate "a left-leaning big spender." One day I was handed a speech draft declaring that the *Washington Post*'s Watergate coverage—admittedly intense and often partisan—was based on the alleged personal hatred publisher Katharine Graham felt for Nixon.

"I'm not saying this stuff," I responded. "I don't care where it comes from. Unless you can confirm the source, I won't make any charge."

That November Nixon won by the expected landslide. What should have been a joyous election night party at the Shoreham Hotel was instead a bittersweet moment. In his victory speech, Nixon neglected to mention any of the regular Republican organizations that had contributed to the sweep. Within days, rumors of an imminent shakeup at the National Committee began circulating.

With a reelection fight of my own coming up in 1974, I had already decided to leave the chairman's job and the arduous travel schedule that went with it. The White House staff reached the same decision, only they had a different timetable.

Two weeks after the election, I joined Attorney General Richard G. Kleindienst for a helicopter ride to the presidential retreat at Camp David in the Maryland mountains outside Washington. If he's going up for the hanging, I thought, they're probably going to hang me too.

"Did you bring enough rope for us both?" I asked Kleindienst.

When the time came, I was ushered into Aspen Lodge for an awkward conversation. Nixon began by telling me I'd done a hell of a job. "I'm proud of you, Bob." He autographed a map charting the hundreds of thousands of miles I had traveled as national chairman, and presented it to me with a Camp David jacket.

Then came the hangman's noose.

"I know after all this you probably want to move on to something else," Nixon said.

"Well, I sure don't want to be chairman till '74," I told him. "But I would like to leave later on. You know, stick around for a little while and have some fun with the job."

Haldeman entered the room, and I felt like the condemned man facing his executioner. Talk turned to 1974. Nixon wanted to help me get reelected. Fresh hints were dropped. Finally, I was asked for names of a potential successor. On my way out, Nixon suggested that I drop in at a nearby cabin and greet his friend Bebe Rebozo.

It took a few more days for me to realize that though I hadn't been the victim of a hanging, I had been pushed off the mountain. At John Mitchell's urging, I went to New York early in December to sound out United Nations Ambassador George Bush about the chairmanship. I'd heard that Bush wanted to be number one somewhere, a desire that couldn't be accommodated at the Pentagon or anywhere else in the Nixon Cabinet. The only alternative was the National Committee.

So I was out, Bush was in, and Nixon was presumably mollified.

The more I thought about it, the more prearranged the whole thing seemed. I had nothing against Bush. What angered me was the callousness of a White House staff that demanded loyalty but failed to return it. Regarding their handling of the whole transition as shabby, I resolved to go quietly—but on my own terms.

Again I turned to Bryce Harlow. My trusted friend and broker drew up a parting agreement under which the President pledged to campaign for my 1974 reelection and assist in raising campaign funds. Like so much else in the unhappy days that followed, time rendered the document and the promises it contained inoperative.

Traditionally, a victorious party chairman occupies a prominent spot in the festivities surrounding a presidential inauguration. In the old days, he used to have a place in the inaugural parade right behind the winning candidate. Not so on January 20, 1973. That day, Robin and I rode down Pennsylvania Avenue in just about the last car in the parade. George McGovern was probably ahead of me. It was a final, intentional snub from CREEP's Jeb Magruder and his boys.

By the spring of 1974, the sands were running out on Richard Nixon's presidency. Impeachment talk was rife on Capitol Hill. Public revulsion over abuses of power lumped together under the umbrella of Watergate threatened disaster for Republicans in the upcoming midterm elections.

Kansas Democrats had not elected one of their own to the United States Senate since the Depression year of 1932. William R. Roy hoped to break the jinx. A forty-six-year-old doctor from Topeka, Bill Roy had every reason to feel optimistic. He had knocked off three-term House member Chester Mize in 1970, turning himself overnight into a force to reckon with in Kansas politics. Roy enhanced his standing two years later when he withstood the Nixon landslide and won a second term with 61 percent of the vote.

By concentrating his energies on broadly popular issues like public health and the environment, Roy impressed many voters as a thoughtful, nondoctrinaire liberal. The politics of antipolitics was his stock in trade. It was a popular stance to take, especially amidst the continuing fallout from Watergate.

My own problem that year went beyond the Nixon scandals and the guilt-by-association tactics used by the opposition. Even without Watergate, the headlines were doing nothing to bolster Republican prospects. The first Arab oil embargo was sending shock waves through the American economy, and agriculture was being particularly hard hit. Inflation was a topic of popular conversation, along with gasoline allotments and rising unemployment. A mood of national frustration bordering on helplessness, the first forerunner of what Jimmy Carter would later call malaise, was eroding public confidence and traditional voter allegiances.

All this would have a much greater effect on elected officials than we knew at the time. Both the Senate and politics generally were rapidly changing. What had once been a genuinely deliberative body, almost an American House of Lords, was being dragged kicking and screaming into the modern era. Doors were coming off committee rooms and private offices. Television increased the visibility of senators and, with it, the demands for direct contact with the voters. Gone was the day when a Frank Carlson could survive politically by going back home only a couple of times each year. In its place was a more representative democracy, the exact opposite of the secretive mentality that had given rise to Watergate.

Campaigning had also become more expensive. Most candidates will tell you that the only thing they dislike more than spending campaign funds is raising them. But this was also part of the new politics. By the middle of January 1974, I was forced to raise a $250,000 war chest. By November I'd have to spend more than all my previous campaigns combined had cost.

Nineteen seventy-four was the first Dole campaign in which we had a paid, professional campaign manager and staff as well as consultants, pollsters and ad men. The overhead was substantial. Worse, volunteer workers were being turned off by the out-of-state professionals who, for all their technical and organizational skill, couldn't match the Kansans' knowledge of or sensitivity to the local electorate.

The campaign went into a tailspin. Polls taken in August showed me trailing Roy by thirteen points. We were $100,000 in debt, and new bills were coming in daily. Roy's broadcast offensive was exactly that—offensive. "Dr. Bill Roy, a *respected* voice for Kansas," it intoned in coded allusion to Watergate. Roy said that, as national party chairman, I either had known about the break-in before it happened or should have. He stuck to this line even after Senate Watergate Committee Chairman Sam Ervin went out of his way at a Washington press conference to exonerate both me and the Republican National Committee of any Watergate involvement.

On August 8, 1974, Richard Nixon resigned the presidency to make way for Gerald Ford. The new President entered office on an almost euphoric tide of national goodwill. It was a mood that quickly dissipated. Less than a month after Ford's inauguration, his pardon of Nixon touched off a storm of protest. A snap poll of Kansas voters showed opinion running 52–40 percent against the pardon, a margin that widened over the next week.

Ford's move was as courageous as it was politically risky. One immediate effect was to lessen the new President's effectiveness on the 1974 campaign trail. Inadvertently, he set off a fresh round of Watergate innuendo that endangered Republican candidates everywhere.

In the middle of this supercharged atmosphere, I decided to switch campaign managers late in August, giving Kansas Lieutenant Governor Dave Owen overall responsibility for my campaign. Owen's first priority was to counter Roy's negative television spots, which before August we had left unanswered. Roy's strategists had combed *The Congressional Record* and sifted through hundreds of legislative tallies. Isolating votes for their maximum potential damage, they fashioned a series of specific charges. Bob Dole voted against farmers. Or the handicapped. Or the elderly. If I had believed what was in Roy's ads, I'd have voted against me, too.

Owen was unhappy with the advertising we were running, and, on his own initiative, he went to a Kansas City television station and hired an announcer whose voice dripped sarcasm. The announcer sat on a stool, turned full face to the camera and detailed Roy's liberal voting record and his reliance on campaign contributions from organized labor. With the tape in hand, Owen telephoned the Boston-based ad agency that had been brought in during the campaign's late stages and told them what he wanted to do. They begged him to delay for twenty-four hours the airing of the homemade spot.

The next day a special-delivery package arrived at campaign headquarters. Inside was a tape of a proposed commercial. It featured my face, gradually obliterated by graffiti—or mud—while a voice-over detailed and then refuted Roy's allegations. "All of which makes Bob Dole look pretty good," ran the tag line. "All of which makes Bill Roy a liar."

Owen exploded with anger at the last phrase. Within minutes he was on the phone to Washington, where he tracked me down on the Senate floor and read the ad copy to me. It was my turn to hit the ceiling. I was already suspicious of television's distorting power and wasn't thrilled about repeating Roy's charges, even in self-defense. Nor did I like the idea of my video image being spattered with mud. And the word "liar" was out of the question in describing my opponent.

But we were behind, and Roy *had* repeatedly stepped over the line between legitimate criticism and dirty pool. I let the spot run but insisted that the last line be changed to read: "All of which makes Bill Roy look like just another old politician."

The effect of the ad was felt instantaneously. Tracking polls showed a surge in my favor. Caught off guard, Roy made his Watergate references still more explicit, which only compounded his problem. By the closing days of the campaign he was caught in his own trap.

There were other charges, regarding the issue of abortion. Just a little more than a year before, the Supreme Court had issued its landmark ruling in *Roe* v. *Wade* legalizing abortion during the first three months of pregnancy. The issue was on many minds, and deservedly so. As an obstetrician, Roy had delivered over five thousand infants. Belatedly he acknowledged having performed a few abortions as well. Roy claimed he personally opposed the procedure, justifying it only when the mother's life would be endangered by carrying a pregnancy to term.

In the closing days of the campaign, pamphlets were passed

around some Topeka neighborhoods denouncing Roy and showing graphic depictions of what their authors said was infanticide. Roy's advisers tried to link the grisly literature to my campaign, but failed, simply because no connection existed. But by making such an accusation the Congressman did, quite accidentally, add to the doubts in the minds of many voters, for whom his earlier, nonpolitical image was by now badly tarnished.

The night before the election, I sat in a Topeka hotel room thinking how much harder it would be to pay off a $50,000 campaign debt if I lost. But Kansas voters dispelled my fears while reaffirming my belief in their fairmindedness. Election night was a long one, though. At three in the morning we called every county clerk in the state, routing some of them out of bed, to confirm our vote count against their official tallies. Only then would I go down to the ballroom of the Ramada Inn with my parents and Robin to claim victory.

The final margin was less than fourteen thousand votes. Slender as it was, I took it as personal vindication. I also thought back to my visit to Camp David two years earlier. In handing me my head, Nixon's palace guard may have saved my hide.

I can hardly close this account of campaigning without mentioning the most important campaign of my life. Elizabeth tells the story of our courtship better than I, so let's just say that on December 6, 1975, we were married. Long before that date, friends knew that something was in the offing. According to staffers on the Hill, they could tell by the way I whistled around the office, and the way I refrained from calling them with work assignments each weekend.

It's true that it took me several months to work up the nerve to ask Elizabeth out. But it wasn't that long before I saw in her a genuineness and a sensitivity to others that are rare in power-hungry Washington.

When I asked her about Salisbury, she described it as "a small town of twenty-two thousand."

"You haven't seen a small town until you've seen Russell,

Kansas," I told her. And we agreed right then that the day you forget where you come from is the day you should retire from public service.

Elizabeth comes from a family of perfectionists, so she has a natural tendency to dwell on what she sees as her own imperfections. Over the years I've tried to convince her that life is too short to worry about yesterday, and perfection is an impossible standard. Returning the favor, Elizabeth has shown by example the value of intellectual and organizational discipline that tightly grabs hold of a problem and won't let it go until it's resolved.

Like many men of my generation and background, I've always tended to internalize my feelings. She's just the opposite. Her emotions are more apparent, and no doubt that too has had a beneficial effect on me.

As we got to know each other better, we found that we had enough in common and enough that was different to sustain a lifelong partnership of equals. She's the early bird, up early most mornings to open her Bible or other devotional reading; if it's still dark outside, I figure it's the middle of the night. She's the culture buff; my way of keeping in touch with opera and theater is driving past the Kennedy Center each day. She likes to rehearse a speech, believing that delivery is an important part of the whole effort; I sometimes give a speech only once.

Elizabeth will read everything she can get her hands on, which led me to joke that if something should ever happen to me, the only book I want her opening at my funeral is a hymnal. She keeps notepads all around the house, and not just next to the telephone. I once asked whether she takes notes on wrong-number calls.

Some people have expressed surprise that I'm so comfortable being married to an independent, high-powered woman. I don't know why. I have always been surrounded by resourceful females, starting with my mother, who did so much to keep our family together during the Depression, and continuing on to such current staff members as Jo-Anne Coe, whom I named the first woman secretary of the Senate; Sheila Burke Chew, who serves as chief of my Senate staff; my executive assistant, Betty

Meyer; administrative assistant Chris Bolton; and office manager Joyce McCluney. And I can't leave out the junior Senator from Kansas, Nancy Landon Kassebaum, who has added fresh luster to one of the most distinguished names in politics.

I guess if you look only at our public roles, at the hours we keep and the crazy travel schedules that have us waving to each other in airports en route to the latest road swing, our marriage may appear a bit unusual. On the other hand, as countless professional couples will tell you, our two careers enrich our marriage and make the time we have together all the more meaningful. We speak the same language. We share the same passion for public service.

None of this would matter if we didn't love each other very much. In my case, love is mingled with profound gratitude. Coming off a divorce, living alone and being unhappy with a bachelor's life, many men would be vulnerable to impulsive judgment and a mistaken second marriage. I was saved from all that the day Elizabeth appeared in my office. God was looking out for me then, as He has so often. Through all the years since, she has cheerfully accepted the demands of politics, and I have rejoiced in her graces. I'd say I got the better of the deal.

CHAPTER SIX

Courtrooms, Courtship

After three years at Harvard Law School, I spent the fall of 1965 in the equally exotic culture of the Orient. Instead of returning to Salisbury or Cambridge, I settled into an eighteenth-century house in the Georgetown neighborhood of Washington, D.C. In the evening, my guests took off their shoes and sat on pillows around a low table in the dining room while I served teriyaki and sukiyaki to Japanese koto music. During the day, I left the kitchen and looked for a job through government employment offices.

I soon landed a position at the Department of Health, Education and Welfare. While Bob Dole was voting against the Great Society, I was working for it. Actually, I was not much more than a footnote to its organizational chart. At HEW there were the Secretary, the Assistant Secretary, a deputy assistant secretary—and me. A low General Services rating didn't keep me from stopping Secretary John W. Gardner in the hallway outside his office and asking him questions about Washington and the department's agenda, which he graciously answered.

The job gave me a chance to use some of the skills picked up in my education courses at Harvard, and to act on my growing interest in the rights and potential contributions of disabled Americans. HEW assigned me to plan a conference on education of the deaf, the first of its kind held under government auspices. There were a site to choose, a roster of speakers to organize, and the publication of conference reports to oversee. In the spring of 1967, several hundred participants assembled at Colorado Springs' Broadmoor Hotel.

When the conference ended, so did my HEW responsibilities. I decided to take a month between jobs to learn my way around the courtroom, since I hadn't taken trial practice at Harvard. This would prepare me to handle cases for local indigents, I thought, and do some socially useful volunteer work.

With that goal in mind, I walked into a D.C. night court that had recently been established to handle a bloated docket. Presiding over the arraignment proceedings was a black-robed Captain Ahab named Edward "Buddy" Beard. Outspoken and highly unorthodox, Judge Beard inspired fear among young lawyers. He once invited a courtroom audience to vote on whether it believed a defendant's plea of innocent. At other times Beard asked defendants to define the binomial theorem or to identify the author of the poem "Ozymandias."

"Who are you?" Beard abruptly asked one night, pointing his finger in my direction.

"Elizabeth Hanford."

"What are you doing here? I've seen you here the last three nights."

"I'm observing the proceedings, Your Honor, so that I can take cases."

"Are you a member of the D.C. bar?"

"I am."

"Come up here. I have a case for you."

I couldn't possibly comply with his request, I informed Judge Beard. I wasn't ready. I was still observing.

Judge Beard didn't make requests, he issued commands. "If you're a member of the D.C. bar, Miss Hanford, you are ready to take this case. Come up here."

I looked around for the nearest exit, but then reconsidered. I'm going to have to practice before this judge sometime, I figured. If I'm serious about defending indigents, I can't afford to alienate him. Besides, I might pick up some valuable legal training from this whole crazy venture.

Reluctantly, I approached the bench. Beard handed me the

information slip for my very first case in the courts of Washington. What followed could have come straight out of a TV sitcom.

My client was a Greek national who was accused of petting, and thereby annoying, a lion at the National Zoo. I was taken to a cell block under the courtroom where the defendant was locked up. It was an iron cage, filled with inmates hanging on the bars. From the way these men greeted me, it was clear they weren't used to seeing female lawyers (this was 1967, remember).

"Hey, man, she's your lawyer," someone called out. As the catcalls continued, I made my way to the opposite end of the cell block and met my client, Mr. Marino.

"Now, Mr. Marino," I told him, "this is not the most serious crime. I think I can get you out tonight. But you'll have to come back and stand trial in about three weeks."

Mr. Marino didn't know what I was talking about. He understood just enough English to protest vehemently that he was going to New York and was never coming back, trial or no trial. As I attempted to dissuade him, the court marshal informed me that Judge Beard was ready for me.

"Well, I'm not ready for Judge Beard. Can't you see? We're still trying to communicate."

The marshal told me to come anyway. No one kept Judge Beard waiting.

As I stepped out of the elevator, I was surrounded by a group of strangers who seemed curious about the case and how I would try it.

"It's ridiculous to keep a man locked up on a charge like annoying and petting a lion in the zoo," I said. "If I get him out he's not coming back. So we're going to trial tonight. Even though I've never seen a trial except on *Perry Mason*."

Everyone around me was scribbling in a notepad.

"You're not court personnel," I gasped. "You're press."

Reporters from the *Post,* the *Star* and the *Evening News* kept on writing.

"Don't you dare print what I just said."

By now, the courtroom was packed with two hundred people clamoring for a show. As I took my place at the defense table I glanced over at my adversary from the U.S. Attorney's Office. It was my classmate Lee Freeman, editor of the *Harvard Law Review,* 1965.

When the proceeding finally got under way, I argued that without the lion as a witness there was no way to know whether he had been "annoyed or teased." Freeman advised the judge not to release my client, who a few weeks earlier had climbed into an antelope cage. Beard looked to the defense team. He wanted Marino's word of honor that he would steer clear of the National Zoo. "Say yes," I whispered in Marino's ear, while punching him in the ribs. "Say yes."

By the grace of God, I won the case. "If this ever gets back to the *Harvard Law Record,*" Lee Freeman said between clenched teeth, "I'll know how it got there." I assured him I had no intention of telling anyone at Harvard about that night's judicial burlesque.

The next day's papers noted the valiant lady lawyer whose novel defense had snatched victory from the jaws of defeat. Judge Beard passed me in the hallway outside his courtroom. "Not bad for the first time out of the box," he said.

That was the beginning of a year that was sometimes hilarious, more often heartrending, but never dull. I didn't make any money, but I wouldn't trade the experience for all the gold in Fort Knox. I know on that first night I must have looked like a delicate Southern flower to the onlookers in Judge Beard's courtroom. Beard later warned me that I would see a lot of the underside of urban life in his court. To prove it, he then sent me to the cell block below, where a young man was writhing in the anguish of drug withdrawal. My blood went cold.

Before long, I was defending alleged drug addicts and armed-robbery suspects. I look back now and marvel at the chances I took prowling around some of Washington's meanest streets looking for witnesses. I often met characters like Racehorse Mitchell, a courthouse legend straight out of Damon Runyon. I also ran into other attorneys—Fifth Street Lawyers, we called them—whose specialty seemed to be cynicism. They laughed at my naiveté and couldn't understand why I continued to counsel my clients to believe that people could change if only they were given a chance.

I will admit that what I didn't know would have filled several issues of *True Detective*. One night, just as I began the defense of a streetwalker the judge recognized my client. "Take off your wig," he directed her. When my client did what the judge ordered, I realized I was defending a female impersonator. I turned every shade of the rainbow. The judge took it all in stride. Nothing surprised him. I guess he was used to this sort of thing.

As chairman of the United States Civil Service Commission, John Macy operated as Uncle Sam's chief headhunter. First appointed by John F. Kennedy, Macy became Lyndon Johnson's presidential talent scout, with a computerized file of twenty thousand prospective jobholders. His commitment to public service was infectious. Determined to knock down the stereotype of federal employees as a clock-punching army, he was just as committed to advancing women and minorities in the federal work force.

Macy had served as a juror on the 1965 White House Fellows panel that turned me down. Now, two years later, I took him up on his invitation to drop by the Civil Service Commission.

Someone on Macy's staff told me about "a great job" in the White House Office of Consumer Affairs. This was a logical extension of my year in private practice. It was also a chance to get in on the ground floor of an issue that was sure to excite public and legislative interest for years to come.

The job was literally too good to be true. Because of budgetary pressures, the only way I could fill this particular opening was by convincing another agency to pick up the tab, to fund it out of a payroll separate from the Executive Office of the President. In bureaucratic jargon, that meant I had to find a slot before I could fill it.

Then I remembered that Food and Drug Administrator James Goddard (whom I had gotten to know at HEW) had encouraged me to get involved in the consumer movement.

Goddard quickly agreed to put me on the FDA payroll, and a few days later I marched into the White House to announce, "I come with a slot!"

I reported for work at the Old Executive Office Building, just across the street from the White House, in April 1968. Hubert Humphrey's vice-presidential office was down the hall. From time to time I saw Humphrey, a gregarious man whose natural ebullience seemed dimmed by the angry emotions of the time.

Normally, no season is more glorious than springtime in Washington. Crocuses perfume the air, and a southern breeze carries with it hints of gentler days to come. There was nothing gentle about the spring of 1968, however. In one week, Lyndon Johnson stunned the nation by withdrawing from the presidential race and Martin Luther King was murdered on the balcony of a Memphis motel. In the wake of King's shooting, a spasm of violence spread across urban America. Johnson was forced to call out National Guard troops to quell riots just a dozen blocks from the White House. When Robert Kennedy was assassinated two months later, many Americans feared that their society was coming apart.

Under the circumstances, Washington's social circuit was less inclined than usual to buzz over primary results and campaign scenarios. Most of what I heard in those crowded, tragic days came secondhand. As deputy assistant for legislative affairs, I spent most of my time shuttling between the EOB and Capitol Hill. My boss was Betty Furness, perhaps best known then for a series of television commercials in which she opened refrigerator doors. By 1968, Furness was opening doors on behalf of millions of American consumers. Most important of all, she made certain the door to Lyndon Johnson's Oval Office was open.

That November the federal government changed hands when Hubert Humphrey was defeated by Richard Nixon. After the votes were counted, Betty left and so did her chief assistant, Les Dix. The rest of us stayed on, a crew without a captain, unsure of our place in the newly commissioned fleet.

Several weeks after the election, two men who identified

themselves as members of the Nixon transition team dropped by our EOB quarters. One was Bob Ellsworth, Bob Dole's friend and the future best man at our wedding. Ellsworth clutched a massive volume describing the form and functions of the entire executive branch. His demeanor was serious, a bit accusatory.

"What is this office?" he asked, leafing through the book. "What exactly is it that you do?"

I had a second chance to explain what we did a few days later when I was summoned to meet with Harry Flemming of the White House staff. I half expected to be tossed out of the office. Instead, I got a pleasant surprise. The Nixon Administration was aware of political realities. It had come to power during the heyday of consumerism. By the spring of 1969 twenty-three states had their own consumer protection offices, and together they coordinated over four hundred programs designed to replace the outmoded and socially irresponsible notion of caveat emptor.

Our operation was spared, even though its title would soon change, and, by implication, its standing in the executive pecking order. We became the President's Committee on Consumer Interests, under the guidance of Virginia Knauer, a former Philadelphia city councilor-at-large and director of Pennsylvania's consumer protection bureau whom President Nixon appointed in March 1969.

Because she had very little Washington experience, Virginia kept most of the existing staff. One change she made was to jump me two grades and move me into an office next to hers as her deputy. So began a very special relationship between myself and a woman who would become both mentor and surrogate mother.

Virginia had and has a kind of balance that is rare in Washington. She is a gifted artist and a pioneer in historic preservation; along with her husband, Bill, she restored and opened as a museum a Colonial-era tavern in Philadelphia's Society Hill neighborhood. She has never allowed her love of public life to crowd out her family or her friends, yet, make no mistake about it, Virginia is a great politician. As one of the first Republican women to hold office in heavily Democratic Philadelphia, she was unabashed in her partisanship, but she was thoroughly professional. In Washington she refused to check her conscience at the door—even at the door to the White House. She could be as feisty in arguing consumer interests before Richard Nixon's Domestic Policy Council as she had been in opposing the Democratic juggernaut in Philadelphia's City Hall. She kept her dissents out of the press. And she extended her loyalty to subordinates no less than to the man in the Oval Office.

Virginia wanted me to share in all her experiences. Among other things, that meant hitting the road to sell Administration policies and serving as Virginia's backup on the Cost of Living Council and the Task Force on Product Liability. We attended an international conference of consumer organizations in Vienna and domestic business gatherings coast to coast.

I made my first public speech before a Prairie Village, Kansas, seminar on women and financial credit. Still thinking of myself as a private citizen who just happened to work at the White House, I was surprised when a knot of reporters at the airport bombarded me with questions about legislation I supported making credit available regardless of gender.

The first presidential statement devoted exclusively to consumer issues was published during Richard Nixon's administration. Noted nutritionist and educator Jean Mayer chaired a White House Conference on Food, Nutrition and Health—another first. Joining forces with Dr. Mayer to promote a 30 percent ceiling on fat in hot dogs got us into as much hot water as the hot dogs themselves. The President sided with his consumer advisers against his very agitated Agriculture Secretary, Clifford M. Hardin. "I'll calm Hardin down," Nixon promised Virginia. "You just keep doing what you're doing."

Strictly speaking, our office had no actual regulatory function. Each month we forwarded approximately four thousand complaints to agencies like the Federal Trade Commission or the Consumer Product Safety Commission, or directly to the companies involved. The mail contained a depressing litany of deceptive packaging, shoddy workmanship, and warranties not worth the paper they were printed on.

Both inspired and angered by what we read, Virginia and I sought common ground between the consuming public and product manufacturers. We established a series of Consumer Action Panels in an effort to mediate consumer complaints against industries ranging from furniture and appliances to automobiles and carpets. These early mediation panels, supported by industry as a form of self-regulation, paved the way for current third-party mechanisms to resolve conflicts in the marketplace.

Virginia and I worked hard to convince businesses that responsiveness to consumer needs and complaints would carry commercial rewards. Unit pricing was a typical case. At first chain store executives resisted spelling out for supermarket customers the comparative cost of twelve ounces of detergent. Faced with already thin profit margins, they were concerned about the expense of figuring and posting such information. It took time, but eventually we convinced a few of the largest chains that the cost was small for the consumer goodwill to be gained. Once firms like Safeway and Jewel came around, smaller stores quickly fell into line.

We persuaded manufacturers to date supermarket items for their freshness and to identify the source of fats and oils in their products. Cosmetic firms agreed to list on the label of creams and lotions the full ingredients, including any substances that might cause allergic reactions.

A simple philosophy guided us. For consumers to make wise choices, they must have access to all relevant information. Our advice to the President led to the creation, by executive order, of the Consumer Information Center, based in Pueblo, Colorado, and designed as a clearinghouse for government publications on health, safety, housing and money management. We launched the newsletter *Consumer News* (which cost a dollar a year) and packed it with useful tips culled from federal agencies and the pages of *The Federal Register*.

"Suggested Guidelines for Consumer Education," a curriculum for young people from kindergarten through the twelfth grade, was created under the guidance of our consumer education director, a former Cambridge housemate and a longtime friend named Doris Sasser. I traveled around the country urging that students be taught how to obtain insurance, personal credit, and home mortgages. On college campuses and at law schools I promoted courses in consumer law.

What began as just a job soon turned into something of a personal crusade. Underdogs have always appealed to me. As a public-interest lawyer I had already seen how fraud or deception can victimize the elderly and others too young or impoverished to fight back.

I even experienced a bit of consumer woe myself when furnishing my apartment. General Sherman reached the sea faster than two rolls of carpet ordered from an Atlanta store arrived at my front door. When finally laid down, the carpeting was too small for my carefully measured rooms. Next came two beds, one more than I had ordered. And to top it all off, the store's computer kept sending me someone else's bill.

My experience with the carpet and the beds might easily be dismissed as a comedy of errors, but unfortunately it was being repeated in thousands of other American homes. Few of their owners were laughing.

I had joined the White House staff at a time when consumerism was still an exotic subject in some policy-making circles. At about the same time, I became involved in two other movements with profound implications for the future. One was economic deregulation, a largely uncharted field whose potential was first glimpsed in our office by a young, brainy and obviously prophetic member of Virginia's staff named Jack Pierce. Because Jack wasn't the kind of person who would raise the office's emotional temperature for no reason, everyone paid attention when he said that deregulation was an idea whose time had come. *We* paid attention, anyway. It would take a while yet for Congress to open its windows to the winds of economic change blowing across the American landscape.

Another major change was already under way, challenging the sexual stereotyping that begins at birth, when a pink blanket is used to identify a girl and simultaneously limit the range of opportunities open to her when she grows up.

The women's movement didn't happen overnight, much

less in a vacuum. Thirty years earlier, during World War II, women left their kitchens and worked in munitions plants. A largely female work force built the B-52 bomber. When the war ended and the planes returned to earth, most of their construction crews traded in their overalls for more conventional feminine garb. The new working woman of the early 1970s was no Rosie the Riveter. Instead of patriotism, she had internal drives that propelled her into the work force to excel and wield power. Women who waited longer than their mothers to marry sought the same professional fulfillment as men. And millions more worked out of simple economic necessity.

By 1970, more than 23 million American women were employed full time. Eight million more held down part-time jobs. Forty percent of the female work force was married. A third had children under eighteen at home. Meanwhile, a rising divorce rate was expanding the number of single-headed households, and the vast majority of them were supported by women.

What all this added up to was nothing less than a quiet revolution. Notwithstanding all the economic and demographic trends, however, America's organizational culture remained predominantly male. In the early 1960s, Margaret Chase Smith wittily summed up the difficulty for women in entering politics, when a group of female journalists asked her how she would respond if she ever woke up one morning and found herself in the White House.

"The first thing I'd do is go straightaway to the President's wife and apologize," she said. "Then I'd go home."

We have come a long way in the years since. But even as a fairly high-ranking woman in the Nixon Administration, I still encountered lingering resentment among those who saw women only as envelope stuffers. Oh, sure, we could type position papers, but having those papers ever reflect *our own* positions as candidates and officeholders was the sort of utopian vision best left to a party platform.

The first time Virginia Knauer testified before a congressional committee, I went with her. So did our very able general counsel, Tilly Fowler.

"Mrs. Knauer," my boss was asked in a senatorial baritone, "do you have anything against men in your office?"

Another time Virginia had to leave midway through some testimony before the House Appropriations Committee and its imperious chairman, Representative Daniel J. Flood. When I stepped forward to complete the statement and take questions as prearranged, Flood called a recess. Only he forgot to turn off his microphone.

"Are we going to let this kid take over the hearing?" he was heard to ask.

Most unsettling was the day I hurried to the Metropolitan Club on I Street for a business meeting with a senior partner of the Cleveland law firm of Jones, Day. The doorman stopped me at the entrance.

"You can't go in there," he said.

"I beg your pardon."

"Women are not permitted in the club."

"I'm sorry. I don't think you understand. My name is Elizabeth Hanford, and I'm here to meet with some attorneys from Cleveland. We have an appointment."

"I'm sorry, ma'am. If you were Queen Elizabeth I couldn't let you into the Metropolitan Club."

After a few minutes, the man I was supposed to meet appeared at the door.

"I had no idea," he said, apologizing.

"You can take your choice," I told him, knowing all along that he didn't really have a choice. "I can go back to the office and send over some man. But I can tell you now that he won't be prepared, and I've spent the weekend getting ready for this meeting."

The meeting went on—without me. Joe Dawson, our press spokesman, wanted to put the story out on the news wires, but I convinced him that a front-page dust-up with a bastion of Washington chauvinism would do no good for either my work or Virginia's.

In the summer of 1973, a vacancy opened up on the Federal Trade Commission. Virginia Knauer proposed me as replacement for retiring Commissioner Mary Gardner Jones.

"Hey," she said that July, "you're just the one for this."

Consumer advocates outside the White House were surprised by her suggestion, especially the chairman of the Senate Commerce Committee, Washington State's Warren Magnuson. "Maggie," as he was popularly known, seemed to be a permanent part of the Washington scene, like the Capitol Dome or August heat waves. It was Magnuson's committee that would pass on any presidential selection for the FTC.

In the spring of 1973, Magnuson and other senators had reluctantly confirmed the FTC nomination of Texas lawyer Mayo Thompson. At the time, an implicit deal was made to assure Magnuson that the next FTC commissioner would have more obvious consumer credentials. Enforcing the deal from Magnuson's end of Pennsylvania Avenue was Michael Pertschuk, the Commerce Committee's chief counsel and staff director. Mike was a friend of mine, but he didn't let that color his opposition to Virginia's idea. He told me frankly that groups like the giant Consumer Federation of America and the National Consumer League would see the nomination of any White House insider as a broken promise. He backed his assertion with a laundry list of people and organizations that would have to be won over.

It was a formidable challenge. Virginia suggested that I take a swing around the consumer circuit, beginning with an appearance before the annual convention of the Consumer Federation of America. I should confront issues head on, she told me, even if that meant detailing internal differences between our office and those around the President.

I had my doubts about the propriety, and wisdom, of taking a roomful of strangers into my confidence, many of them openly hostile to the Nixon Administration, but Virginia insisted.

"It's the only thing to do," she said. "Don't worry about me. Just make sure the meeting is off the record. Once you have that assurance, state your views. They may disagree with you, but they'll respect your honesty." Hers was a selflessness rare in Washington.

Walking into the CFA's meeting room in Milwaukee felt a bit like that first night in Judge Beard's courtroom, except that this time I was no novice. There was no real grilling; the meeting was cordial enough. It showed me that communication can often begin in a simple gesture. Even if the walls dividing us were not leveled, they were breached.

I also called consumer advocate Esther Petersen and syndicated columnist Sidney Margolis. These conversations—like discussions with other consumer advocates—were spirited, what diplomats call "frank and constructive dialogue." Soon I was able to give Mike Pertschuk a list of my own.

"Now, Mike," I began, "let me try this out on you." Then I went down my list. It included over two dozen state attorneys general, journalists and organization leaders. When I reached the bottom, there was silence on the other end of the line. But only for a moment.

"You got it," Mike said. Magnuson was going out of town for a few days, and a hearing would be scheduled promptly. According to Mike, there would be no problems.

Being confirmed was relatively simple. Getting sworn into office was another matter. One of my final assignments as Virginia's deputy was a speech in New Jersey just across the river from Manhattan. Coming out of the Holland Tunnel, a drunk driver rear-ended the police car in which I was riding. I suffered a ruptured disc which put me into Georgetown Hospital for a month in traction.

Accident or no accident, FTC Chairman Lewis Engman expected me to carry my load. Fine, I told him, come on out to the hospital and swear me in there. On December 3, 1973, Engman appeared in the doorway of my hospital room, accompanied by other commissioners and staff members.

I took the oath from my bed. We celebrated with quiche and tossed salad, and champagne chilled in a bedpan. Two hours later, everyone else made his way back to the office. I remained in the hospital for another two weeks, enjoying Chesapeake Bay crabs and a full Italian meal. I also boned up on the FTC caseload. It wasn't restful. But it was good preparation for what lay ahead of me.

Virginia Knauer was a natural-born matchmaker. In the spring of 1972 she had asked me to help her get a consumer plank into that year's GOP platform. She arranged for us to make a pitch to Bob Dole, the Kansas Senator who was also Republican Party chairman.

This was the first time I met Bob. When a side door of his office opened to reveal a tall, dark stranger, I thought he was awfully attractive. He claims he wrote my name on his blotter right after that. Maybe so. But I didn't hear from him for several months.

Other suitors were less bashful. About this time I was dating a fellow Southerner. Like the rest of football-mad Washington, he was devoted to the Washington Redskins. It was a passion I didn't share, as he discovered the day he called to tell me he had somehow wangled tickets on the fifty-yard line.

"Thanks," I replied. "It's nice of you to invite me, but I've got so much to do. I'm getting an advance copy of the new Nader report to read this weekend."

My date was aghast. He could go along with Nader six days a week, but the seventh unquestionably belonged to George Allen and Billy Kilmer. Eventually, I agreed to meet him at RFK Stadium. On Sunday he arrived early to load up on hot dogs, programs and other essentials. As the opening kickoff approached, he looked at his watch and scanned the rapidly filling stands for signs of his reluctant date.

He finally spotted me slowly advancing through the crowd. His smile did a vanishing act when he saw the briefcase I was carrying. For the next two hours, I glanced through the Nader report and basked in the sun. I thought it was a pretty good afternoon. He thought it was a pretty poor date.

"I said I would *go* to the game," I told him. "I didn't say I would *watch* it."

I ran into Bob Dole a second time when he and Tricia Nixon opened GOP campaign headquarters a block from the White House. And our paths crossed again at the Miami convention, when we both attended a party thrown by insurance magnate Clement Stone. Not long after that, Bob called me. We talked for forty minutes or so, long enough to discover how many interests and friends we had in common.

A few weeks later I got a second call. We covered new ground, and Bob said it might be nice to go out some evening.

It certainly would, I replied, waiting for him to suggest a time and place. But he didn't.

Third time never fails. After another long conversation, he finally invited me to dinner at the Watergate restaurant. Later Bob told me he had delayed asking me out because he had been concerned about the thirteen-year difference in our ages. And he was a little shy. I liked that. It contrasted nicely with the image some have of Washington as a town full of ladies' men.

He was also straightforward and absolutely honest. On a visit to my parents in Salisbury, he appeared one morning in the kitchen with a towel draped over his right shoulder.

"Mrs. Hanford," he told my mother, "I think you ought to see my problem."

"That's not a problem, Bob," she told him. "That's a badge of honor."

Even today, Bob kids me about forgetting his physical disability. "How am I supposed to hold the nail and hammer it?" he'll say with a smile when I ask him to hang a picture. Someone with his energy and stamina makes you forget that he's limited in any way.

From the first time I met him, I was impressed by his way with people. On one of those trips to Salisbury, Bob invited Mother and a group of her friends to lunch at a local club. He sat at the head of the table surrounded by twenty gray-haired ladies who laughed at his jokes and decided on the spot that I'd be foolish not to marry this man. Bob has always been good at building coalitions.

The Federal Trade Commission is one of the oldest of Uncle Sam's consumer watchdogs. It grew out of the fertile mind of Louis D. Brandeis, the famous "people's lawyer" from Boston who convinced Woodrow Wilson of the dangers of business monopoly. The FTC was chartered in 1914 to probe alleged violations of federal antitrust laws and to issue cease-and-desist orders against corporations found guilty of engaging in unfair methods of competition.

Like so much of Wilson's New Freedom, the FTC was intended to be a bulwark against bigness. It began with the premise that economic concentration could be carried to such extremes as to endanger democracy itself. In the 1930s this assumption led the commission to side with small business against food giants like A&P. Yet the commission's fervor ebbed over time, until critics derided Brandeis' once vigorous agency as "the Little Old Lady of Pennsylvania Avenue."

About the time I arrived on the scene, things were changing again, and for the better, as consumer groups and the organized bar prodded the commission to take a more aggressive stance. In 1974 Congress passed the Magnuson-Moss Act, which dramatically increased the FTC's power by authorizing it to write rules affecting entire industries instead of determining unfair trade practices one company at a time.

My early months on the job were notable for Chairman Lewis Engman's oft-asked question "How much will it cost?" Federal regulators back then weren't accustomed to such inquiries, but Engman wouldn't be put off. An old friend from Harvard Law days, Lew was an effective chairman whose willingness to apply fresh schools of thought to the regulatory field came as no surprise to me. It was Engman, for instance, who institutionalized "cost–benefit analysis" as an FTC policy-making tool. By utilizing the talents of economists, statisticians and others, it was possible to gauge the benefits of government action against their social and economic costs to society at large. Properly conducted, cost–benefit analysis could serve as a check on the long arm of federal regulators.

Additional innovations followed as the FTC became the first agency in Washington to raise the banner of deregulation. The agenda of increased competition and lower consumer prices that I would pursue as Secretary of Transportation had its genesis in my days as an FTC commissioner. Before arguing for more head-to-head competition at agencies like the Interstate Commerce Commission and the Civil Aeronautics Board, we had to get our own house in order. So the FTC launched an exhaustive review, which led to the rescinding of 145 of our rules, some of which regulated industries no longer in existence.

On the surface, such issues may sound dry. From my vantage point, they were anything but. Rather, they were a logical extension of my earlier work on behalf of individuals victimized by discrimination or economic abuse. One early case involved a group of West Coast travel agencies that were taking advantage of distraught people by making false claims on behalf of Philippine doctors. The travel firms proposed to fly desperately ill people five thousand miles and back, to be treated by so-called "psychic surgeons" who removed diseased organs with their bare hands. The FTC quickly put an end to the scheme.

Likewise with owners of a Montana uranium mine offering to transport those suffering from arthritis, bursitis, asthma—you name it—to the bottom of a shaft to inhale radon gas, a substance claimed to have beneficial effects on the nervous system.

Not all my time was spent fighting quack cures. The FTC took an active role in enforcing the Equal Credit Opportunity Act. Women were especially vulnerable; divorce or separation could be a kind of fiscal death. Without a credit record of their own, women were often denied credit of any kind, while the income of working women was commonly discounted by mortgage lenders and insurance companies.

To help women know their rights under the law, we developed imaginative public-service spots which in turn were vigorously promoted by American Women in Radio and Television. One of these ads dramatized the effect on a family when a breadwinner disappears—vanishing from the picture on the screen and leaving a gap in any woman's future. We convened FTC workshops on women in business, and I invited female colleagues at the FTC to regular "networking" sessions in my office.

Another priority was the elderly. I never forgot the excellent care my Grandmother Cathey received in a North Carolina rest home. From visits I made to her, it was a short step to arguing the need to investigate complaints against other, less reliable facilities. The result was a grim education in deceptive claims regarding nursing-home services and contractual disclaimers relieving the homes of responsibility for patients' health, safety or property.

And there were reports of some nursing homes receiving

kickbacks from pharmaceutical and other suppliers and mis-handling patients' money and valuables. Surprisingly, the com-mission staff showed little initial interest in pursuing an investigation of such reports. When I called in the director of the Bureau of Consumer Protection for "a little talk," the staff's attitude underwent a sudden and welcome change. More im-portant, the stage was set for changes in the nursing-home industry.

Generally speaking, I saw the commission as a chance to bring about lower prices for consumers, to ensure better-quality goods and services, and to expand the choices available in a free, competitive marketplace. One of my proudest moments came in leading the charge to overturn an old common-law rule that posed dangers to consumers who bought on credit, and especially to the poor and disadvantaged. The so-called "holder-in-due-course" doctrine took away their only remedy against schlock merchants who refused to honor their con-tracts.

Under the old rule, when the consumer purchased an item on credit, the merchant was allowed to sell the customer's note of indebtedness to someone else, making it impossible for the consumer to withhold payment in the event the product failed to work. The seller had no incentive to honor the warranty or resolve the problem. Our decision changed all that by requiring finance agreements to include a written statement preserving consumers' rights against the original seller.

There were times—and the change in this old doctrine was one of them—when service on the commission satisfied a deeper need, which I tried to communicate to college audiences wherever I went. In an age of massive, overpowering institu-tions—big business, big labor, big government—it was essen-tial to let the individual know that his voice still counted, that there was an alternative to the apathy or cynicism that inspired many Americans to turn inward during what Tom Wolfe la-beled "the Me Decade."

I believe now what I believed then. Perhaps no one in our society is more unjustly maligned than the bureaucrat. Even the phrase has become a pejorative. Taxpayers don't like the way their money is collected. Local officials and individual recipients are critical of the way government returns their money. And almost everyone has something unkind to say about mail delivery.

Woodrow Wilson used to say that government had to borrow all the brains it could get. It still does. Now more than ever, we need the energy, the drive and, most of all, the idealism of young Americans. I tell youthful audiences they can find no higher calling in life than that of public service. They may not get rich, but they'll enrich the lives of countless others. Along the way, they can raise society's sights and elevate its standards. And when the time comes to look back, as inevitably it will, they can take pride in having been an active part of the struggle of their times. Because of them, the world is a little better.

August 8, 1974, was wet and dreary in Washington. On this final day of Richard Nixon's presidency, my mother looked out my FTC window at rain-slicked Pennsylvania Avenue and said, "All of Washington is crying today."

My thoughts were with Bob, whose reelection campaign might easily be damaged by Nixon's downfall. We had grown much closer in the two years since our first meeting. I admired Bob's strength of character, his intellect, his incisive mind and, of course, his sense of humor. He was someone I could look up to but also be a peer to.

We had so much in common, not least of all careers that were distinct but in some ways overlapping. Clearly, I was never going to be the kind of wife who worried about my husband being home in time for dinner. Luckily, Bob didn't want that. Now, as then, one measure of our love is the freedom we give each other to pursue professional interests, without jealousy or competition. (Of course, he says I steal his best jokes. And he keeps threatening to give my recipe for pie crust to the Federal Highway Administration.)

By the summer and early fall of 1974, I was leaving my phone on when I turned in for the night. At one or two in the morning Bob would call me long distance. After fifteen hours on the campaign trail, with another day like it soon to begin, hearing my voice gave him something to look forward to each day, he said.

That October I was invited to join a group of young American political leaders on a trip to Japan for three weeks. When I told Bob, he said I should take advantage of what sounded like a great opportunity. "You'll probably learn a lot," he added.

Only later did it dawn on him that I would be away beginning the day after the election. That night he called from Topeka. "I'm looking forward to celebrating with you when I get back to Washington," he said.

"Don't you remember?" I told him. "I'm leaving for Japan tomorrow!"

"What?"

When I arrived home from the trip and found a bottle of champagne and a dozen red roses, I knew that things were getting serious. Bob said he had just wanted to make sure he had a job before he popped the question. He never got down on his knees. Come to think of it, I don't even remember a formal proposal. We just gradually began to think of the future as something we wanted to share. We were happier together than apart.

We were out walking one day when a friend of mine approached us and expressed the hope that I would keep my own name after our marriage. She went on at length about my having worked long and hard to develop a career and a professional identity. Surely I didn't want to give all that up, she continued.

"I think we want to have the same name," Bob shot back. "I don't care if it's Bob Hanford or Elizabeth Dole, we want the same name."

Our wedding was scheduled around the congressional calendar. We settled on a Saturday in December 1975. Since Bob and I each had an ailing father, we decided to have a small, private ceremony, followed by a large reception at the Washington Club on Dupont Circle. I looked at several churches before choosing the Washington Cathedral's Bethlehem Chapel. It is the oldest part of a church that had been under construction since 1907 and originally intended as an American Westminster

Abbey. Woodrow Wilson had been entombed in a crypt under the chapel floor, as had other statesmen and heroes. I was less concerned with its historic associations than with the Gothic chapel's intimacy. I fell in love with it, and have gone back often.

President Ford would be in China on December 6, so he entertained us at the White House a few days before. Richard Nixon called to invite Bob and me out to San Clemente for a cup of tea. Consumer Product Safety Commissioner Barbara Franklin told me I could call her if I ever needed advice on safe cribs or toys.

A Washington astrologer took one look at my palm lines and announced, "To have a successful marriage you will have to be a lamb in politics and a lion at home. You are both romantics with strong minds and you ought to rule the home and he the rest." My horoscope for December 6 urged me to pay special attention to "public relations, legal affairs, co-operative efforts, marriage."

At a wedding breakfast at the F Street Club, there was a reproduction of *The Congressional Record* on each guest's plate. Included in the "Extension of Remarks" was a suggestion already made by my colleagues at the FTC: "I move to amend the Robinson-Patman Act to render the Dole-Hanford merger a combination in the public interest, and not in undue restraint of trade."

A few minutes before 6 P.M., I stood outside the Bethlehem Chapel, reading over my marriage vows. Bob decided to wing it. The ceremony was delayed for a few minutes by the cathedral's organist, who seemed determined to perform a concert instead of just playing the Wedding March. As soon as Dr. Elson, the Senate chaplain, stemmed the flow of music, the fifteen-minute service began. At the first ministerial pause in the vows, Bob jumped in with a hearty, if premature, "I do."

Our honeymoon was cut short by the sudden death of Bob's dad, who had stayed on in our Watergate apartment. I felt cheated of the years I could have enjoyed with a man whose warmth and kindness had deeply impressed me.

A month later, I had a chance to test Kansans' response to

their newest adopted daughter. I needn't have worried. Three hundred and fifty people came out in zero temperature to greet Bob and me one evening in Hays. They confirmed what Bob had already told me: Kansas isn't a place on the map. It's a state of mind.

CHAPTER SEVEN

Ramrod and Rainbow

BOB

Finality is not the language of politics.

—BENJAMIN DISRAELI

There's an old rule in American politics that says you don't run for Vice President. Neither do you run away from the job if it's offered. Franklin Roosevelt's first Vice President, John Nance Garner, once described the job as not worth a pitcher of warm spit, but it has long since ceased to be a national joke. By 1975 there was even an official residence for the nation's second-highest office. Alexander Throttlebottom, the hapless Veep of musical comedy, wouldn't recognize the rambling, turreted structure perched high on a hill overlooking Washington's Embassy Row.

Gerald Ford's Vice President, Nelson A. Rockefeller, disliked the place, preferring his elegant Foxhall Road mansion. He helped with the refurnishing of the house, but he refused to spend more than a few nights in it.

Accommodations were the least of Rockefeller's disappointments in a job he had rejected at least once before Ford called in August 1974 and persuaded him to take it. It seemed at first to be a perfect match: Rockefeller's international experience and administrative background balancing the down-home appeal of a former Michigan congressman untested in the global arena. The two men admired each other; each wanted their political partnership to be successful.

Despite all the changes that have transformed the modern vice presidency, the office remains a hostage to fortune. No one who occupies it can do more than a President desires or the rest of the executive branch will allow. Rockefeller wanted to break that historic mold. As head of the White House Domestic Council, he expected to be a key policy-maker, implementing an ambitious agenda drawn up by his personal secretariat.

It didn't work out that way. The Council of Economic Advisers and the Office of Management and Budget thought Rockefeller's ideas were too expensive for a conservative Administration trying to patch a hemorrhaging federal budget. Politics submerged policy-making. For twenty years Rockefeller had battled the Republican right, and his name had become synonymous with an Eastern establishment that was distrusted by grass-root Republicans in the South and the West. Fairly or not, by 1975 New York's four-term Governor was seen as a political liability in the very regions where the GOP staked its future.

That November, Rockefeller took himself out of the running for 1976. Prior to his announcement, the Vice President had let it be known that the only way he would stay on in the job was if his responsibilities were broadened to include those of White House chief of staff. He would serve in a second Ford term, Rockefeller made clear, only as a kind of deputy president. That way he could finesse White House organization charts.

Rockefeller's departure was not enough to prevent a stiff challenge to Ford's presidency from the right. On March 2, 1976, the President chalked up a narrow victory over Ronald Reagan in the New Hampshire primary. A week later he won in Florida, and on March 16 he took Illinois' big delegation by a decisive margin. Anticipating an early end to Reagan's insurgency, Ford got a severe jolt on March 23. North Carolina Republicans rallied to the former California Governor, whose bristling rhetoric appealed to their suspicions of Secretary of

State Henry A. Kissinger, détente with the Soviet Union, and proposed treaties that would relinquish U.S. control of the Panama Canal.

The Reagan campaign, energized by its North Carolina victory and by a series of televised attacks on Ford's foreign policy, was able to shake off defeats in New York, Wisconsin and Pennsylvania. On May 1, Reagan swept all of Texas' one hundred delegates, setting the stage for a protracted round of trench warfare leading up to the August convention.

When Kansas held its state convention in May, friends advised me to stay away. I had been mentioned as a possible running mate, and they were afraid I would alienate partisans in both camps, dooming whatever slight chance I might have of being on the ticket. But there are times when silence is not golden, just yellow. As I told the delegates in Topeka, one reason the people of Kansas had voted for me in the past was that I never reneged on a commitment. I wasn't about to start now. On the first ballot, Kansas would be with Ford.

On July 26, Pennsylvania's moderate Republican Senator Richard S. Schweiker sent shock waves through the party when he accepted Reagan's offer to be his running mate. Schweiker's announcement shook delegate loyalties, but not the way Reagan strategists had envisioned. Within twenty-four hours former Texas Governor John Connally got off the fence and publicly endorsed Ford, as did Mississippi's Clarke Reed, whose support was crucial to winning that state's thirty delegates. Schweiker's home state held firm in its commitment to Ford.

Ford and his managers had spent so much time on the fight with Reagan for the nomination, they had given little thought to putting together an organization for the fall campaign against the Democratic nominee, Jimmy Carter, or to selecting a vice-presidential running mate. A couple of weeks before the convention, I was asked, along with a dozen other candidates, to send financial and medical records to the White House. When we got to the convention in Kansas City, I spoke to a few strategically placed opinion-makers like former Defense Secretary Melvin R. Laird. I asked Laird whether he would do me a favor by raising my name in press speculation—I might run for reelection in Kansas someday and it would sound impressive back home.

I also talked with my old friend Lyn Nofziger, then working as Reagan's press secretary. I knew that Ford and Reagan had agreed to meet as soon as the presidential balloting was concluded. If Ford won, he was sure to ask Reagan who he thought should be his Vice President. Could Reagan say something nice if my name came up? Lyn jokingly offered me the job, saying that all I had to do was jump ship and board the Reagan campaign.

Monday, August 16, was opening day in Kansas City's Kemper Arena. As temporary chairman, I welcomed delegates with a verbal blast at Jimmy Carter, who was asking voters to elect him on trust alone. The speech was well received by delegates who agreed on little else. It also appealed to Ford's personal combativeness.

Several factors were coming together to influence the vice-presidential selection. Ford was well aware of the Midwestern farmers' resentment over the 1975 embargo on grain sales to the Soviet Union. Carter was strong in the South, and his running mate, Senator Walter F. Mondale of Minnesota, was there to hold wavering liberals in line. Ford knew that the Farm Belt was essential if he was going to win the 270 electoral votes he needed in November. I had the good fortune of having been born in Kansas, and I could talk the language of farmers whose daily existence depended on faith, hope and parity.

Ford wanted a running mate with whom he was philosophically and personally compatible, someone who would be able to discuss a wide array of issues knowledgeably and who could heal wounds left by the divisive primary contest with Reagan.

On the eve of the convention, presidential advisers urged boldness, but polling data modified this counsel. If Ford chose John Connally, for instance, he would make a bold grab for Texas, but he might also turn off voters who were suspicious of Connally's big-business image. Another Texan, Anne Armstrong, who was now ambassador to Great Britain, would dramatically shuffle the deck. She would certainly throw Carter off stride. But Ford pollsters had found resistance, especially among Republican women, to the idea of a woman on the ticket.

According to their numbers, Howard Baker would add less Southern strength than might be expected from his Tennessee roots. Treasury Secretary William E. Simon was too much of a Washington insider. Former Deputy Attorney General William D. Ruckelshaus had no clearly discernible political base. Besides, his name would never fit on a campaign button.

On the convention's second night, delegates defeated a Reagan-sponsored rules change that would have compelled Ford to name his running mate before Wednesday night's presidential balloting. With that, the die was cast for the President's first-ballot nomination twenty-four hours later. As soon as his victory was official, Ford and a few advisers went to Reagan's Alameda Plaza hotel suite for their prearranged meeting. Ford threw out half a dozen vice-presidential possibilities. Reagan responded favorably to my name.

Elsewhere around Kansas City, Reagan diehards were trying to force their man on the ticket despite his protests. Their predawn rebellion dramatized the party's internal divisions and raised the pressure on Ford to select a running mate acceptable to the right.

At ten-thirty Thursday morning, the phone rang in our hotel suite. A White House operator was on the other end.

"Hello, Bob. This is Jerry Ford."

"Nice to hear from you, Mr. President."

"Bob, I've given it a lot of thought and I'd like you to be my running mate. We've known each other for a long time. You know the Midwest and the Farm Belt. You can hit the ground running. You've got the experience to be President. We've got a way to go, but I know we can do it. What do you think?"

I thought it over for about a second. "If you think I can help. Certainly, Mr. President."

There was a brief visit to the Fords at their hotel, which included a quick, cautionary warning about my occasionally caustic humor. There was nothing wrong with having a little fun, Ford assured me. "Just be careful what you say."

ELIZABETH

The Federal Trade Commission is a semijudicial body, so it has a calendar of oral arguments and weekly conferences where cases are decided. By July, commissioners are in the middle of round-the-clock opinion writing, interspersed with budget meetings for the coming year. August is a vacation month, and a welcome escape from the heavy early-summer work load and Washington's brutal heat.

August 1976 was going to be different. How different I had no way of knowing when Bob and I arrived in Kansas City. If we could just get through convention week, I told myself, we could go away and collapse on a beach somewhere.

Gerald Ford had other plans. Bob has given you his version of that frenetic morning; let me give you mine. In Kansas City we stayed on the seventeenth floor of the Muehlbach Hotel, where Harry Truman had sweated out election night 1948. John and Nellie Connally were next door. Early Thursday morning, August 19, while the rest of the city rubbed sleep from its eyes, reporters gathered in the corridor outside our door.

"Bob," I said, "I hear people out in the hall. I'll bet it's the press."

"What?"

"There's a crowd outside the door. I think they're reporters."

"Elizabeth, put your ear up against the door. See if you can hear what they're saying."

At first I could make out only a low, indistinct babble. Then I heard Bob's name. Someone else repeated it.

The phone rang. It was ABC's Bob Clark, wanting Bob to verify the news.

"What news?" Bob asked.

"Come on, Senator. Are you kidding me? I've been told that you're Ford's pick."

Ford's pick. The words barely registered. Just enough to send alarms out in all directions. My emotions were definitely mixed. Of course I was proud of Bob and happy about his achievement, but I also felt that a distinct change was about to occur for a couple only recently married. The honeymoon was over.

Within minutes, a group of Secret Service agents came to our room to slip a protective cordon around us and bestow official names. For the next ten and a half weeks, we were Ramrod and Rainbow. Thoughts of a tropical beach were dropped for more immediate concerns. Who would place Bob's name in nomination? Who would second it? Where could we find someone to translate his speech for hearing-impaired viewers?

Reporters had some questions of their own. "I think my own career is a pretty good testament to my belief that women should be able to develop their full potential," I told them. "Above all, they should be able to *choose,* whether it's a career, or the role of homemaker and mother, or both. Choice is what it's all about."

Early in our relationship, Bob had encouraged me to continue my career. Now outside forces threatened to take matters out of our hands. Briefly, it appeared as though I might be forced to resign from the FTC. Deputy White House counsel Ed Schmults did some hasty research and reported back that a leave of absence would satisfy legal requirements under the Hatch Act. I wrote a letter to the commission that same day, returning my post–August 19 salary to the Treasury to be applied to the national debt.

I tried unsuccessfully to reach my family in Salisbury. Newsmen had more luck. By midafternoon they were traipsing through the backyard at 712 South Fulton Street and snapping pictures inside the house. Finally I got through to my brother in Charlotte. He was all ready to head to Salisbury and protect our elderly parents from the demands of instant celebrity.

"You know," I told him, "they've never been through anything like this before." Neither had I.

That night the bands playing and the roar of the crowd

made me forget for a moment polls showing us thirty-three points behind the opposition. They were enough to make me dismiss the Democrats' five-week head start and GOP organizational unpreparedness caused by a divisive primary fight. Maybe we *could* pull off the biggest upset in the history of American politics. The mood carried over into the next day. Ford decided to launch his campaign immediately in Bob's hometown of Russell, Kansas. It was a symbolic way of reassuring farmers that the President meant what he said when he promised no future grain embargoes.

It was also one of the emotional highlights of my life. The logistics of mounting a presidential visit on twenty-four hours' notice are daunting, especially when the nearest airport capable of handling Air Force One is seventy miles from the scene of the rally. Somehow, everything came together.

There were ten thousand people packed tightly on the courthouse lawn when we arrived a few minutes after noon. The Russell High School band played "It's a Grand Old Flag." Volunteers handed out hot dogs, and supporters waved home-made signs welcoming the first President to visit Russell since Theodore Roosevelt stopped off at the train depot one day in 1905. Elderly people sat in lawn chairs down front, and farmers in pickup trucks completed a scene straight out of a Norman Rockwell poster.

August 19 would have been Doran Dole's seventy-sixth birthday. This made the occasion all the more poignant. Bob began his speech by describing the telephone call from the President and how he had weighed his response "for about one minute." He recalled his county attorney days, and an even more distant era when Russell rallied around him when he most needed help.

"I am proof that a person today can come from a small town and doesn't need wealth and material things to move ahead," he said. Looking out over the crowd, he saw familiar faces from an earlier time. They touched something deep inside him, something he could not hold back.

"If I have had any success," he told his audience, "it is because of the people here. I can think of all the times the people of Russell helped me when I needed help." He paused, and put one hand to his forehead. Tears rolled down his face. When he spoke again, it was in a near-whisper.

"That was a long time ago, and I thank you for it."

I had a catch in my own throat as I sat ten feet away, wanting to go to him. Glancing over at President Ford, I saw him almost imperceptibly shake his head. But an instant later Ford himself rose to his feet, leading ten thousand people in a spontaneous ovation.

The moment passed as quickly as it came. But from then on, observers began to describe what they called "a new Bob Dole." He was the same man I had known for four years.

After the rally, Bob's mother invited the President to her house for some refreshment before the Fords went on to Vail. Someone had taken visitors through the house earlier in the day and had forgotten to put Bina's spare key back in its usual place. After a frantic search, I found the missing key behind a drainpipe, but not before a crowd of onlookers gathered to see the President of the United States locked out of the house whose doormat read, "Welcome to the Home of the Doles."

BOB

Russell's pleasure was not universally shared. Tom Wicker described me in the *New York Times* as "the most distinguished Republican vice presidential nominee since William E. Miller." The *Washington Post* said I was "Ronald Reagan's gift to the party." Considering how much conservatives longed for the vanquished challenger, the *Post*'s observation was more complimentary than critical.

Post columnist Mary McGrory was typical of Washington pundits who expressed "shock and dismay" over my selection. Others reacted in their own way. Minnesota GOP Chairman Chuck Slocum thought I was a combination of Bob Taft and Don Rickles.

"We've got righteous Jimmy, dull Walter and stuffy Jerry," said Slocum. "At least Bob Dole will add some zip to the campaign."

Carter pleaded indifference to my nomination, telling re-

porters in Plains, Georgia, on August 20, that he would let
Walter Mondale or his press secretary, Jody Powell, respond to
any charges I might make. Having established his above-the-
battle stance, Carter unsheathed a silk-covered stiletto. He
would not make an issue out of Watergate, because, he said,
the American people were well aware which party was responsible for the scandal.

One reporter asked Carter whether he was being fair in his
constant referrals to "the Nixon-Ford Administration." Wasn't
that only an attempt to link the incumbent with "an unsavory
name?"

"It's not my fault that Nixon's unsavory," Carter retorted.

In the same press conference, Carter said that in my 1974
campaign against Bill Roy I had called Roy an "abortionist."
(This was news to me.) "But I don't begrudge Senator Dole or
any other candidate the right to be combative and aggressive
and to raise issues that might be politically advantageous to
them."

Carter's performance that day was typically adroit. Democratic rivals had spent a frustrating primary season trying to
put a glove on the Georgian who placed emphasis on the at-
mospherics of trust to the exclusion of substantive policy discussions. Now it was my turn to shell a few peanuts, to see
whether Carter could catch hardball as well as he pitched.

Ford spelled this out on August 26, when I went to Vail
for a series of strategy sessions. He and his top advisers had
decided that the incumbent should stay in the White House
Rose Garden for as much of the campaign as possible and that
I would be sent out into the briar patch, to rally Republicans,
placate farmers, and poach on Carter preserves in the South
and border states.

"You're going to be the tough guy," Ford said.

There were only sixty-seven days until November 2, and I
had no campaign organization in place, no staff, no schedulers.
The latest Harris Poll said we had to convert 350,000 voters a
day in order to win. The first step was to reassemble a Republican Party shattered by Watergate. Fortunately, there were
plenty of issues to draw on. Carter was pledged to carry out the

Humphrey-Hawkins Act, a legislative witches' brew that committed the federal government to tax and spend whatever was necessary to get the jobless rate down to 3 percent. By contrast, the Republican platform called for an end to deficit spending and proposed tax cuts to stimulate private investment and job formation. Democrats demanded a comprehensive, federally funded program of national health insurance; we favored catastrophic insurance extended through private companies.

The most striking differences were over defense. Carter-Mondale wanted an immediate cut of five to seven billion dollars in the Pentagon budget. At a time when the Kremlin was in the midst of a massive military buildup, we believed that would send the worst possible signal to the men in Moscow.

One day after Carter spoke to American Legion convention delegates in Seattle, I gave them a very different message. Better to spend billions for defense, I told the Legionnaires, than to lose one life on a foreign battlefield. On the highly charged issue of what to do with Vietnam draft evaders and deserters, I contrasted Carter's offer to issue a blanket pardon with Ford's conditional amnesty in which draft evaders would perform public-service jobs in order to regain U.S. citizenship.

Later that week, I dogged Carter's trail again, catching him in a flip-flop on grain embargoes at the Iowa State Fair. I tried to dent the Georgian's hold on his home region by linking him to the Democratic platform and to big-spending Democrats in Congress, his running mate included. Walter Mondale's 1975 rating of 94 percent from Americans for Democratic Action gave me plenty to talk about in Dixie.

Mondale and I had served together on the Senate Finance Committee. Our differences in committee as well as on the floor made us one pair of senators who could be absent for months and never be missed; in most cases when I voted yes, he voted no, and vice versa. Mondale's opposition to military spending was as reflexive as his support for domestic programs like Humphrey-Hawkins and court-ordered busing. He had voted against the antiballistic-missile system, the B-1 bomber, the Trident submarine and the cruise missile.

Meanwhile, I was busy putting together a campaign orga-

nization. Before leaving Kansas City, I had reached out to the
Reagan camp. Lyn Nofziger accepted an invitation to go on the
road with me. "We won't win," he told a friend at the time,
"but we'll have a lot of fun." Larry Speakes came over from the
White House, where he had been press secretary Ron Nessen's
deputy, to handle the journalistic road show. Noel Koch, a
deputy assistant secretary of defense and Nixon speechwriter,
took on writing chores. Dave Owen was my White House liaison and all-around troubleshooter. Besides Nofziger, old Reagan hands like Charles Black and Paul Russo pitched in. So did
Tully Plesser, a New York–based pollster who had helped out
in my 1974 Senate race.

There's a simple formula for national campaigning: up before dawn each day, into a motorcade to catch an airplane
waiting to whisk you to three media-market cities, more motor-
cades and flashing lights—anything to get a cameraman to snap
your picture or a network anchorman to put you on the evening
news for ten seconds.

Nothing about the 1976 campaign was simple. Things
were done on short notice, like turning the plane around in
midair one day and heading for Denver, where Ronald Reagan
and I had a pleasant if unexceptional meeting. I was willing to
go the extra mile—in this case about five hundred extra miles
—to get Reagan and his followers to support the ticket more
actively.

Politics is not a job for insecure people. On the night of my
nomination, half of America didn't know my name. The other
half thought I was something to drink. On the campaign trail I
was variously called Bob Doyle, Bob Dale and Bob Daley. I
spent an hour one morning stranded at a horse farm in Lexington, Kentucky. I like horses, but they don't vote. In Boston the
press bus got stuck coming out of a tunnel. Later that same day
I was scheduled to visit a carnival in Trenton, New Jersey.

At Trenton the plan called for me to ride in a car escorted
by an American Legion honor guard around an oval track next
door to where the carnival had set up shop. Advance men dis-
appeared behind the stadium stands to rustle up a crowd. They
came back discouraged. Everyone was having too much fun at
the carnival and no one wanted to stop throwing money into

bottles to listen to some politician. By the time I got to the stadium it was practically deserted, so I rode around waving at empty bleachers for ten minutes. The one good thing about the event was that it came too late in the day to make the network news broadcasts.

At the Southern 500 stock-car race in Darlington, South Carolina, I maneuvered myself next to Jimmy Carter, who was also there that day. "I'm more of a stock-car fan than I was yesterday," I assured the huge crowd. Big deal. Carter one-upped me by promising to invite all the drivers to the White House.

"It's going to be a busy place," I remarked.

Early in September, we got our first real break: Carter's famous interview with *Playboy* magazine in which he said he had "lusted in his heart" and in which he also harshly criticized Lyndon Johnson. Johnson was still revered in Texas, and polls showed Carter's once commanding lead in the West and the border South melting away.

Just when the campaign was shifting our way, a mid-September flap arose over press reports that I had received an illegal 1970 campaign contribution from Gulf Oil lobbyist Claude Wild, Jr. To back up my denials of any illegality, I invited the *Washington Post*'s Walter Pincus to review my past campaign records. Pincus spent two days poring over papers on Capitol Hill. The story collapsed. But in the meantime I had suffered through a week of intensely critical reporting.

Nelson Rockefeller offered some friendly counsel. "I never read anything about myself in the papers," he told me during a swing through upstate New York. "My advice to you is to do the same. Otherwise you'll spend half the day reading the criticism and the other half reacting."

Rockefeller gave me more than advice. The Vice President sent Jerry Waters from his staff to smooth out a ragged scheduling operation. This freed me to concentrate on Carter, Mondale, the Farm Belt and discontented Republicans. On September 18 I met with Ford and his campaign manager, Jim Baker, at the White House. The President wanted me to take the gloves off and really go after Carter. He wasn't the only one. That same week, *Time* assessed my performance so far as surprisingly tame. Instead of "a tabby cat," said *Time,* voters expected a display of slashing partisanship. When were they going to see it?

If I'd had my way, the answer would have been no time soon. My near-defeat in 1974 had led me to some soul-searching. Ideally, 1976 should have been an affirmative campaign, a party-building exercise taking advantage of the national optimism surrounding the Bicentennial and Ford's restoration of trust to a tarnished presidency. I would have liked to make more appearances in urban neighborhoods, on college campuses and among audiences rarely reached by Republicans. But the first principle of campaign scheduling is that you go where the ducks are, particularly when you're far behind.

Occasionally, there were times when everything clicked and the campaign soared to emotional heights. I'll never forget the day in late September when I visited with disabled members of what I called "my community" in Hollywood, Florida. I referred to myself in terms similar to the ones used at the Democratic convention by Barbara Jordan, whose spellbinding oratory and articulate performance on the House Judiciary Committee that voted Richard Nixon's impeachment had thrust her onto the national stage.

According to Jordan, the greatest thing about the convention that nominated Carter-Mondale was her own highly visible leadership position. She had come full cycle; black America had come full cycle.

"And I would like to think," I told the group in Florida, "that when I stood up in Kansas City I might have given hope to someone, some person or group of persons, who had reservations about whether anyone with a handicap could succeed. If you can use me in the next six weeks, use me. If you can use me in the next four years, that would be even better."

ELIZABETH

Bob had commented that our life together would never be dull, but there was no way he or anyone else could have prepared me for the fall of 1976.

Members of the Federal Trade Commission were supposed
to be apolitical. Joining the FTC was like taking the veil. The
first inkling that all this would change for me came in Seattle a
few days after the convention. While Bob addressed the American Legion convention, I visited the FTC's regional office,
where I stood out like a fifth ace in the pack. According to the
commission's scrupulous code, I was no longer a government
professional. As of August 19, I was the wife of the Republican
candidate for Vice President.

There was nothing in my past experience to ground me in
politics. I had never given a political speech. And with so many
demands over the previous weeks, with a staff to hire and a
schedule to arrange, the last thing in the world anyone had
thought about was what the candidate's wife should say.

I wasn't presumptuous enough to think the voters were
electing me, any more than they were deciding between Betty
Ford and Rosalynn Carter. They wanted to know what Ford
and Carter would do for America, not what I thought about
the Humphrey-Hawkins Act or the Angolan resistance. But as
an independent career woman, and an FTC commissioner with
ten years of government experience, I wasn't going to spend the
whole campaign answering reporters' questions with a demure
"I don't do issues." *I did do issues.* Six days a week. The genie
couldn't be put back into the bottle.

It was an awkward situation all the way around. Bob jokingly referred to me as his Southern strategy. But for the first
week or so after the convention I pretty much played the traditional political wife, standing at my husband's side and smiling
for the cameras.

I was caught between conflicting emotions. Bob wanted
me to campaign with him. Hoping to give whatever moral support I could at what was bound to be a difficult time, I didn't
want to leave the side of the man to whom I'd been married less
than a year. But I also agreed with campaign veterans who
downplayed media interest in candidates' wives and families.
At the same time, I was under pressure from women at the
Republican National Committee and elsewhere whose political
activism predated my own. The best way to help Bob, they
argued, was to carve out a separate campaign schedule and

cover as much territory as possible. My instincts told me they were right, so Bob and I attempted a compromise. We went to the same cities, split off on separate agendas and joined up again in the evening.

One thing about a campaign. You cherish more than ever the rare moments you have together. When the door of your hotel room closes behind you, you kick off your shoes and savor the exquisite feeling that for the next few hours your life is your own. And certainly, after sixteen hours of speechmaking and press interviews, you are not going to review the intricacies of Bob's farm policy.

Instead, I listened to his speeches closely for a few days, got the gist of what he was saying and where he was putting his emphasis. Finally I told everyone that the time had come for me to go out on my own. Bob thought it was worth a try. But he also gently warned me not to expect too much media attention.

One of my earliest stops was Baton Rouge, Louisiana. I'll never forget it. Bob was due to pass through town the very next day. When he arrived, he was handed a local newspaper whose front page featured four pictures of his wife—with news stories discussing the issues. Real issues.

"Well," I asked him that night, "what do you think now?"

"Why aren't you headed for the airport?" he said.

Not all my events were headline-makers. I fed peanuts to an elephant in Huntsville, Alabama, joined a kazoo band in Edwardsville, Illinois, went to a Bohemian mushroom festival in a Chicago suburb and later that same day marched in Newark's Columbus Day parade. It was like a civics lesson you can't possibly get in the classroom or in Washington.

Politics blends high drama with low comedy. In Houston, Nellie Connally told me of having been struck by camera equipment as eager newsmen rushed to tape her husband for the evening news. She had once been left behind in a strange city when the Connally campaign express roared off without her.

That has never happened to me, but I have had my share of mishaps. I don't like surprises. I want to prepare for things, to organize and, if possible, to manage a situation. Controlling a national political campaign, especially one put together as hastily as Ford-Dole in 1976, is out of the question. It's like riding a tiger. You hold on for dear life or else you get devoured.

You learn to improvise. Once, asked to deliver a speech to a West Palm Beach, Florida, chamber of commerce, I discovered that I was booked instead into a joint appearance with Jimmy Carter's son Jack. I had thirty seconds—the amount of time it took to escort me to the podium—to adjust to the change in format.

On another day in Florida I covered five cities, giving speeches and press conferences and visiting senior citizens and Republican women's groups. Everywhere I assured my audience that win, lose or draw in November, I had no intention of living off a dole. By this time I had taken up Bob's habit of skipping meals to circulate through the crowd and thank people for coming. At lunch that day, a woman took my hand and asked me where in the world I got the energy to do what I was doing.

"I get it from you," I told her.

It was true. Something about a campaign sweeps you up on an emotional current and hurtles you from one situation to the next. That something is the high-voltage support that charges a live audience and inspires a candidate. I hope the day never comes when television substitutes for face to face contact with the voters.

The televised debate has become a standard of modern presidential campaigns. More citizens watch these encounters in a single evening than turn out to see a candidate in six months of whistle-stopping, which explained the Ford camp's eagerness to lock horns with Jimmy Carter. Coming out of Kansas City so far behind, White House strategists hoped the debates would level the field of competition overnight. They viewed a one-on-one debate as Ford's best shot at making Carter the issue.

Also, 1976 was the first time vice-presidential candidates debated each other on television. Ford suggested it within twenty-four hours of Bob's nomination, and Bob agreed. But as the October 15 confrontation in Houston drew near, it seemed to me that too little time had been set aside for preparation. We had originally planned to prepare one afternoon a week, but that had gone by the boards because of increasingly heavy travel schedules. Bob was inundated with briefing books detailing Mondale's Senate voting record. I doubted whether anyone could master a foot and a half of paper while campaigning all day and half the night.

Three days before the debate, Bob flew to Marysville, Tennessee, to keep a campaign commitment to an old friend, Howard Baker. On the way back to Washington, I was determined that Bob would have a little peace and quiet in which to work. I didn't want him badgered by a whole lot of people with magic formulas for victory in Houston. But they wouldn't leave him alone. So I did something I had thought about doing for a long while: I blew my stack and ordered everyone out of Bob's private compartment. Unfortunately, there was nothing I could do about the bad cold Bob had picked up in Tennessee, or the briefing books that continued to arrive.

BOB

Since Vice Presidents don't make policy, vice-presidential candidates have to be careful how they make news. I discovered this for myself after telling an audience at an agricultural event in Mankato, Minnesota, that if Ford was reelected he would raise farm price supports. Later, the President informed me in unmistakable terms that from then on he would make any such announcements himself.

As far as the debate went, I didn't expect the seventy-five-minute clash with Mondale in Houston's Alley Theater to generate many headlines. I knew it would be a chance to score some points with groups crucial to Republican success. I went in with a simple strategy: to appeal to conservatives by criticizing Mondale's voting record and going after Carter as a litmus liberal whose promises would add a hundred billion dollars to the federal budget, forcing higher taxes while short-changing military preparedness.

Shortly before eight-thirty, Mondale and I shook hands and took up our places at lecterns precisely seven and a half feet apart. Unlike the earlier debates between Carter and Ford, the Houston ground rules allowed for a freewheeling exchange on any number of topics. In my opening statement, I set the tone of the evening by praising Ford's proven leadership, raising doubts about Carter's qualifications and labeling Mondale a big spender on everything but national defense.

Mondale, besides promoting the usual Democratic shopping list of federal programs, promised to play a major role in government reorganization. I responded by saying that I hoped his government shake-up wouldn't be patterned on Jimmy Carter's reorganization of Georgia's executive branch, in which the state Agriculture Department had been reorganized right out of existence.

The early stages of the debate seemed to drag. Mondale looked nervous, and I should have smiled more. (At least, that's what the campaign consultants said afterward.) But I felt pretty good about the way it was going. I hammered away at Carter's spending plans and the renewed inflation that was sure to ravage low-income Americans if even half the Democratic platform was enacted. I suggested that Carter needed three presidential debates so that he could state his three positions on each issue.

But I tripped up badly later on. In briefing books from the Republican National Committee there were references to the GOP as the party of peace. I had used the line many times in the past. Out in Kansas, and all through the Middle West, Democrats like to accuse Republicans of causing depressions, and Republicans respond by pointing out the wars we've gotten into under Democratic administrations. This is treacherous ground. I should have been more careful in approaching it at all, but I resented the fact that Carter and Mondale were scoring points by referring to "the Nixon-Ford Administration." They also blamed Nixon and Ford for Vietnam, which is at the least a highly novel interpretation of history. I should have kept the two issues separate. But I jumbled them together, arguing that Republicans generally were no more to blame for the excesses of Nixon and his courtiers than Democrats were to blame for the 1.6 million American lives lost in twentieth-century warfare.

As a result, I left the impression that I thought both World

Wars, Korea and Vietnam were "Democrat wars." Mondale jumped at the chance to label me a hatchet man. For good measure he tossed in a jab at Ford's pardon of Nixon, and said I had "probably the worst record" in the Senate on tax loopholes.

I don't know how many people Mondale and I kept away from the Friday-night football game, but no one said we put them to sleep. When the debate ended, the President called me. "Your performance was superb," Ford said. "You hit hard but fair." Nelson Rockefeller phoned with similar words. So did Mel Laird and others who were not usually my staunchest admirers.

Bob Healy, writing in the *Boston Globe,* said I had been assigned Jimmy Carter as a target and had "chewed him up." Polls taken immediately after the Houston confrontation showed a 6 percent surge of support for Ford-Dole among the voter audiences we had targeted. Everywhere I went, the crowds were noticeably larger and more enthusiastic than before. Yet to this day all that some voters remember about my 1976 campaign is a single remark, a poorly phrased argument that canceled out ten weeks of constructive campaigning and overshadowed the thirty-one points we made up in the polls. Given television's power to form instant identities, I had no reason to expect anything different. I was in the big leagues now and would be held accountable for whatever I said, just as Jimmy Carter would be for his reference to "ethnic purity" and Jerry Ford was for asserting that Eastern Europe was free of Soviet domination.

The only way to justify a mistake is by learning enough to avoid its repetition. Win, lose or draw, the 1976 vice-presidential debate taught me to think twice before saying something that might appear insensitive or call into question the patriotism of any American. There is nothing partisan about war or the sacrifice that attends it.

I saw Ronald Reagan again during the first week of October in New Haven, Connecticut, where he was visiting his son at Yale. Reagan's Secret Service agents were gone, and in place of the dozens of newsmen who a few weeks earlier had hung on every word he said there was a single local reporter. It was a poignant reminder that power in a republic is a temporary thing.

In the campaign's closing weeks, I concentrated on the agricultural Midwest and South, where polls showed us gaining fast. After telling farmers that the original grain embargo had been caused in part by labor leader George Meany's endorsement of longshoremen's demands to utilize U.S. shipping capacity, I added that if Carter was elected the White House would have two hot lines—one to Moscow, the other to AFL-CIO headquarters.

The stretch run to the election was frenzied. A typical day began with a walking tour of Sioux City stockyards in a snowstorm. Lunch was in Corpus Christi, dinner in Louisiana's bayou country. In a voice cracking with fatigue, I reminded voters that our candidate's name wasn't Ford-Nixon; it was Jerry Ford.

Everywhere I cited Ford's accomplishments: cutting inflation in half, reducing unemployment, maintaining a trade balance with foreign nations in the black, and, most important of all, restoring public trust in government. Jimmy Carter talked trust; Jerry Ford had earned it.

Airport for airport, rally for rally, Ford matched my pace, visiting seventeen states during the campaign's last ten days. On the Thursday before election day, he called me at 5 A.M. Mountain Standard Time with news too good to put off. A new Gallup Poll that showed us in the lead for the first time all year would be published that weekend. The one-point margin was as thin as December ice, and other surveys by Harris and Roper continued to show Carter clinging to a slim advantage.

Still, the momentum was with us. "I know you must be exhausted," Ford told me. "But we're going to make it, Bob. You're doing a great job. Keep it up, and I'll see you back here on Tuesday."

On Monday, the first of November, I campaigned in five Midwestern states. It was a fitting climax to a ten-week odyssey covering forty-four states and 62,000 miles. As I flew back over the eastern half of the United States, the skies were cloudless. I wanted to believe that Gallup was right—but there were other, less encouraging numbers that weekend.

Government statistics released in the campaign's closing days suggested at least a pause in the economic recovery. Inflation appeared to be reheating, and unemployment hovered stubbornly close to 8 percent. The new reports could not have come at a worse time. According to Lou Harris, the percentage of voters who credited Ford with pulling the country out of recession slipped to 47–41 negative that last weekend. We also took a pounding on the Nixon pardon. In a single week, public disapproval of Ford's action had widened from 55–34 to 57–32. That might not seem like much, but in such a close race the slightest shift could make the difference in key states of the industrial Midwest and the border South.

On the morning of November 2, a Secret Service agent confidently said, "You're going to win. You're never going to drive a car again." Publicly, I predicted a sharp drop in the price of peanut butter and a corresponding rise in pineapple futures. But I had been through too many campaigns to feel as optimistic as I sounded.

ELIZABETH

We spent election night with the Fords at the White House. Bob detected trouble early on. Carter's sweep of the South sealed our fate, and sent us on our way home long before the result was official.

Hope dies hard, however. As late as Wednesday afternoon, Bob asked me to call Bryce Harlow about voting irregularities. He wanted Harlow's opinion about doing a recount that might reverse Carter's razor-thin margins in Ohio, Missouri and Hawaii. Ford scotched the idea.

That afternoon Bob got up from a sickbed (he had finally given in to a bad case of flu) to host a party for reporters who had covered the campaign. He was interviewed by Barbara Walters, who boldly inquired whether he thought he was re-

sponsible for Ford's defeat. Bob answered her with more restraint than I would have been able to muster.

"Elizabeth," he told me a few days later, "I couldn't have
gotten through this without you. We gave it our best shot.
That's all that counts. Now there's just one thing for me to do,
and that's go back and be the best United States senator I can."
As usual, my husband looked forward, not back. There was no
depression, no second-guessing. He must have felt an ache to
come so far and finish so close, but he concealed it with a
stoicism rooted in his hospital days and the buttoned-down
emotions of Kansas.

BOB

If you want to find out who your friends are, lose an election. For the first few days after November 2, I was consoled
by sympathetic messages. But as it dawned on people just how
close we had come to winning, they needed to blame someone.
Barbara Walters wasn't the only one to assign me responsibility
for the loss. It's said that when you're the cutting edge of a
campaign, *somebody* has to get cut. I tried to make a joke out
of that saying, telling people that I had been told to go for the
jugular and I did—my own.

One day I was alone in the Senate dining room when Hubert Humphrey sat down at my table. "How are you doing,
Bob?"

"Fine, Hubert. I'm hanging in there."

"Bob, I've been where you are," Humphrey said. "I know
what you're going through. Some people around this town have
awfully short memories. They forget how much ground you
made up in the polls. All they can say is, 'Why didn't you carry
Ohio?' Well, you did everything they wanted you to. They assigned you the Farm Belt, and you carried it for them. You did
one hell of a job."

Humphrey's old antagonist, Richard Nixon, called with a
similar message. "It's scapegoating time," he said. As if I needed
reminding. Nixon told me to forget about the Monday-morning

quarterbacks and the temptation to dwell on what might have been. Move on: that was Nixon's message. Before hanging up he reminded me that I had an obligation to support the man who would be President after January 20, 1977.

During the campaign, I had been pretty rough on Jimmy Carter. Over the next four years I wouldn't shy away from criticizing the Carter Administration's handling of economic and foreign policy. For all his talents, and they included a formidable intellect, Carter seemed oddly miscast in an office that demanded inspiration even more than administration.

Carter scattered his energies, trying to do too much on too many fronts. I also think he misread public disenchantment with the so-called imperial presidency. Walking down Pennsylvania Avenue on Inauguration Day, selling the presidential yacht *Sequoia,* carrying his own bags, wearing a cardigan sweater for a nationally televised address—these were all minor bits of political theater, but as image-making they trivialized the most powerful office in the world. Presidents from Franklin Roosevelt to Ronald Reagan have demonstrated that the American people have a hard time accepting the leader of the free world as one of the boys.

I prefer Harry Truman's view. Truman never forgot where he came from. But no matter what those around him thought of Harry S. Truman of Independence, Missouri, he never let them forget that the office he held deserved their respect.

Carter's failure to adopt the folkways of Capitol Hill was less crippling than his philosophical isolation from the Democratic Old Guard. Elected without a strong ideological base, he put all his eggs into the basket of competence. This made him doubly vulnerable when events slipped out of control and the early promise of Carter's leadership gave way to presidential complaints about a national malaise.

History will credit Carter handsomely for his peacemaking efforts in the Middle East. And if Democrats break free of the New Deal's grip and pursue more centrist policies, Carter may yet be seen as a man ahead of his time.

My personal contacts with Carter were limited. Early in the Senate debate over ratification of the Panama Canal treaties which would turn over control of the canal to the Panamanians in the year 2000, he phoned me with a message of thanks for the Ford-Dole ticket's support of the treaties.

"Mr. President," I said, "I don't recall taking a stand."

"Would you like me to send up the Joint Chiefs to brief you?"

"Oh, I'm not that important."

"Oh yes you are," Carter insisted.

His call was premature. When I failed to get what I thought were necessary guarantees of U.S. military and shipping rights through the canal, I opposed the treaties.

Travel can be as broadening for politicians as for other tourists. In the late seventies I was on the road more than Charles Kuralt.

In Jerusalem, I reassured Prime Minister Menachem Begin and Golda Meir that the United States would never pressure Israel to negotiate with the Palestinian Liberation Organization until the PLO renounced terrorism and accepted Israel's right of existence. After replacing New York Senator James L. Buckley on a commission overseeing compliance with the human-rights provisions of the Helsinki Accords, I gained fresh, painful insight into the anguish of Soviet Jews, intellectual dissidents and other victims of official persecution in a society where anti-Semitism is rampant and the only religion tolerated is orthodox Marxism. When the Carter Administration campaigned against human-rights violations in the Third World, I sponsored amendments blocking international lending assistance to the notorious Marxist regimes in Vietnam, Cambodia and Cuba.

I was just as active at home. As the ranking Republican on the Senate's Nutrition and Human Needs Committee, I fought for food stamps, Meals on Wheels, and women and children's nutrition programs. I criticized Carter's energy policies as unduly harsh on the poor, proposed a catastrophic-health-insurance program and introduced a plan to help American families save for a child's college education with the help of federal tax credits.

"Republicans need to make the extra effort to erase the

lingering image of our party as the cadre of the elite, the wealthy, the insensitive," I told an Atlanta gathering of black Republicans. "Our job now is to demonstrate our concern to blacks and others who doubt our sincerity."

Long before Ronald Reagan proclaimed his "New Beginning" in January 1981, I was part of congressional efforts to rewrite the tax code. In 1978 we enacted a major cut in capital-gains taxes. A year later, Colorado freshman William L. Armstrong joined me in proposing a law requiring a balanced federal budget. In losing, we started a dialogue that continues to this day.

I went a step further and introduced a constitutional amendment mandating a balanced budget except during wartime or a congressionally designated emergency. Year after year, it gained greater support as the American economy slowed and middle- and low-income workers suffered the biggest drop in purchasing power since the end of World War II.

Subsequently I tried to amend a bill raising the national debt ceiling with a provision to tie personal-tax rates to changes in the cost-of-living index. Other members of Congress had proposed this most fundamental of tax reforms; Ed Brooke, Jim Buckley and Bob Griffin had all done so before me. But now they were gone. Congress needed to be told that it couldn't go on forever practicing pickpocket government and that's exactly what indexation was meant to halt.

The idea came from economist Milton Friedman, who objected to a tax code that in effect punished workers who received a cost-of-living adjustment or a merit raise. If a raise kicked them into a higher bracket, they found that instead of getting ahead they were lucky just to keep their heads above water. By letting inflation and "bracket creep" do their dirty work, Congress was able to count on a cool $10 billion in extra revenues each year to spend to its heart's content. Barely offsetting this were periodic "tax cuts," usually timed to coincide with election campaigns. These were as fraudulent as they were politically attractive.

Although indexation lacked a Senate majority at the time, the political dialogue was beginning to reflect ideas Ronald Reagan would implement during his presidency. By 1985, tax indexation would be law, and the tax code itself would be poised for massive overhaul. Words once banned from Washington's polite conversation, words like "profit" and "incentive," would guide Congress' reform efforts.

By then, too, I had begun to construct working alliances with my colleagues on both sides of the aisle, putting into practice the lessons of twenty years in Congress. Hubert Humphrey and I became sparring partners on the Senate Agriculture Committee. We also became close friends. Whether it was words or federal dollars, Hubert was never stingy. One morning in committee, when he was well into a stem-winder on how much we needed higher dairy price supports, I pulled a glass of milk from under my desk.

"Here, Hubert, wet your whistle," I said.

For once, even Hubert was speechless.

But not for long. After we had settled on a support price that was less generous than he wanted, Hubert promised me he was going out to his place at Waverly, Minnesota, to tell his cows what Bob Dole had done to them that day in committee.

By the middle of 1977, Hubert was spending less time in Washington and Waverly and more in New York's Memorial Sloan-Kettering Cancer Center. I often talked with him on the phone during his stays there. Some people say the Senate is like a club, but at its best it's more an extended family. It certainly was throughout Hubert's long illness. He had the courage of a prizefighter, and I marveled at the way his spirits never drooped. Before he entered the hospital for the last time, I introduced legislation naming the new Department of Health and Human Services building on the Mall for him.

And when I spoke at the annual Gridiron Dinner in January 1978, I couldn't leave the podium without paying tribute to the happiest warrior in American politics. "He died January thirteenth," I said, "but we don't have to believe that if we don't want to. His legacy ennobles us, teaching us that nothing is so temporary as political animosities, nothing so cleansing as forgiveness, and nothing so vital to the proper governance of this great people as a capacity for laughter and a loving heart. That's really what it's all about."

ELIZABETH

In 1977, the Federal Trade Commission, to which I re-turned after the election, got a new chairman—not Bella Abzug, as had been rumored, but Mike Pertschuk from the Senate Commerce Committee. The scrappy, outspoken Pert-schuk had something in mind to offend practically everyone from advertisers to used-car dealers. When one FTC antitrust ruling threatened to disrupt long-established patterns of bot-tling and distribution in the soft-drink business, industry rep-resentatives asked Congress to review our decision. I wrote the opinion in the case. Bob was part of the Senate majority voting to overturn it.

That June, just prior to a Senate vote on the matter, Bob and I laid out our differences over a proposed consumer-protec-tion agency before the American Advertising Federation. I thought such an agency would consolidate the overlapping work of twenty-six separate consumer offices, and serve as a permanent advocate for economic deregulation inside the fed-eral establishment. He dismissed the CPA as overly intrusive and costly. I couldn't resist a gentle tweaking of my husband's strong pro-business stand. Bob had been delayed, I told the crowd, because he had to stop by the Chamber of Commerce to pick up his speech.

A few days later we repeated our public disagreement on ABC's *Good Morning, America*. As I was listing the reasons why an agency should be established, Bob interrupted.

"If I could just get a word in," he said.

"But I'm trying to make my point," I countered.

I clocked it later, to see whether I really hogged most of the time. (I didn't.) For about twelve minutes the program's host looked on as we went at it. We got a flood of mail after that show. One lady wrote Bob that if he ever wanted to get anywhere in politics, he had better get his wife to shut her mouth. Others praised my courage and endorsed my position. One viewer expressed hope that our "marital differences could be resolved."

Over the next year, Bob moved closer to announcing his

candidacy for the presidency in 1980. As he did so, my professional status became the subject of intense debate. Before I resigned from the FTC in March 1979, Bob and I talked it over at length. He exerted no pressure, unlike some of my women friends who thought I was mistakenly putting my own career on hold for his presidential ambitions.

I didn't see it that way. How could I sit out one of the great experiences of my husband's life, virtually saying to him, "Good luck, Bob, and I'll see you when it's over"? A career is more than a paycheck: it's a series of learning opportunities. A national political campaign, with all its potential for growth as I discussed issues across the country with the press and the public, would be an unparalleled learning opportunity. I didn't rush to judgment. But I had no trouble making up my mind either.

Before leaving the commission, I took care of some unfinished business. In a January 1979 speech to the National Association of Home Builders, I warned of a consumer revolt that was brewing and strongly urged members to have their industry enforce private warranties against shoddy construction and other new-home defects. Or else the Federal Trade Commission would take action.

One California builder at the convention said my comments were as welcome as a belch in a choir loft. But in the years since, more and more builders have committed themselves to providing buyers' protection plans for homeowners. I had singled out in my speech the Home Owners Warranty (HOW) program, which safeguards owners against defects for up to ten years, as an imaginative example of self-regulation. Today, over twelve thousand builders belong to HOW. The number of homes that HOW insures has more than doubled since 1979. I'll take that progress any day over a standing ovation.

BOB

On May 14, 1979, when I went home to Russell to announce my candidacy for President, four thousand people filled the streets around City Hall. On the fringe of the crowd were a few members of the American Agricultural Movement. AAM was used to being on the fringe. Earlier that year it had staged a highly publicized "tractorcade" in Washington to dramatize the plight of farmers and to pressure Congress into giving them immediate relief.

That morning in Russell, AAM posted a pair of signs on tractors parked near the courthouse lawn. "Where Was Bob in Washington?" they read.

It was an ironic complaint. Being in Washington *was* the problem in my 1980 campaign. Part of it, anyway. In truth, it was Ronald Reagan's year. In the meantime I was busy with work on the Finance Committee, while also keeping an eye cocked on home-state politics, where the calendar forced me to weigh running for reelection to the Senate against a long-shot bid for the White House.

Sometimes I think I never really ran for President in 1980. Certainly few people seemed aware of my candidacy at the time. There was a lot of talk about the five M's: money, manpower, management, media and momentum. While my campaign wasn't broke, it was on the verge of qualifying for food stamps, and I was too occupied with Senate business to pay much attention to campaign management. Although I was ranked third in New Hampshire (behind Ronald Reagan and Howard Baker) in the fall of 1979, any momentum I had soon dissolved in the media attention focused on George Bush after he upset Reagan in the Iowa caucuses.

My one hope was to pick up Reagan's supporters if he faltered. Friends questioned the realism of that scenario. Looking back I can see why. In any event, with me in Washington plugging away on legislation, the brunt of the campaigning fell on Elizabeth.

ELIZABETH

One story sums up some of the frustration of the 1980 campaign. Bob was scheduled to speak to a gathering in a key farm state, but at the last minute he was unable to leave the Senate, where he was heavily involved in efforts to repeal the carryover-basis provisions. The language was arcane but the effect of repeal would be to save farmers and small-business owners from paying massive additional taxes.

I offered to speak in his place. Sorry, they wanted Bob Dole or nobody. Wives didn't count. I reminded them that carryover basis was their organization's top legislative priority. "Where would you like him to be?" I bluntly asked one of the group's officials. "Here or in Washington?"

"In Washington, of course."

"Then why can't I take five minutes to describe his farm program and his twenty-seven years of support for farmers on the House and Senate Agriculture Committees?"

"I'm sorry, Mrs. Dole. The rule is no surrogates."

That night Bob flew out, to receive passing mention at a dinner sponsored by the farm group. Before dessert was served he was on his way back to Washington, where he arrived at two in the morning. A few hours later he was on the Senate floor.

BOB

I pulled out of the 1980 presidential contest at about the time Elizabeth passed me in the polls. My Senate race was looming. For a few weeks I toyed with the idea of leaving politics altogether. I imagined my name on the door of some Washington law firm. Nine-to-five days. Weekends around the house. I didn't have to be a senator.

I did want to be a player, though. Back in the Finance Committee that fall, the opening rounds of the Carter–Reagan bout reminded me just how much I would be missing if I walked away from Capitol Hill on the eve of a Republican restoration. After committee members approved a 10 percent personal-tax cut in line with the GOP platform, the Democratic leadership (and the Carter White House) made sure the bill never made it to the Senate floor.

Following Ronald Reagan's nomination at the Detroit convention, I concentrated on my Senate reelection fight. Elizabeth joined the Reagan campaign as head of Voter Groups for Reagan-Bush and traveled extensively as part of a GOP Truth Squad taking aim at Jimmy Carter's record. On the night of November 4, Reagan's landslide showed up early. The same was true of my own win among the voters of Kansas.

The real election drama in 1980 centered on an unexpected race for control of the Senate. For Howard Baker to replace Democrat Robert Byrd of West Virginia as Majority Leader, Republicans had to pick up eight new seats. Before that Tuesday, almost no one in Washington expected a shift of such magnitude. But as the night went on, and one incumbent Democrat after another tumbled in the Reagan onslaught, the improbable became the inevitable.

Around two in the morning, Baker called me.

"I've been checking races around the country," he said, "and if current trends hold, there's going to be a Republican Senate next January. And you're going to be chairman of the Finance Committee, Bob."

"That's great news, Howard. One thing, though—who's going to tell Russell Long?"

On Wednesday morning, I met the press in Topeka. Reporters expecting an ebullient performance were disappointed. One even complained that I hadn't cracked a single joke. Why?

"All of a sudden," I told him, "I realize that we're going to have to deliver. And it's a lot harder to deliver than it is to criticize."

The campaigning wasn't over yet. Between election day and the inaugural, Reagan had a Cabinet to choose, and a government to staff. Senators were generous with advice. One Western colleague of mine suggested names for eight Cabinet positions. Asked by the Reagan transition team which of his candidates was the most important, he replied, "All eight."

I had a contender of my own. He was John R. Block, a hog farmer who doubled as director of the Illinois Department of Agriculture. I thought it would be a welcome change to have a farmer with dirt on his hands running federal farm programs.

Elizabeth had brought Block to my attention. She had come to know him during the Reagan campaign as an articulate spokesman for free-market farm policies.

Several weeks went by, and one slot after another was filled. Treasury went to a Wall Streeter named Donald T. Regan, State to Alexander M. Haig, Commerce to a Connecticut CEO named Malcolm Baldrige, Defense and Justice to Californians who were also longtime associates of the new President. The Reagan Administration was beginning to look positively bicoastal.

I took a map of the United States and drew a big red circle around the middle. I sent it to my colleague Paul Laxalt, a close friend of Reagan's who was helping with the Cabinet selections. The map was accompanied by a note that said, "Paul, that blank space is what's referred to as the Midwest."

A few days later John Block was named Secretary of Agriculture.

CHAPTER EIGHT

Team Players

BOB

*At first I intended to become a student of the
Senate rules and I did learn much about them,
but I soon found that the Senate had but one
fixed rule . . . which was to the effect that the
Senate would do anything it wanted to do
whenever it wanted to do it. When I had
learned that, I did not waste much time on the
other rules, because they were so seldom
applied.*

—CALVIN COOLIDGE

In January 1981, Republicans took control of the Senate
for the first time in a quarter century. For me and others in the
new majority it meant a chance to show that we could deliver
more than speeches. Instead of railing against government, we
were the government. When you're in the minority, you have
the option of standing on the sidelines; when in doubt, you can
always vote no and put out a press release. This may be enough
to stay in office, but it isn't leadership.

Part of the challenge we faced was to make the creaky,
tradition-encrusted Senate respond to the conservative mandate
of 1980. It wouldn't be easy, since Senate rules are hand-

tailored for obstruction and delay. It's easier to keep something from happening there than to make it happen. And for all the speechmaking and debate on the floor, most of the real discussion takes place off the floor. Outside forces tend to set our agenda, forcing members to react more than they anticipate. If the Senate ever resembled a club, those days are past. Elizabeth has pointed out that members' wives are probably closer to one another than are their husbands. Partisanship and ambition can frustrate collegiality, and it's tough to find time in which to nurture close friendships.

Some senators choose to observe the political process more than they participate in it. Some are reflexive presidential supporters, taking their cue from the West Wing of the White House. Some are themselves potential Presidents. Nearly all are dedicated men and women, required to master subjects of enormous complexity under intense pressure and constant deadlines. Seniority is far less important today for a senator's advancement than is plain hard work. To make your mark, you have to know what you're talking about, be honest with your colleagues and live up to your commitments. In the Senate as anywhere else, you become a leader by knowing where you want to go, and by persuading others to follow you.

Ronald Reagan came to Washington with that kind of personal vision, as well as the leadership skills to implement it. His presidency would be a turning point in public policy and in public attitudes toward conservatism. Before January 1981, American conservatives were caricatured as little old ladies in tennis sneakers looking for Communists under their beds and fluoride in their water. Or we were lampooned as overstuffed men in batwing collars who never did anything for the first time and who were afraid to look at a new moon out of respect for the old.

Reagan changed all that. His conservatism was an instrument for reform, a dynamic substitute for government that measured compassion by what it spent and not by what it bought. Reagan understood that voters didn't want an economist in the White House. They sought leadership to inspire a common effort for the common good. Government is about hope, not budget formulas, aircraft carriers or UDAG grants. Hope had run out for those who were weary of Jimmy Carter's malaise and misery index. Their rejection of the status quo paved the way for the Reagan Revolution.

They had to start the revolution without me. I was out of commission for a few weeks in February and March 1981, recovering from an operation to remove a kidney stone. One day the new President helicoptered out to Walter Reed Army Hospital for a visit and a little missionary work. Reagan brought with him George Gilder's book *Wealth and Poverty,* a provocative history of capitalism that held a place in the library of supply-side economists beside Arthur Laffer's napkins.

I didn't tell Reagan, but I was already reading Gilder's book in my hospital room. I didn't *have* to tell him of my personal loyalty or of my gratitude at being part of a congressional majority for the first time in my career.

Reagan and I had a lot in common. We both grew up in small towns in the Midwest. We preferred straight talk to bureaucratic mumbo-jumbo. We liked a good joke. And we found it hard to stomach the feeling of self-importance that thrives inside the Capital Beltway and regards the rest of America— the real America—as if it were a suburb of Washington, D.C.

I made it clear to Reagan that day at Walter Reed that I would be his ball carrier on the Senate Finance Committee. I might not always be able to run straight downfield. Sometimes I would have to change course a little, follow my own pattern. That was a matter of tactics. What counted was that we were both on the same team.

Nevertheless, I had my doubts about supply-side economics, which seemed to vary depending on who was describing it. Mathematicians aren't the only ones who would like to square the circle. If there was a magic formula that would give us lower taxes, all the benefits voters clamor for and every weapons system on the military's wish list, politicians would have figured it out years ago. The reality is otherwise.

As the new chairman of the Finance Committee, I faced my own reality. Replacing a legendary figure like Russell Long was a bit intimidating. Long had dominated the most powerful committee in the Senate for fourteen years, wielding a gavel as if he had been born to it. In a way he had been: Russell was the son of Louisiana's famous Kingfish, Huey P. Long.

Russell's resourcefulness had led to all sorts of Senate folk tales. There was his 1965 race for majority whip, for example, in which he needed a vote from South Carolina's Olin Johnston. Johnston coveted Russell's Senate desk, which long before Huey owned it had been the property of the Southern firebrand John C. Calhoun. Long casually remarked to Johnston that maybe he would like to have this little piece of history. The desk switched hands; Long won the election. Afterward, someone asked him what Huey would have thought of his tactics. "He would have understood," said Long.

No one understood the Senate better than Russell Long. Scheduling legislative markups, often late at night and close to deadline, was a Long forte. Once, during final consideration of a 1978 tax bill, a junior committee member asked for explanation of the pending roll call. "If everyone knew what they're voting on," Russell cracked, "we'd never get out of here."

He had a point. The Finance Committee oversees roughly half the federal budget. No other arm of Congress touches as many lives or has the potential to ruffle as many feathers. Because members deal with such high-visibility issues as taxes, Medicare, Social Security and trade, getting a quorum is seldom a problem. Long had a reputation for making his committee work on a reasonably bipartisan basis. Filibustering was unheard of, in part due to committee rules that gave the chairman the power to decide when debate had run its course.

Watching Long operate was an education in itself. Some chairmen call meetings; others orchestrate them. Russell was of the latter school. The ability to conciliate differing viewpoints is at least as important for success on Finance as knowledge of the federal tax code. For all the power granted him by formal rules, a chairman leads by consensus, not command. Those were lessons I intended to put to use during my own term in the chairman's seat.

In the early weeks of the Reagan presidency, the committee's eleven Republicans resembled a theatrical cast on opening night—a little nervous and not quite sure of their lines. Our first vote was on Don Regan's nomination to be Secretary of the Treasury. By custom, when the committee staff director runs down the list of members for their votes he calls for the chairman's vote last. This time, Russell Long voted twice—once when his name was read and again when he heard the words "Mr. Chairman."

Realizing his mistake, Long joined in the laughter. "I not only vote with my chairman," he quipped, "I vote for my chairman."

My Senate predecessor, Frank Carlson, once told me about the time he received two telephone calls from the same chamber of commerce within an hour. In the first, someone demanded economy in government; in the second, someone demanded Carlson's support for a federally funded water project. Carlson chuckled over the story and what it said about human nature. David A. Stockman would have missed the humor.

A congressman from a safe district in Michigan when Reagan named him director of the Office of Management and Budget, Dave Stockman was a thirty-four-year-old closet zealot in a Prince Valiant haircut who saw the Reagan Revolution as a national means test. Like nearly everyone who dealt with Stockman, I was impressed by his intellect and numbers-crunching skills. As if he didn't know already, the budget director soon had plenty of evidence to confirm that one man's boondoggle is another's sacred cow, and that it's easier to eliminate waste, fraud and abuse in speeches than in the federal budget-making process.

The White House had decided that its first priority would be reductions in spending. Assuming that Congress went along with nearly $50 billion in proposed budget cuts, the Administration could fulfill its promise to lower personal-tax rates and make it easier for business to write off capital investment.

One of the real heroes of that momentous session was Budget Committee Chairman Pete V. Domenici. Even before Domenici's colleagues formally took up the Reagan budget, storm signals were flying on the House side of Capitol Hill. Representative Jack Kemp of New York and other supply-siders claimed that their 30 percent tax cut would generate enough economic activity to pay for itself. Kemp predicted that any significant effort to reduce federal spending would lead to blood on the floors of Congress.

Kemp was right about one thing. The proposed spending cuts—most of which weren't cuts at all, but merely reductions in planned increases—touched off a public outcry. Some of the most fervent protests came from old friends and allies. The Veterans of Foreign Wars sent me a stiff letter about belt-tightening in veterans' programs and reminding me of the group's support in prior campaigns.

As a life member of the VFW, I have tremendous respect for its members and leadership. Even so, I could hardly conceal my surprise and disappointment when an organization whose members had distinguished themselves by service to their country in the past failed to see the importance of the current battle. My own duty was to control the growth of federal spending. Things finally became so confrontational that I decided it was best to return the VFW's 1980 campaign contribution—five hundred dollars, as I recall.

We made history on a daily, almost an hourly, basis in 1981. One afternoon in May, I excused myself from a discussion of food stamps in the Agriculture Committee to run over to Finance. "We've got a little package of budget cuts to consider," I explained. The "little package" covered twenty-four single-spaced legal-size pages. It sliced $22 billion from federal spending over the next two years, exceeding the White House's own request by a billion dollars.

Cutting taxes should be easier than cutting programs. But when the Finance Committee took up the original White House proposal, the only consensus on supply-side theory was negative. There was widespread agreement on the need to boost personal savings and encourage investment. The same was true of curtailing estate and gift taxes and applying tax indexing to safeguard workers' incomes against inflation.

There was the rub. Even with the budget cuts, there

wouldn't be enough money in the pot to pay for all these specifically targeted incentives and still afford Roth-Kemp in its most generous form. Across the Hill, the House Ways and Means Committee also had a new chairman. Tough as nails and tested in Richard J. Daley's Chicago, where no prisoners are taken and no quarter given, Democrat Dan Rostenkowski had as much to prove to his troops as I did to mine.

After weeks of jousting, I knew Rosty might go along with a two-year, 20 percent tax cut, something I mentioned in a White House meeting with the President, his chief of staff, James A. Baker III, and Baker's pragmatic second, Richard Darman. I was barely back in my office when a White House messenger delivered a note from the President ruling out any such measure.

I told Reagan there was no way I could marshal eleven votes in the Finance Committee for his original version. To break the impasse, the President suggested that committee staff members get together with their counterparts at Treasury and try to work something out. A weekend of round-the-clock negotiations produced a modified tax cut of 25 percent, to be phased in over three installments starting on October 1, 1981. The plan was next broached to conservative Democrats in the House, self-proclaimed Boll Weevils, who along with Republicans were looking for ways to frustrate efforts by the House Democratic leadership to delay, reduce and restructure the Reagan tax cuts. By the time I went public with the new formula at the end of May, it had already been embraced by Reagan loyalists in both houses.

The ground was laid for congressional acceptance of a bill to the White House's liking, despite a last-minute bidding war with Rostenkowski, House Speaker Thomas P. "Tip" O'Neill and others. On July 23, 1981, the House voted to cut personal taxes by 25 percent. A final package that emerged from conference included individual retirement accounts and some generous ornaments that real-estate and other business interests could hang on their Christmas trees. Only later would anyone ask out loud whether the Economic Recovery Tax Act of 1981 was too much of a good thing.

After the vote, Reagan called me from Air Force One en route to the West Coast. The President asked whether there was anything he could do to thank me for my work in committee and on the floor. I said there was. He could telephone my mother, who was in the hospital. Reagan placed the call within an hour. It was a characteristic gesture from one whose political instincts were equaled by his personal thoughtfulness.

ELIZABETH

In December 1980, Jim Baker asked me to become head of the White House Office of Public Liaison.

OPL was descended from an earlier Office of Public Affairs, which had been created during the Nixon Administration by White House counselor Bryce Harlow to tap the energy of organized Americans. As post–New Deal government took on the appearance of a broker state, Harlow saw the possibilities that modern communications offered for mobilizing grass-roots support behind a President's policies. At the press of a button in a Washington office, an avalanche of mailgrams or telephone calls from interested citizens could be directed at members of Congress. Subsequent administrations built on Harlow's original idea.

By Jimmy Carter's time, the Office of Public Affairs had become a mirror of the Democratic coalition, with separate operations addressing issues of concern to women, blacks, Hispanics, labor, business and consumers. Each one had an equal place at the bargaining table where public policy was crafted and past loyalties were rewarded. Under such a setup, White House staffers tended to become caseworkers for the groups they represented. Jim Baker had something else in mind. In Baker's view, we shouldn't be playing divide and conquer—let alone divide and be conquered *by*. Because economic reforms would dominate Ronald Reagan's first year in office, it was essential that Public Liaison rally the organized public around *our* agenda.

My staff would be half as large as that of my Carter Administation predecessor, Anne Wexler. What we lacked in numbers we would make up in versatility. For example, I asked Morton Blackwell to come on board to work with religious organizations and the defense community. As the youngest delegate supporting Barry Goldwater at the 1964 GOP convention, Blackwell had gilt-edged conservative credentials. But as a friendly emissary to right-to-work groups, Morton didn't always see eye to eye with Bob Bonitati, our labor liaison who had been a leader in the professional Airline Pilots Association (AFL-CIO) before joining Public Liaison.

I was fortunate to land Red Cavaney as my deputy. Red had been connected with the White House since the early 1970s, when he helped with Richard Nixon's travels and directed Gerald Ford's advance office. His later forays into issue work brought Cavaney to the attention of Jim Baker, who in turn recommended him to me. Red and I hit it off from our first meeting. Not the least of his professional assets was a range of contacts, developed over his earlier White House stints, that made him a walking Rolodex.

One of my associates once remarked that the atmosphere around the White House was like the men's locker room at Burning Tree Country Club. There is a jackets-off, loose-tie informality that goes with the long hours, the high pressure and the slangy irreverence of the political fraternity. The language is politician's shorthand—colorful and to the point.

One morning at the regular eight o'clock staff meeting in the Roosevelt Room, I took a head count. There were thirty-two men in the room. And me. From grade school through the FTC, I had gotten used to firsts, but this was the first time in my career I ever felt sensitive to being "the woman" in a government setting.

Truth be told, my gender was less an obstacle than my marriage. In those early weeks, a lot of people inside and out of 1600 Pennsylvania Avenue shook their heads in disbelief when they were told that Bob and I didn't regularly exchange strategic information over dinner. After all, they reasoned, he was writing tax laws and I was promoting them as the Administration's number-one priority.

Bob laughed it off, bragging that he got more calls from the White House than anyone on Capitol Hill, even if most of them were from his wife telling him what to put on the stove for dinner.

With me it was different. Business lobbyists would call my office hoping to get me to put in a word on their behalf with the Finance chairman. I had a stock reply: Call the Hill yourself.

I initially hoped to discuss in depth with Bob his work and its implications for the Reagan program. At Jim Baker's request I passed on an occasional message from the West Wing. But I discovered soon enough that Bob didn't want to talk shop extensively at home. He got plenty of that during the day. Just as quickly, I came to share his desire for an oasis from the job, one neutral zone that was more or less off limits to tax-leasing and the latest budget battle with OMB.

An exception occurred in the fall of 1981, when the Reagan Administration was backed against a wall over a controversial multibillion-dollar arms deal with Saudi Arabia. The dispute centered around five sophisticated early-warning planes known as AWACS. Around seven one evening, Red Cavaney, business liaison Wayne Valis and I were parceling out the names of undecided lawmakers, among whom Bob Dole's was prominent. The session came to an abrupt end when I said I was going home to cook dinner.

"Gee, that sounds nice," said Valis.

As a matter of fact, I told them, I planned a thick steak, candlelight—the whole nine yards.

"That's great, Elizabeth," said Valis. "Sounds really romantic. But isn't this a bit early for you to be going home? Don't you want to finish targeting these senators?"

"Wayne," I said, "you don't seem to understand. Tonight, Bob Dole is my target."

When I accepted Public Liaison, I didn't know much about the office or its functions. Today I still think very few people understand what it does, or fully appreciate its vital role in building support for a President's programs.

From prior experience, I had some definite ideas about

how I wanted the office organized. You can rush from meeting to meeting at the White House, confusing activity with achievement. I didn't want to fall into that trap, so I asked my staffers for regular written reports, in part to insure accountability but, more important, to force everyone to think strategically as well as tactically. The reports, in turn, were the basis for what we called Red Flag Warnings. Each week, I collected red flags—prospective political problems—and passed them on to Jim Baker. The system gave us a chance to anticipate trouble and hopefully to avoid it altogether. "There is no better way of solving a problem," I told my staff, "than learning of it early rather than late."

If the White House were a business, Public Liaison would be the marketing and sales division. Our job was to make sure the West Wing's ivory-tower types stayed in contact with the world beyond the gates, that organized groups had their views heard and considered, and that once official policy was determined it was supported. Failing this, we hoped to neutralize opposition at the grass-roots level.

We did our market research by bringing in groups from outside, often to meet with the President. In a typical day these might include the Hispanic Chamber of Commerce, the International Longshoreman's Union, the VFW, Hadassah and the Business Roundtable.

Success at OPL can be measured with two yardsticks. The positive one gauges close legislative victories in which your efforts may have made the difference. Everyone understands winning. The other, less obvious, method is to list all the things that could have gone wrong but didn't, thanks to your efforts. It's like holding your finger in the dike: after two thousand meetings that we set up in the White House, no one has embarrassed the President with an unguarded comment or an outright attack. It's sticking to a script, but allowing enough spontaneity for a genuine two-way communication between the man in the Oval Office and the millions who put him there.

There's something about the White House—what with the marine in formal dress who salutes arriving visitors, the presidential seal over the West Wing entrance, the Secret Service agents and the historical objects lining the hallways leading to the Oval Office—that inspires reverence. It's the closest thing we have to a royal residence.

I was always struck that people who beat their breast in my office would fall into an awed silence the moment they were ushered into Ronald Reagan's presence.

I remember an industrialist who, outside of presidential earshot, voiced stinging criticism of certain budget proposals.

"But that's not what you told the President when you saw him earlier this afternoon," I said.

"Don't be silly, Elizabeth, I wasn't going to say anything *to the President.*"

Sometimes it was hard to get visitors to say anything at all. At one of the first meetings we arranged, the President pointed a finger at a visitor sitting a few feet away and said, "I'd like to hear your views. Tell me what's on your mind." The man went white as a sheet.

Ordinarily, President Reagan had an almost magical way of putting people at ease. I once brought in a white-haired Alabamian named Billy Stimson who represented the National Forest Products Association. Like the President, Stimson had been part of a World War II cavalry unit.

"Mr. President," said Stimson, "as one old cavalryman to another, I just want you to know that our cart has gone off the road and into a ditch. And we are here to ask for your help in putting our poor spavined horse back on his feet."

Stimson's appeal for tax relief and lower interest rates summed up what we were working for in the spring and summer of 1981. From the start, Public Liaison's schedule was dominated by the Reagan economic program. Coincidentally this meant that Bob and I were both coalition-building: while he was seeking fifty-one votes for the Reagan package on Capitol Hill, I was organizing popular support through OPL's far-flung network.

It takes a lot of work to arrange for a paper rainfall to hit Capitol Hill. And timing is essential. The whole effort—sending a message from the White House through trade associations and companies and finally to families and neighbors—takes off and you cross your fingers in hopes it returns to Capitol Hill at just the right moment in Congress' schedule. Fortunately, we had good intelligence sources on the Hill.

By the summer of 1981, Congress was considering the Reagan budget and tax cuts. With the President's superb ability to elicit public support, OPL was able to muster the combined resources of over a thousand trade associations, companies and citizen organizations. In order to test our developing coalition, word was passed that Jim Baker and I would like to see copies of specific legislative alerts being sent to grass-roots America. Then Jim and I followed through with random phone calls to thank organization and business leaders for their help. In no time at all, the Washington underground was carrying the message: Dole and Baker are taking names and want to see your homework.

When the Great Communicator turned up the heat on Congress, we were ready. Organizations like the U.S. Chamber of Commerce, the National Association of Manufacturers and the National Association of Wholesale Distributors blitzed Capitol Hill with mailgrams and postcards timed to coincide with each televised presidential appeal. The National Federation of Independent Business alone spent $175,000 per onslaught.

Dozens of companies included endorsements of the Reagan tax cut in their dividend envelopes. There was no way investors could miss the connection between Ronald Reagan's agenda and future prosperity.

Not everything was smooth sailing. One day OPL sponsored an event addressed by the Reverend Leon Sullivan, a Philadelphia minister who would later enlist corporate America to help end racial exploitation of South African workers. A big man with a voice to match, Sullivan is a shrewd idealist, well versed in how the political game is played. At a Roosevelt Room meeting attended by reporters, he expressed concern over the possible impact of Administration budget cuts on the poor. Yet he also promised to cooperate with White House efforts to plug holes in the social-safety net by utilizing private-sector resources. Sullivan was perfectly sincere, unlike some who said one thing in the Oval Office and another a half hour later on the White House driveway. He didn't mean for his comments to be taken as criticism. But he had no more control over press reaction than I had over the *New York Times* Op Ed page.

Long before Donald Regan invented the White House Shovel Brigade, I oversaw the West Wing Fire Patrol. We put out brushfires before they turned into infernos. Ronald Reagan was our fire chief. I'll never forget the afternoon he dropped by a Rose Garden event with a grin on his face, for our third encounter of that day.

"Elizabeth," he said, "we've got to stop meeting like this."

Day after day, in ceremonial sessions like this one, at substantive meetings on the issues and through behind-the-scenes persuasion, we fashioned a popular mandate for change.

The final test came in July 1981. Three days before the vote, President Reagan went on television with a last-minute call to arms. Over the next seventy-two hours, more than a million messages demanding enactment of the President's three-year, 25 percent tax cut inundated Capitol Hill.

Outflanked, outgunned and outmaneuvered, Tip O'Neill called it "a telephone blitz like this nation has never seen." Another member of O'Neill's leadership team marveled at the orchestration of public opinion. "The deals we could withstand," he told the *Washington Star,* "but not that damn Alexander Graham Bell."

BOB

Practical politics consists of ignoring the facts.

—HENRY ADAMS

For the Reagan Administration, 1982 was a time of testing. Economic recession pushed unemployment to a postwar record. Night after night, television beamed pictures of soup lines and shuttered factory gates into millions of homes. Not since the electronic eye made Vietnam America's first living-room war had viewers seen such a barrage of highly emotional images.

The problem went deeper than that, of course. Financial markets that were made skittish by the rising federal deficit weren't about to reduce interest rates. Resurgent Democrats talked about annulling the 1980 election. It wasn't an idle boast. Unless the economy improved by November 1982, the Democrats might regain control of the Senate, scuttling the third year of the Reagan tax cut and throwing into doubt the rebuilding of America's defenses after a decade of neglect.

All this was on my mind during the winter of 1981–82. Oddly enough, it seemed that whenever I spoke out against the deficit, somebody criticized me for lacking vision. I was called a latter-day Hoover, a green-eyeshade conservative who had attended too many chicken dinners and delivered too many austerity lectures to appreciate the new economics.

If the old-time religion says you can't endlessly spend more than you take in, then old-time religion is good enough for me. The real lack of vision was in those who buried their heads in the sand by refusing to confront the deficit. Their thoughts seemed fixed on the next election when they ought to have been thinking about the next generation, including seventy million or so baby-boomers who will have to wear the financial strait-jacket fitted by elected officials addicted to credit-card government.

It was as if Washington had a new beatitude: Blessed are the young, for they shall inherit the national debt.

Real vision tries to reconcile people of seemingly opposite views, whatever the obstacles or the political risks. Yet early in 1982 politicians of both parties appeared determined to validate Henry Adams' cynical maxim by ignoring the economic facts of life. The White House understandably didn't want to tinker with a tax cut that was just beginning to take effect. Congressional Democrats, still smarting from their losses the previous summer, were in no mood to cooperate on a deficit-reduction package that included further spending cuts.

There was a vehicle for responsible action in Congress' own budget resolution, which called for spending reductions of

$280 billion over a three-year period, and nearly $100 billion in new revenue. New revenue didn't have to mean new taxes, much less a reversal of the personal-tax cuts enacted the previous summer. Before doing anything else, I thought, we ought to collect what was already due. So Iowa's Charles E. Grassley and I introduced a package of tax-compliance measures designed to retrieve a large chunk of the estimated $100 billion that was owed annually but that went unreported to the IRS. In doing so, Chuck Grassley and I foreshadowed the sweeping tax-reform program of 1986 that put an end to the abuse of tax shelters while directing investment toward more productive channels.

What followed was a predictable game of chicken. Members of Congress, after all, are only human. They prefer handing out benefits to enforcing fiscal discipline. Revenue bills are supposed to originate in the House, but Dan Rostenkowski preferred to let the Senate Republicans take the heat on this one. He'd wait to see what we came up with before committing himself. Russell Long told me bluntly not to expect help from Finance Committee Democrats unless Republicans put together a plan that would pass muster with the White House.

Knowing that our ability to govern was being tested, I invited other Republicans on the committee to an economic conclave in a second-floor hearing room of the Dirksen Senate Office Building. Over the next three days and nights a rare team spirit grew up among Rockefeller Republicans like Rhode Island's John Chafee and New Right activists like Idaho's Steve Symms. There wasn't a single leak from our meetings, despite a near-suffocating mob of reporters and lobbyists in the hall outside.

While I was walking down the corridor one evening, someone remarked that every one of the $200-an-hour lobbyists camping outside our door was wearing Gucci shoes.

"They'll be barefoot in the morning," I replied.

A deliberately informal atmosphere inside the hearing room didn't mask the difficulties confronting us. Unlike the situation in the summer of 1981, we faced choices much harder than how much money to give away.

As far as the original three-year tax cut was concerned, I wouldn't consider repealing it, delaying it or rewriting it. Instead, we removed a few ornaments from the 1981 Christmas tree. We cut back on some generous provisions dealing with business depreciation. We also restrained an accountant's dream called safe-harbor leasing that cost the Treasury $22 billion. The provision allowed profitable companies to reduce their tax bills, sometimes to the vanishing point, by purchasing investment tax credits from money-losers. It may have been a great deal for someone like General Electric or Occidental Petroleum, but it wasn't so hot for the average taxpayer.

Will Rogers used to say that the American tax code produced more liars than anything but golf. Jimmy Carter called it a scandal. Anyone who truly cared about fairness would object to a system so riddled with loopholes that it looked like Swiss cheese and smelled like Limburger.

The result of our work, the Tax Equity and Fiscal Responsibility Act of 1982 (TEFRA), brought the deficit down by nearly $100 billion, with barely 10 percent of the money coming from new taxes. The rest resulted from closing some of the more offensive loopholes and enforcing compliance with existing taxes. One of the smallest revenue sources in TEFRA caused us the biggest headache. The White House, having said no to a gasoline tax, sent Finance Committee Republicans scurrying to embrace an idea straight out of the Administration's own budget proposals. Withholding 10 percent of interest and dividend income was a concept initially broached by Don Regan's Treasury Department. The President himself signified his approval in calls to committee members, pointing out that withholding could be worth as much as three or four billion dollars a year.

Such numbers carried little weight compared with the popular uproar generated by angry bankers. Needing eleven votes on the committee to pass withholding, I finally convinced Hawaii Democrat Spark M. Matsunaga to side with Republicans (all except John Chafee, who had already printed 1982 campaign brochures boasting of his earlier opposition to tax withholding). Inexplicably, Treasury balked at granting a minor tax break to the Hawaiian sugar industry; I balked back at Treasury.

Withholding secured, the White House signed on with us for the whole TEFRA bill after receiving assurances that spending cuts would predominate in the final package. The President afterward complained that he didn't get three dollars in budget reductions for every dollar of new revenue. As far as the Finance Committee was concerned, we reduced spending on programs within our jurisdiction in line with the three-for-one formula. Other major areas of the budget, including defense and federal pay, also met White House targets. As later estimated by the Congressional Budget Office, the Administration itself could have achieved the majority of the savings without congressional action, mostly through managerial reforms and reduced interest on the debt.

Throughout June and July of 1982, I was shelled from all sides. Democrats wouldn't accept a tax-reform package that bore a Republican imprint. The Guccis were out in full force, and so were supply-siders quick to accuse me of betraying the Reagan Revolution. They called me a closet liberal. I was certainly no liberal. Nor was I a lemming.

A dramatic confrontation occurred late on the night of July 22. Senators adopted by a lopsided margin Arkansas Democrat David Pryor's amendment striking out part of TEFRA requiring restaurants to report waiters' tips up to 7 percent of gross sales. Weary but happy, the Guccis went home to celebrate. I had anticipated something like this happening, and had asked Finance Committee staffers to draw up a list of "dogs and cats" —revenue raisers we could add on the spot. It was after two o'clock in the morning when I struck back with my amendment to replace $2.8 billion by cutting in half the deductibility of business-entertainment expenses.

For years liberals had been denouncing the three-martini lunch. Here was a chance for them to put up or shut up. It was a revealing debate. Ted Kennedy suggested that another way to make up the lost revenue was to do away with the third year of the Reagan tax cut. But Kennedy was in the minority, and the three-martini-lunch amendment carried the day, 57–40. Once the sun came up over Washington, Gucci jubilation turned to alarm. By the time the bill reached conference, restaurateurs were offering to report tips up to 8 percent of gross sales in exchange for restoration of the status quo on entertainment expenses. I was more than happy to accept their offer.

The final showdown over TEFRA involved North Carolina Senators Jesse A. Helms and John P. East, both Republicans. Accepting an increase in cigarette taxes was no way for either of them to win votes in the nation's number-one tobacco state. Helms softened the political impact by limiting the tax hike to three years. He then promised to support the final bill if his vote meant the difference between victory and defeat.

Despite Reagan's personal intervention and a round of last-minute phone calls from the White House, Howard Baker was still trying desperately to plug holes in Administration ranks. In the predawn hours of July 23, Baker stood at the entrance to the Republican cloakroom, reminding Helms of his pledge.

"Jesse, we need your vote."

"I can't do it, Howard."

"We need your vote, Jesse."

"It's political suicide, Howard."

"We need your vote now, Jesse."

Silently, Helms made his way onto the floor. At the call of his name, he responded "Aye." So did John East. Together they made the difference, as TEFRA passed, 50–47. Not one Democrat broke party ranks to vote for the bill. (With the Democrats now in control of the Senate, I can't help but remember that day whenever I hear my Democratic friends promote a bipartisan approach to the budget.)

That same week the stock market took off, soaring over three hundred points by the end of the year and launching the great bull market that took it to unprecedented heights over the next five years. Interest rates headed south. The recession bottomed out in November and began reversing itself the next month. Voters, reassured that the deficit was being addressed, returned to office the same number of Republican senators we had going into the election. And GOP losses in the House were

far less severe than might be expected. Of even greater importance over the long haul was the fact that TEFRA helped the
Republican Party retain its historic reputation for fiscal integrity. To lose that would be a body blow.

Another heated debate taking place simultaneously with
TEFRA involved extension of the 1965 Voting Rights Act.
Civil-rights groups argued that electoral results were enough to
show violations of the original statute, by excluding minorities
from office. Opponents, including Attorney General William
French Smith, insisted that legal action must be based on evidence of a deliberate intent to discriminate.

For weeks those of us on the Senate Judiciary Committee
tried to decide between "results" and "intent." As one of a
handful of uncommitted members, I was ideally positioned
to play the honest broker's role. Beyond attempts at compromise, I had my own obligations to consider. Kansans have a
special view toward human rights, one rooted in the agonies
preceding statehood in 1861, when opposing bands of Free
State Jayhawkers and pro-slavery Bushwackers made "Bleeding Kansas" a dress rehearsal for the American Civil War.
After the war, the state welcomed tens of thousands of black
"Exodusters" from the impoverished South. It led the Union
in approving a constitutional amendment giving blacks the
vote.

From a practical standpoint, there was no way the President could refuse to sign an extension when it reached his desk.
Here, then, was a chance for me to allay conservative fears
about quotas and to strengthen the bill. Along the way Republicans might also win some credit from traditionally suspicious
blacks and Hispanics.

With the help of Chuck Grassley and others in the conservative mainstream, on May 3 the Judiciary Committee adopted
my amendment that accepted results as a valid criteria for legal
action while specifically ruling out proportional representation
as a remedy for voter discrimination. The 14–4 margin was
large enough to prevent opposing lawmakers from burying the
bill in oratory. That same day, Reagan hailed the action and

pledged his own support for a twenty-five-year extension of the Voting Rights Act.

Actions like this led to speculation about "the new Bob Dole." According to popular theory, Elizabeth was responsible for my sudden mellowing. Armchair psychologists reversed the old adage to suggest that "bedfellows make strange politics."

With all due respect to Elizabeth, it would be unusual if age and experience hadn't broadened my perspective. In truth, most of those who talked about a new Bob Dole hadn't known the old one very well. What had changed was not my character or my personality but my role in the Senate, where success is impossible to achieve unless you have the votes on your side. In January 1981 I became part of a majority, in position to put forward a constructive program and to line up the votes for its enactment.

Something else. Shuttling between the Agriculture and Finance Committees gave me an unusual perspective. As a fiscal conservative, I believe that the best form of social justice is having a job in the private sector, with a real paycheck that isn't dependent on the whim of some congressional committee or vulnerable to shifts in a sluggish, overtaxed economy.

Let's face it, however: some people have nowhere to turn but to government. Much of my work on the Agriculture Committee revolved around the legitimate needs of these people. In Finance, the special pleaders are well heeled, well connected and wall to wall. Not so in Agriculture. There's no Poor PAC to remind us of all the fatherless families struggling to maintain their living without sacrificing their dignity. Poor people don't have lobbyists who take congressmen and their staffs to lunch on K Street.

In the closing months of 1982, bankers everywhere targeted me for an avalanche of postcards and personal appeals, all calling for repeal of 10 percent withholding on interest and dividends, appeals that I resisted. Old friends in the industry did everything but take back their toaster. It didn't matter so much for big banks: they had computers and personnel to comply with withholding requirements. Smaller financial institutions, by contrast, found the additional cost and paperwork burdensome.

The issue came to a head for me early in 1983, at a meeting of the Kansas Bankers Association in Dodge City. Waiting for me outside the room were two severely disabled young people with their parents. Tim was in a special wheelchair, unable to move anything except his eyes. Carla was only slightly more mobile. Both wanted to talk to me about help in gaining greater access to a more physically independent lifestyle. So often in politics, you're at the mercy of your schedulers. But sometimes instead of racing ahead to the next meeting, you need to slow down and talk with real people who have real problems.

On my way back to Washington I kept thinking about Tim and Carla. What they faced was far more serious than the loss of a few tenths of one percent of compound interest. Back home, I sat in our bedroom and told Elizabeth how deeply moved I had been by this encounter. "I've been meaning for years to start a foundation for disabled persons," I said, "and I haven't done it. This is the time."

Since then, the Dole Foundation has raised over $3.5 million to address issues like job training and placement for disabled workers. One of the foundation's grants has assisted New York City's National Theater Workshop for the Handicapped teach its members advanced communications skills. In Kentucky, a challenge grant paved the way for a fast-food restaurant that employs the mentally retarded. Exceptional children in Virginia are being helped to adjust to the working world. Seattle students are being taught campground-management skills. Two dozen epileptics once thought of as unemployable have been trained for work through the Epilepsy Foundation of Ohio.

In the end, bank withholding was largely repealed. But I didn't lose, because out of that fight came the impetus for the Dole Foundation, which, through the generous support of thousands of donors, has invested in the most precious capital of all—human potential.

ELIZABETH

Congressmen weren't the only ones who liked the 1981 tax cuts better than their 1982 sequel. Part of my job at Public Liaison was to convince businessmen that the ultimate bottom line was a sound national economy. And it wasn't easy getting captains of industry to embrace a package whose benefits, unlike its costs, were theoretical.

Jack Albertine was an exception. As head of the American Business Conference, Albertine represented some of the country's most dynamic firms—tomorrow's IBMs.

"Jack," I told him, "we need a leader."

"Well, Elizabeth, it's not as if we were talking about cutting taxes."

"No, Jack, we're not. But you know as well as I do that we've got to get the deficit under control. The only way to convince the markets we mean business is by removing some of the Christmas-tree ornaments. If we don't do it now, interest rates will stay up. And you can forget about a growth economy."

Albertine paused for a moment. "But, Elizabeth, I haven't even seen the full bill."

"If it's any consolation," I said, "I haven't seen it either. But I will. And soon. And then I'm going to need you to lead the charge."

"Oh, what the heck, Elizabeth," sighed Albertine. "Count me in."

I also signed on Prudential's Bob Beck. Beck joined us even though he'd been warned that TEFRA might cost his company as much as $200 million. Reporters asked him why.

"It's good for America," said Beck, "and whatever is good for America will be good for Prudential."

Throughout this period, I worked to pave an avenue of trust between the White House and the business world. Loyalty, after all, is a two-way street. And the Prompt Pay Act of 1982 gave me a chance to return the support of businesses much smaller than Prudential.

For years, vendors doing business with the federal government often waited six months or more for payment. Once the 1981–82 recession hit, cash flow became a life-and-death matter for thousands of small and medium-sized firms. A drive was launched on Capitol Hill to require Uncle Sam to reimburse vendors on time or pay an interest penalty like any other customer. I supported the legislation as an exercise in elemental fairness and argued the points within the councils of government.

To say that not everyone in the Administration shared my logic is an understatement. Don Regan claimed it would cost too much. So did the Office of Management and Budget, the Pentagon and practically every agency that had ever bought goods and services with taxpayer dollars.

I arranged a meeting for Mike McKevitt of the National Federation of Independent Business with the President. The session was held in the Roosevelt Room, a few steps from the Oval Office. Besides the President, McKevitt and myself, those around the table included Don Regan, Dave Stockman and Stockman's deputy at OMB, Ed Harper.

McKevitt came right to the point. "Mr. President," he said, "we have a problem. As a businessman, I have to pay my bills on time. As a citizen, I *certainly* have to pay my taxes on time. [Don Regan was starting to squirm in his chair.] But, Mr. President, when the federal government owes me money, it can pay whenever it feels like. And there's not a thing I can do about it."

"That's wrong," the President said. "I came here to change things like that."

"Mr. President," said McKevitt, "I know a perfect way you can do just that. We have legislation pending on the Hill that would take care of the problem once and for all."

"I can't imagine any reason why we wouldn't support it," said Reagan.

I glanced over at the Secretary of the Treasury, who looked as though he were about to detonate. Regan cleared his throat.

"Mr. President," he said, "there are some technical problems with the bill—"

Reagan cut him off. "I'm sure we can work them out, Don.

The important thing is that we support the concept. We certainly don't want people calling Uncle Sam a deadbeat. Do we?"

Heads nodded all around. The Prompt Payment Bill was on its way to prompt enactment.

Coming on top of our other victories, this latest skirmish enhanced Public Liaison's credibility at both ends of Pennsylvania Avenue. I now felt able to offer bolder counsel at senior staff meetings. Like pressing presidential pollster Richard Wirthlin to sample public reaction on two fronts where the Administration seemed vulnerable. One was fairness. Administration budget cuts were widely portrayed as the thin end of a wedge dividing the poor—especially poor women—from the rest of society. The other issue haunting Republicans was the gender gap. Wirthlin's surveys subsequently confirmed that many Americans saw a White House tilt toward affluent white males. Left unaddressed, fairness and the gender gap could constitute a one-two punch against every GOP candidate in the upcoming elections.

In the 1980 campaign, President Reagan had gone out of his way to assure women voters that although he opposed the Equal Rights Amendment, he was committed to rooting out vestiges of discrimination in the legal code. Carrying out a campaign promise, the Reagan Administration established a Legal Equity Task Force, followed by the Fifty States Project—both intended to uncover discriminatory language in federal and state statutes.

Clearly, more had to be done. In August 1982 I was made head of a White House Coordinating Council on Women which was charged with increasing opportunities for women both within the Administration and in the country at large, the latter through presidential initiatives, directives and specific legislative proposals. The Administration also sponsored legislation that would make it easier for mothers to collect billions in court-ordered child-support payments. And Social Security laws were redrawn to equalize benefits for widows and widowers.

When Bob Dole introduced his own package of pension-law reforms, it revived the talk about the two of us working as some kind of political tag team. These people didn't realize how little time we had to compare notes. Nor did they understand how we can compartmentalize the issues we're working on. At one point during the negotiations over the 1983 budget, Bob said to me one evening, "Elizabeth, I'm not going to be able to talk to you about what I'm doing."

And he didn't. But then, he wasn't the only one of us with official secrets.

Early in his presidency, Ronald Reagan told me about the strains he had felt as governor of California. "Each morning began with someone standing before my desk describing yet another disaster," he said. "The feeling of stress became almost unbearable. I had the urge to look over my shoulder for someone I could pass the problem to. One day it came to me that I was looking in the wrong direction. I looked up instead of back. I'm still looking up. I couldn't face one more day in this office if I didn't know I could ask God's help and it would be given."

My own spiritual journey began many years ago, in a Carolina home where Sunday was the Lord's Day, reserved for acts of mercy and my grandmother's unforgettable Bible stories. Mom Cathey was such a perfect role model it was only natural that I should want to follow in her footsteps.

From an early age I was active in the church. But as we move along, how often in our busy lives something seems to get in the way of a more than ritualistic faith. It may be money, or power, or prestige. In my case, it was career. More specifically, the Holy Grail of public service became very nearly all-consuming. I was satisfied with nothing less than my best. Understandable enough but, as you can imagine, it becomes pretty demanding when you're trying to foresee every difficulty and realize every opportunity. It's even harder on those around you. My work left little time to be a friend to friends, let alone to the friendless.

Ironically, this form of perfectionism, so different from my grandmother's selfless spirituality, began crowding out what Mom Cathey had taught me were life's most important objectives. Sunday had become just another day of the week. Grad-

ually, over a period of years, I realized that though I was blessed
with a beautiful marriage and a challenging career, my life was
close to spiritual starvation.

I prayed about this and, no faster than I was ready, I believe God led me to the people and the experiences that would
transform my life. Mine has not been a road-to-Damascus experience, but a continuing search for guidance and the true
perspective that comes with the strengthening of faith.

Growing up in Salisbury, I had cherished the ties that bind
a permanent congregation. It was a feeling I missed in the non-
denominational atmosphere at Duke and Harvard. Then, at the
Foundry Methodist Church on Washington's Sixteenth Street,
I found Ed Bauman, a caring, sensitive pastor who urged me to
join a spiritual-growth group that tried to relate personal faith
to everyday experience. Each Monday night I left the White
House and went to a church near Dupont Circle. I climbed a
flight of stairs to a second-floor room sparsely furnished with
an old couch and some chairs. The nine members of the group
ranged in age from thirty to sixty-six. Our occupations and our
politics were eclectic.

Soon I was sharing feelings that I would never have expressed to White House colleagues. We all felt a common need
to stretch spiritually. Each of us was looking for answers,
and depending on the others for help in phrasing the right questions. During these Monday-night meetings, for example, I
came face to face with a compulsion to do things right, and
the companion drive to constantly please. Gradually, I began to redefine perfectionism the way my grandmother had
taught it. Some people define strength as independence, self-
reliance and resourcefulness, but I have learned that real
strength, inner strength, comes from a dependence on the
one source who can replenish life with the power that comes
from above.

I've also discovered that Sundays *can* be set aside for spiritual and personal rejuvenation without disastrous effects on
your work week. With our frenetic schedules, Sunday is more
precious than ever to Bob and me. In the morning we go to the
services at Foundry Methodist. Later we might have brunch

with friends or just relax with the Sunday papers and a good book.

I'm a long way from where I want to be. At times I have even wondered whether I am trying to tackle spiritual growth with that same perfectionist zeal that prompts a man to pray, "Please, Lord, give me patience—and I need it right now!" One of my most cherished possessions is Mom Cathey's Bible. I love to read notes she wrote in its margins when she couldn't sleep some nights, including this notation next to Psalm 139: "May 22, 1952, 1:00 A.M.—my prayer: 'Search me, O God, and know my heart—try me, and know my thoughts. See if there be any wicked way in me, and lead me in the way everlasting.' "

My grandmother has never exerted more influence than she does today, when I am reminded that what we do on our own matters little—what counts is what God chooses to do through us. Life is more than a few years spent on self-indulgence or career advancement. It's a privilege, a responsibility and a stewardship to be met according to His calling.

This came home to me with special force in early January 1983, when President Reagan invited me to join his Cabinet as Secretary of Transportation. I didn't go to political advisers for counsel. I talked it over with Ed Bauman and others from the Monday-night group. Jenna Dorn, who then worked for Senator Mark Hatfield and would later become my strong right hand at DOT, said I had no choice but to accept. "Think what it would mean for women!" she exclaimed.

Ed Bauman echoed her advice. When earlier rumors about a Cabinet appointment reached us, Bob and I had talked it over. He said it was a natural progression, and encouraged me, even though it might cause occasional conflicts with his Senate agenda or his prospects as a candidate for national office.

Since I knew he would approve, I decided to surprise him. But Jim Baker leaked the news to Bob, whispering in his ear at a meeting of the presidential commission on Social Security, "You might want to turn on the TV at eight o'clock tonight. I have a hunch you'll be interested in what the President has to say."

I went straight from the presidential press conference

where my appointment was announced to my Public Liaison office. For the next two hours I called associates in the business, labor and other constituent communities with whom I had worked in the past and whose cooperation I would need at DOT. For most of the evening, Bob sat nearby, enjoying my excitement and the whirlwind of activity.

My confirmation hearing was set for January 16, 1983. Bob introduced me to members of the Senate Commerce Committee. As for himself, he said that he could identify with Nathan Hale. "I only regret that I have but one wife to give for my country's infrastructure."

BOB

You know what leadership is? It is the ability to get men to do what they don't want to do and like it.

—Harry S. Truman

The pace of American democracy is often likened to the tortoise, but popular government resembles the turtle in another way. The only way to make progress is by sticking your neck out. That's what I did on Social Security throughout Ronald Reagan's first term. For my efforts I almost got my head chopped off.

In the spring of 1981, the Reagan Administration proposed a scaling back of Social Security provisions dealing with student benefits and burial payments. The Administration also called for substantial penalties on early retirement, a thorough review of disability cases and the elimination of a $122-a-month minimum benefit going to three million recipients.

The sweeping changes produced near-panic on Capitol Hill, where almost no one wanted to confront the subject. I instructed staff members to quietly devise a long-range plan anyway, one that could satisfy both the retirees who received Social Security benefits and the wage earners who paid for them.

When Spencer Rich of the *Washington Post* wrote a front-page story detailing the staff's work, any chance we had for an early rescue attempt went out the window. In September 1981 Reagan backtracked on the issue of minimum benefits. He invited leaders of both parties to join him in "removing Social Security once and for all from politics." To begin the progress, Reagan appointed a national commission to examine the system's weaknesses and report its findings back within twelve months.

The blue-ribbon panel is a staple of modern government, one that Reagan would employ to win backing for his Central American policies and the MX missile. It is also an acknowledgment of political gridlock by representatives who are unable to make representative government work.

I was one of seven lawmakers named to the National Commission on Social Security Reform. The chairman was Alan Greenspan, Gerald Ford's favorite economist and now chairman of the Federal Reserve Board. On the other side, to watch out for labor's interests, was AFL-CIO president Lane Kirkland. Tip O'Neill was represented by former Social Security Commissioner Robert Ball, and the ageless Representative Claude Pepper of Florida carried the banner for the organized elderly. Rounding out the roster were emissaries from the business world led by Prudential's Robert Beck.

Tip O'Neill had his own solution to the Social Security crisis: eliminate Republicans from Congress. Commission members paid less attention to party standings than to a different set of numbers. Social Security would soon go broke. According to demographers, when the baby-boom generation reached its peak earning power in the 1990s, the system would be in good health—but next month was another story. Social Security was paying out $30,000 more a minute than it took in, forcing it, late in 1982, to dip into reserves for $17 billion.

Raise taxes. Cut benefits. We had to find a compromise in there someplace.

The Reagan Administration properly refused to accept new payroll taxes. Republican commissioners reminded those across the table that under the Carter Administration in 1977 a sched-

uled series of payroll-tax increases that added up to the largest
tax bill in U.S. history had been enacted to rescue the system—
and here we were, five years later, trying to stave off total
collapse. The problem could not be solved by taking $100 bil-
lion out of general revenues, as some suggested. We didn't *have*
any general revenues—only a general debt. Politically and financially, however, there was no way to raise the $150 to $175
billion required to put the system on a sound footing through
benefit cuts alone.

As the December 31 deadline neared, the commission was
stalemated. Reagan reluctantly extended its life by two weeks.
But neither the White House nor Tip O'Neill was anxious to
embrace a compromise that had something in it to offend nearly
everyone. So long as the President and the Speaker stayed aloof
from the negotiations, commissioners resembled a pair of ball
teams that had the talent to win but lacked a star pitcher.

What happened next bears little resemblance to the orderly
processes described in civics books. The Ninety-eighth Congress convened for the first time on January 3, 1983. That
morning, Daniel Patrick Moynihan came up to me on the Senate floor. He had read an article I'd written on Social Security
for the *Washington Post* and had been encouraged by its description of "relatively modest steps" needed to save the system.

"Are we going to let this commission go down the tubes
without giving it one more try?" asked Moynihan.

"Let's talk," I said. "Let's get ahold of Ball." Robert Ball
was O'Neill's representative.

The next day, Ball, Moynihan and I met in a Finance Committee hideaway office. The results were promising enough for
me to alert Alan Greenspan, and Moynihan invited Republican
Congressman Barber B. Conable of New York. Our major
stumbling blocks were payroll-tax increases and corresponding
benefit cuts. Ball's solution to the first was to move up the
already scheduled tax increases, which he would offset with tax
credits for employers. When Claude Pepper showed flexibility
on cost-of-living adjustments, the way was cleared to overcome
the second hurdle.

Forty-eight hours later, we brought the White House into

the negotiations. On the evening of January 5, Jim Baker convened the Gang of Seven—the original nucleus, plus Dave
Stockman and himself—at his Foxhall Road home in northwest
Washington. It was the start of an eleven-day marathon, conducted without staffers and under strict security. One morning
I spotted in my rearview mirror a posse of reporters hot on my
trail, but I managed to ditch them.

There was no way to blunt press curiosity about what was
going on at Baker's house. Few people at the time caught the
irony that a commission created because Congress wished to
delegate its decision-making power had now delegated its authority to the Gang of Seven. Such are the birth pangs of public
policy.

On January 13, in a San Francisco speech, Baker floated a
trial balloon based on our talks. He said Reagan might accept
some acceleration of already scheduled payroll taxes as long as
they were balanced by spending reforms. The Administration
pulled back from its opposition to taxing Social Security benefits of upper-income recipients. The logjam was breaking.

On Saturday, January 15, 1983, the Gang of Seven reas-
sembled at Blair House. Bob Ball served as go-between with Tip
O'Neill, who was playing in a West Coast golf tournament.
While Ball talked by phone with O'Neill and others, I crossed
Pennsylvania Avenue to have lunch with Jim Baker and the
commission's trio of business representatives. Over a bowl of
chili in the White House mess, Bob Beck and his colleagues
agreed to give a little to save a lot.

Later that day, Ball, Greenspan, Moynihan and I worked
out the final settlement in an hour. A light snow was falling
when we left Blair House. Reagan and O'Neill had both indi-
cated they would accept whatever we came up with, just as long
as it was adopted by a large majority.

Greenspan explained the details of the compromise to the
rest of the commission. No one was ecstatic over a package that
would postpone cost-of-living increases due July 1, 1983,
would accelerate the schedule of payroll taxes, and would give
a tax credit for workers and employers to help offset any economic dislocation caused by the change. The retirement age

would gradually be raised from sixty-five to sixty-seven. Upper-income retirees would pay income tax on half their Social Security benefits.

Still, it was the best a democratic government could do. The final vote was twelve in favor, three opposed. Greenspan called Baker at the White House, and Ball telephoned O'Neill. By nightfall, the President and the Speaker were in agreement for the first time.

The *Los Angeles Times* said it best: "The commission's job was to save the system by showing how its books could be balanced without hurting the 36 million retired Americans who depend on its checks each month. It has done that job well. It is now up to Congress to show the same political maturity in implementing the proposals that the commission showed in shaping them."

In March, Congress accepted the *Times*'s challenge. Reagan signed the bill into law on April 20.

I received a letter from Claude Pepper: "We could never have produced the solution without your skill and sincerest desire to see that our Commission make a meaningful contribution to the saving of Social Security. You never lost hope and faith in our accomplishing the immeasurable task of saving Social Security as a sound and solvent institution for the next seventy-five years."

In the midst of Social Security bailout negotiations, I accepted an invitation to speak at the capital's annual Gridiron Dinner. It seemed a good time to place Washington's breathless self-obsession in perspective, so I quoted words Justice Oliver Wendell Holmes had used half a century earlier: "We are the leaders of the whole stream of life. We lead it in the same sense that small boys lead a circus parade when they march ahead of it. But if they turn down a side street, the parade goes on."

Turning to President Reagan, I congratulated him for leading the country well and for avoiding policy side streets. "And I take heart from the knowledge that whatever you or I or any one of us may do, the American parade will go on, propelled by a vision two centuries old—the dream of an inclusive soci-

ety, where individual rights are wedded to social responsibilities, and freedom to choose means obligation to serve."

The biggest laugh of the evening came at the end of my
remarks. I flatly stated that under no circumstances would Dole
be a candidate for President in 1984.

Elizabeth jumped to her feet.

"Speak for yourself, sweetheart," she said.

CHAPTER NINE

Two Lives,
On the Run

ELIZABETH

On February 7, 1983, I became the newest member of
President Reagan's Cabinet. Bob assured reporters that there'd
be no problem distinguishing our professional roles: as Finance
Committee chairman, he was in charge of loopholes; as Secretary of Transportation, I was in charge of potholes.

Potholes would be the least of my concerns. Among its
many responsibilities, the Department of Transportation chan-
nels highway funds to the states, regulates the movement of
hazardous materials and inspects commercial and private aircraft. It wages war on illicit drugs at sea through the Coast
Guard and campaigns against drunk drivers on land. Promoting
commercial development of outer space, DOT is one branch of
government for which the sky is no limit.

Drew Lewis, my predecessor, left some very large shoes to
fill. Besides the administrative challenges that come with
100,000 employees and a $27 billion budget, there were con-
flicting demands from auto executives, railroad unions and congressional chairmen, for whom Cabinet officers come and go
while the seniority system is forever. Finally, my years as Secretary would coincide with a dramatic period of transition, as
industries accustomed to four decades of Washington's economic oversight were forced to adjust to a freer, more competitive climate.

My first week in office provided a taste of crisis management when independent truckers went on strike over heavy-vehicle taxes. By the time long-distance haulers were back on the road, I had identified $70 million to restore Washington's venerable Union Station, closed for five years due to congressional mismanagement. When reopened in 1988, this historic landmark will house dozens of shops, restaurants and theaters and a first-class transportation center. I would also need to implement complex congressional legislation doubling federal funds that assist states in repairing highways and transit systems.

In developing a broader policy agenda, I contacted former Secretaries and other respected members of the transportation fraternity. One of them cautioned me to stay away from public-safety issues, which he thought would only bring political trouble. Whenever there's a disaster in the air or on the ground, you can count on emotional media coverage, he said, and everyone will turn to the Transportation Secretary for explanations. Good news, on the other hand, barely gets yawning respect.

I didn't take the advice. In the limited time I'd have to serve, I could think of no greater satisfaction than knowing that my efforts might contribute to the saving of lives. Safety across all modes of transportation would be a dominant theme of my tenure. First, I asked to review what was on the drawing boards and in the research labs. One promising highway safety idea was an additional brake light to be mounted at the base of a car's rear window. The new light had been through five years of successful tests on taxis and police cars, so I took it off the shelf and made it standard equipment for 1986 vehicles. The device cost consumers less than twenty dollars a car, but studies have shown that when all cars are equipped with the tiny lamp we can eliminate some 900,000 rear-end crashes annually.

A much more difficult challenge arose from a long-standing dispute between government officials and leaders of the auto and insurance industries over air bags and other passive restraints in new cars. The passive-restraint requirement, known as Rule 208, had been reiterated by the Carter Administration, rescinded in the early months of the Reagan presidency, and appealed all the way to the Supreme Court. In the summer of 1983 the Court remanded 208 with specific instructions for additional departmental review. It was time once and for all to settle the issue. For nearly twenty years, while the lawyers argued and the politicians debated, people had been dying on the highways.

We knew from previous tests that air bags alone wouldn't stop the carnage. Although they provide excellent protection in frontal crashes, they are not much help in a rear-end collision or a rollover. They were also expensive, but even when prices came down, it would still take a decade or more to equip the entire American automotive fleet with air bags. Safety belts, on the other hand, were proven lifesavers and already standard equipment. So at the same time that I arranged for five hundred government vehicles outfitted with air bags to continue testing, I also attempted to involve the American people themselves in the decision-making process through their state legislators.

The goal: to save as many lives as possible, as quickly as possible, and break the long stalemate with a sound regulation that would stand up on appeal in the courts. Under the plan we devised, unless by 1986 two thirds of the population was covered by state safety-belt laws that met federal criteria, manufacturers would have to install automatic passenger restraints of their choice in at least 10 percent of all '87-model cars. This figure would rise in successive years until it reached 100 percent in model-year 1990.

State legislatures held the option. There were no sanctions to compel state action, other than market forces and popular demand. Since this unprecedented offer was announced in the summer of 1984, twenty-nine states and the District of Columbia have taken me up on it. As a result, hundreds of lives are being saved and crippling injuries prevented for the first time in the twenty-year history of Rule 208. In keeping with our schedule, a quarter of all 1988 cars are equipped with passive restraints.

Preserving air bag technology was another major goal. An incentive in Rule 208 encouraged manufacturers to select air bags over automatic belts on the door; as a result, ten automobile manufacturers will soon offer air bags as an option. Detroit is discovering what we've been preaching for years: safety sells.

And future car buyers will be able to choose from a wider range of safety options.

It's a bleak truism that tragedy often precedes reform. A drunk driver snuffs out the life of a child—and public outrage leads to tougher laws and stiffer sentencing. Take it from one who lost an uncle to a drunk driver: the human costs can scar a family for generations.

Of the more than forty thousand Americans who die each year on the nation's highways, at least half lose their lives in alcohol-related accidents. Over 300,000 people are seriously injured, many maimed for life. While you can't begin to calculate the grief and suffering experienced by crash victims and their loved ones, taxpayers fork up billions of dollars annually to pay the medical expenses and rehabilitation costs of these victims.

Ordinarily, the state governments set traffic law. But when there's no uniform minimum drinking age, teenagers are tempted to drive across state lines to take advantage of more liberal laws next door. These in effect become "blood borders," inducements to drink and drive. The problem was serious enough that in 1984 President Reagan and I championed legislation encouraging states to raise their drinking age to twenty-one. Today forty-nine states have this law on their books.

I have used the bully pulpit to wage my own war on drunk driving, insisting we'll continue to fight until we get every drunk driver off the American road. Citizen activists like Mothers Against Drunk Driving (MADD) have raised the national consciousness and it has been my privilege to join them in this effort. Americans, I now believe, are unwilling to tolerate lax laws or lenient judges. Due in part to a substantial decline in drunk driving and a three-fold increase in the use of safety belts since the first state law was passed, the last two years have produced the lowest fatal accident rate in history. Encouraging as this trend appears, now is no time to rest on our laurels.

In all my efforts to promote safer transportation, I tried to respect individual choice. But what happens when an individual's behavior becomes a public menace? In January 1987 an Amtrak train carrying passengers from Washington to Boston derailed outside Baltimore. Sixteen bodies were pulled from the twisted wreckage. Blood tests of the brakeman and the engineer of the Conrail train involved in the accident revealed traces of marijuana. If the rail unions had had their way, those tests would not have been permitted. For twelve years the unions had stalled efforts to test workers for alcohol or drug abuse. Then, eleven months before Amtrak's *Colonial* went off the tracks, we succeeded in implementing the first drug-testing procedure of its kind in railroad history.

It came none too soon. Of the first eight hundred employees tested after accidents, 5.1 percent showed alcohol or drugs in their system. This was more than enough to convince me that DOT should be the first civilian department to undertake the most effective deterrent, random drug testing. Not surprisingly, the decision didn't make me the most popular person around.

Public safety is a public trust. If you work in a cockpit or an engine room, you are responsible for the lives of your passengers. There is no escaping that responsibility. As Secretary of Transportation, I had to be able to look people in the eye and assure them that I'd done everything possible to give them what they expect and deserve—a drug-free transportation system.

Random testing is a sensitive issue, to be handled with maximum regard for individual dignity and privacy. Under our rules, tests had to be confirmed by a method that is virtually foolproof, and even then we asked a doctor to tell us whether there could be *any* reason to throw out a positive reading.

I believe that the most compassionate way to help an employee with a problem is rehabilitation. The idea wasn't to fire employees but rather to help those with a drug-abuse problem break free of their dependence. What could be more sensitive? My senior staff and I were among the thirty thousand DOT employees to be tested. The rest were in safety- or security-related positions—air traffic controllers and railroad inspectors, for example. I moved next to extend testing to those we regulated, such as pilots, maintenance crews, truckers, rail engineers and brakemen.

When I arrived at DOT, early in 1983, the economy was just coming out of recession. Later that year, as the President's tax and budget policies took hold, fuel costs dropped and airline deregulation belatedly realized its promise. Even the aviation industry was surprised by the surge in passenger traffic. Millions of people who never thought they would have the money to fly were taking advantage of lower fares. According to a recent study by the Brookings Institution, the combination of lower fares and more frequent flights has resulted in consumer savings of at least $6 billion annually.

Success can bring problems of its own, however. In this case, they included undeniable strains on the air traffic system. In essence, we had an aviation industry that was on the verge of explosive growth, surprised by this rapid surge, and hobbled by the ball and chain of a federal bureaucracy, the FAA, that was ill prepared to stay ahead of the growth curve. The challenge we faced was to get that bureaucracy to respond to a dynamic market while also making the world's safest air system still safer. It was a task of the highest order, one that will require the vigilance of future Secretaries of Transportation.

One of my first actions as Secretary was to immediately order fourteen thousand "white glove" inspections affecting 374 separate airlines—inspections over and above those already scheduled. Next came a comprehensive eighteen-month probe of general aviation and a vigorous examination of the FAA.

I then established a panel of technical experts and program analysts, a Safety Review Task Force. As it embarked on its first of a series of investigations across the transport spectrum, I delivered these simple marching orders: Tell us what we need to do differently; what we can do better. Skeptics who expected us to give an official whitewash of the FAA were surprised by the panel's first report, and the shake-up that followed. One of the first recommendations was a massive overhaul of the FAA's system of inspecting aircraft.

Astonishing as it sounds, we discovered that the FAA inspector handbooks hadn't been changed in twenty-eight years. So we rewrote the handbooks, and before long we rewrote the rule books, as part of a complete overhaul of FAA inspection procedures. Inspectors would now be reassigned periodically to prevent a buddy system from growing up between them and the inspected carriers. Methods of hiring and training personnel were updated, and the entire inspector work force was increased 60 percent. We levied the largest fines in history, including $9.5 million against one carrier.

This was just the start of the FAA's makeover. Over the next three years the number of air traffic controllers grew by 24 percent, with an additional 860 hirings called for in my final budget request. While overall funding for DOT actually shrank during my tenure, I secured a 50 percent increase in money for the FAA. Even during a time of fiscal austerity, I was able to persuade OMB to accept a $1 billion shot in the arm in fiscal year 1988, only to see accounts for vital equipment and salaries cut by the House of Representatives.

It was pretty frustrating to hear House members blame the Reagan Administration for not spending enough money on aviation safety, and then, when the TV lights went off, see them slice millions from my budget, stalling key components of a ten-year, $12 billion modernization of the National Airspace System. The NAS is the most complex nonmilitary program of its kind since Project Apollo put a man on the moon. NAS will double U.S. air capacity, because it relies on a new generation of computers that can handle four times the informational load and ten times the operating speed of current equipment.

Perched on the frontier of advanced technology, the NAS will also generate a string of new safety features. Commercial jets which I've required to carry anticollision warning devices will benefit as well from advance warnings of wind-shear conditions—those sudden, often violent shifts in wind speed or direction that pose special dangers for any aircraft at takeoff or landing. The NAS will include weather printouts for cockpit crews, vastly improved radar for controllers, and landing systems with three times the precision of anything used in commercial aviation.

In all the headlines about congested skies, our steady progress on NAS has been all but lost. So has an unsurpassed safety record. By the time I left DOT, 85 percent of the mammoth NAS was under contract and many hundreds of pieces of hardware were already in place. And the last three years have been the safest in aviation history. In 1986, for instance, 394 million passengers flew 302 billion miles on scheduled U.S. carriers without a single fatality. General aviation and commuter lines reported their safest years as well.

None of this obscures one inescapable fact of life in official Washington: nothing happens as fast as you want it to. There are all sorts of procedural roadblocks. For example, it took months to issue a simple requirement that pilots of small aircraft must turn on their transponder, an identifying device that informs ground controllers of a plane's presence in the area. We first had to draft a proposed rule in the FAA bureaucracy; then we had to contend with cost–benefit analysis necessary to ensure the rule's survival in court, OMB reviews and a lengthy public comment period. Such is the necessary price we pay for participatory democracy.

Before I proposed several measures to ensure that small aircraft do not cross paths with commercial airlines over the nation's busiest airports, cautious members of my staff warned me that some aviation interest groups would come off the wall. And, sure enough, the letters poured in, encouraged by full-page newspaper ads paid for by special interests alarmed over changes in the status quo. It was pretty much what I had come to expect. You take tough action, you get a reaction. All in a day's work.

A different kind of turmoil was brewing on the nation's runways, among weary travelers waiting for flights and baggage. I'm a frequent flyer myself and I've experienced my share of canceled flights, misplaced garment bags and nervous checking of my watch. One of the worst hours of my life was spent at Dulles Airport, trying to figure out some way to get to Philadelphia in time to attend the funeral of Virginia Knauer's son. I got there just as Virginia was leaving for the cemetery.

At such times, it's little consolation that weather is responsible for 70 percent of all delays. There's not much we can do about that, but we could and did move on a number of fronts to ease airport angst. By adding a dozen more flight paths, the FAA reduced delays in the congested skies around New York City by 40 percent. "Tiger teams" were sent out by the agency to visit individual airports and come up with measures suitable to each site. We couldn't wait for the NAS and other budget increases to address long-range problems. The problem existed *now,* when airlines were scheduling more flights during popular times of the day than air facilities could possibly accommodate.

I asked rival carriers to voluntarily adjust their schedules, suspending antitrust provisions long enough to get more than a thousand flights spaced out to consumer advantage. After hearing repeated complaints of delays, cancelations and lost baggage, we slapped one airline with a $250,000 fine. Still other investigations led to tough settlement agreements at numerous airports and to a new rule requiring airlines to inform travelers of their on-time performance and baggage complaints. The information made available under this "truth in scheduling" provision will let consumers see which airlines have the best records, and by their choices they will promote better service.

Since leaving the department, I've noted with more than passing interest significant improvements in airline schedules. For the summer of 1987, delay figures were down considerably from levels of the previous year, and in the month of September delays dropped 41 percent from the previous September level. It's been a source of special satisfaction for me to observe the fruits of our labor, the results of seeds sown many months earlier.

Transportation has always been a largely masculine domain. There aren't many female faces among the truckers, ship captains, railroad engineers and highway construction crews who made up my department's natural constituency. Ironically, since the Coast Guard drops anchor in DOT waters, I am the first woman ever to head a branch of the U.S. armed forces.

At first, this took a little getting used to on both sides. Before I visited a ship, my staff would be peppered with questions by admirals wanting to know whether I objected to being helped from my car, and how I felt about the ritual boarding ceremony.

Old salts must have been a bit shaken (I know I was) when an unscheduled visit to a Coast Guard cutter was added to a Florida schedule and I found myself precariously climbing a gangplank in my three-inch-high heels. There was no choice but to hand my pocketbook to a saluting officer of the deck as I hoisted myself up one ramp across the water and down another. "Here," I said to him, "please hold this." After being piped aboard, I made things even worse by referring to topside as "upstairs."

Back on land, it was revealed that only 19 percent of the DOT work force was female. What had it been in 1967, when the department was established? I asked. The answer: 18.5 percent. Minority workers had also been overlooked. I told a departmental women's breakfast that some changes would be made. Having heard similar vows in the past, employees had learned not to put much credence in them.

To counter the skeptics, I asked DOT women themselves to help us find ways to boost midlevel employees into senior management positions, and to give women in secretarial and clerical slots a chance to broaden their professional horizons. The result was a ten-point program that attracted the attention of other Cabinet members and even the Canadian government. It has boosted by several percentage points the number of females in a 100,000-member work force. Of equal importance, it has raised the confidence and the job prospects of thousands of women, many of them in the air traffic control system. Not long ago, a pilot told me that in his approach to a major U.S. airport he had heard three distinct voices over the air traffic control system. Women's voices. And DOT is proud to be one of the first in government to operate a day care center for the benefit of working mothers.*

We've taken some giant strides in the twenty years since a few Nixon Administration female appointees established a support system called Executive Women in Government. In those days the first question most bosses asked was "Can you type?"

---

*We have come a long way, but there's a way to go yet. Not long ago a stewardess approached me on a plane and whispered into my ear the comment put to her by a male passenger a few rows back: "I hear that Secretary Dole's wife is on board."

Today, many of the bosses are women and some of the typists are men. Diversity is the hallmark of the modern American woman. We wear the robes of a judge, the face mask of a surgeon, the pinstripes of a banker. We teach on campuses, peer through lab microscopes, design buildings and run businesses. Some of us write the laws that other women enforce. Some build rockets for others to ride into space. The most energetic of all run a home and raise a family. No role is superior to another.

Never having had children myself, I'm lucky to have Robin, who is much more than a stepdaughter, and a pair of nephews close enough to be like sons. John, a young minister, works in the Senate on issues of international religious liberty, and Jody is the fourth generation of Hanfords to enter the family business.

Given the predominance of two-income couples in today's society, there is nothing about the division of labor in the Dole household that isn't repeated in millions of American homes every night of the week. Just ask the makers of Lean Cuisine. Fortunately, I have the soul of a short-order cook, as well as a small library of thirty-minute-meal cookbooks. "Don't spend all that time in the kitchen," Bob tells me whenever I propose to cook him a full-course meal. "Let's go out so we can talk."

Thinking back to election night, 1980, I can recall a bitter-sweet feeling that outside forces were taking control of my life. It wasn't just the frantic schedule—the 8 A.M. appointments at the hairdresser, complete with phone calls taken under the dryer. And how many nights I'd have eagerly traded dinner in a hotel ballroom with a couple thousand people for an evening at home with my husband, or the chance to watch television and ride the stationary bicycle that's set up in our small apartment.

Did I say *small?* When first married, we put off looking for a house. There'd be time for that later, we told ourselves. Twelve years have passed, and I'm still yearning for a fireplace and for a little backyard in which to commune with nature.

My advice to any dual-career couple is to have as many special times as you can, and not allow work to crowd out the really important things in life. Bob and I don't get to travel together as much as we would like, but we look for every opportunity. When Bob's on the road, he sometimes sends me flowers. He follows my schedule as closely as his own. Before I left town, he's been known to call my staff and ask what kind of plane I'd be using, to make sure it had two engines and two pilots, and to check up on weather conditions.

Whenever we're apart, we burn up the telephone wires. At home, we write lots of messages. I remember one time when Bob flew into town late at night, long after I was asleep. I had addressed the White House Conference on Small Business earlier in the day. On my way out the door the next morning for an early TV show while he still slept, I remembered that he was to speak to the same audience that day. Hurrying back inside, I left a note on the bathroom mirror: "Don't use the joke about making the bed—I already used it."

The bed joke is part of the very public private life that we lead. *People* magazine had included with its profile of Bob and me a photo of us making the bed together in our Watergate apartment. A few days after the magazine hit the newsstands, Bob got a letter from an irate California Republican. The man said he had nothing against a female Cabinet officer. His complaint was strictly personal. "Senator Dole," he wrote, "my wife saw that picture of you making the bed, and now she has *me* helping make the bed. Please, Senator, you've got to stop doing all that work around the house. You're causing problems for men all across America."

"You don't know the half of it," Bob wrote back. "The only reason she was helping make the bed was because they were taking pictures."

I got my chance to return the ribbing when I was invited to match wits with former trade ambassador and Middle East negotiator Robert Strauss at the 1984 Gridiron Dinner. I was uniquely qualified to pass judgment on air bags, I reminded the audience; after all, I'd been driving around with one for years. I also recalled a recent interview in which a reporter had asked Bob whether being married to a powerful woman ever made him feel a bit emasculated.

"Hold it, cupcake," I had interrupted. "I'll take this one."
Bob laughed harder than anyone else.

BOB

*If you would test a man's character, then give
him power.*

—ABRAHAM LINCOLN

Like most conservatives, I put great stock in self-reliance,
but experience has shown me that there's no such thing as an
entirely self-made man or woman. A government program
called the GI Bill of Rights allowed me to complete college, the
only one of four children in my family to do so. Without the
encouragement of a Washburn law librarian who didn't even
belong to my party, I might not have entered politics. And if it
weren't for Hampar Kelikian, my life would have been very
different indeed.

Everyone wants to make it on his own, but not everyone
can. Maybe there aren't enough jobs where a person lives.
Maybe the schools aren't as good, or he hasn't had the breaks
you or I have. Homeless people didn't just show up yesterday
on the grates of America's cities. As Russell County attorney, I
used to get called in the middle of the night when some poor
guy had been found off the side of the highway, sleeping in a
car with his entire family. Saddest of all, the local welfare office
often paid just enough to move the family on to the next town.

Conservatism means different things to different people.
To me, it's a creed of opportunity, rooted in the ability of
seemingly ordinary people to achieve extraordinary things. This
explains my support for civil-rights legislation, as well as the
1983 bill making the late Dr. Martin Luther King, Jr.'s, birthday a federal holiday. I'm a conservative Republican, King was
a liberal Democrat, but the ideals I defended in the mountains
of Italy forty years ago included the rights for which King
fought on the streets of Birmingham and Selma.

Opponents of the bill said King was too controversial, or

claimed that a new federal holiday would be too expensive. As the bill's floor manager, I took a different stand in leading off final debate on October 3, 1983:

"A nation defines itself in many ways; in the promises it makes and the programs it enacts, the dreams it enshrines or the doors it slams shut. . . . Thanks to Dr. King . . . America . . . wrote new laws to strike down old barriers. She built bridges instead of walls. She invited the black man and woman into the mainstream of society—and in doing so, opened the way for women, the disabled, and other minorities who found their own voice in the civil-rights movement.

"There is nothing partisan about justice," I reminded my colleagues. "It is as conservative as the Constitution, as liberal as Lincoln, as radical as Jefferson's sweeping assertion that all of God's creation is equal in His eyes. . . ."

Ten days later, the Senate overwhelmingly approved the bill. The King holiday celebrates much more than one man's life. It reaffirms America's age-old commitment to human freedom. In our own time, freedom-loving people of both races have carried out one of history's great social revolutions. In doing so, they have reaffirmed America's status as the world's foremost developing nation. We are developing still, something we ought to think about every January 15.

Freedom is a gift from God, not government. It is indivisible. To have it for ourselves, we must demand it for others. That conviction, and our willingness to act upon it, has made America a beacon in the night of tyranny, and a source of inspiration to oppressed people everywhere: to boat people who fled Indochina after Communist rule turned that region into a vast prison camp; to Filipinos who poured into the streets of Manila demanding an end to Marcos' corruption and a return of political liberties; to courageous Salvadorans who defied the death threats of Marxist guerrillas and stood in the tropical sun for hours to vote in El Salvador's election.

Freedom is not easily won in the modern world. In Nicaragua, those who stand up for human rights must battle a repressive dictatorship that openly boasts of suppressing the Catholic Church. In Afghanistan, the Soviet puppet regime fights its opposition with toy bombs that kill and dismember children. In Angola, Jonas Savimbi's democratic resistance forces do battle with tens of thousands of Cuban mercenaries sent at Moscow's request.

From the rain forests of Cambodia to the streets of Port-au-Prince, Haiti, freedom's forces are on the march. For the first time, most Third World guerrilla movements are fighting to overthrow Communism so that they can replace it with democracy. In our own hemisphere, American support has gone to Nicaragua's freedom fighters so that pluralistic democracy might be given a chance in that unhappy country as it has been throughout much of Latin America.

We haven't always explained our goals as well as we should have, but that doesn't detract from the moral justification of U.S. policy in that region. Much more is at stake than Swiss bank accounts or forgetful White House assistants. Central America is in our geopolitical backyard. There is no place there for a Soviet client state, let alone one sworn to subvert its democratic, peaceloving neighbors. The threat is real, the challenge undeniable. American credibility and American security are on the line. If we believe our assertion that freedom is a universal right, we will break out of our natural insularity and reject the isolationism of those who want to hide behind the Atlantic, the Pacific—and the Rio Grande. We won't lock our doors or close our eyes to the world we live in, nor should we have to send our diplomats to beg assistance from foreign sultans when members of Congress tie the President's hands.

Opponents of U.S. aid to the Nicaraguan resistance assume a moral equivalence between the contras and the Sandinista regime in Managua. Just how wrong they are came home to me with dramatic force during a visit to Central America in August 1987. Along with four other Republican senators, I made the trip to sound out leaders in the region about prospects for a negotiated peace based on a plan initiated by Costa Rican President Oscar Arias and finally initialed by Nicaraguan strongman Daniel Ortega.

In between constructive talks with Honduran President José Azcona and would-be peacemaker Arias, we arrived in

Managua August 31. None of us had any idea whether Ortega would even receive the delegation. But a short bus ride brought us to an old country club on the city's outskirts, its grounds lined with antiaircraft guns. There we cooled our heels for half an hour, before being ushered into a room full of media people.

I waited for the press to snap their pictures and leave, allowing Ortega and the rest of us to have a private discussion of the Arias plan and our concerns about Nicaraguan subversion in the region. Ortega had other ideas. With the media present and a nationwide audience listening in via Radio Managua, the "Comandante" began by ridiculing a recent broadcast to his country by the President of the United States. "And how are the contras doing after receiving President Reagan's radio message?" he asked sarcastically.

I interrupted Ortega's anti-American harangue by pointing out the military assistance his own regime was getting from the Soviet Union and its allies. According to Ortega, the Soviets, the Cubans and the Bulgarians were on hand to help the people of Nicaragua. "Well, we're helping the contras," I told him.

After further sparring over human-rights violations, I asked Ortega point blank, "Do you want to talk about the August seventh peace initiative or do you just want to have this pep rally?"

Democratic Congressman Peter Kostmayer, a last-minute addition to the meeting, jumped in to assure Ortega: "You have to do much less than you could imagine to stop contra aid." Ortega pricked up his ears as Kostmayer mentioned a few steps, like reopening the newspaper *La Prensa,* allowing the Catholic Church to resume uncensored radio broadcasts, and releasing some jailed opposition leaders.

"It'll take more than that," I interjected. "There's got to be a total democratization."

Ortega eventually calmed down enough to stop making speeches and start a dialogue. But it was obvious that there would be no agreement that afternoon. Ortega convinced me more than ever that he would never turn his back on his masters in Moscow and Havana or drop plans to export his revolution throughout Central America. Why else would a nation of 2.4

million people support a 150,000-man army? As for internal reforms, I've never known a Marxist to voluntarily relinquish power.

Yet everything I saw—the thumbs-up signs we got from average Nicaraguans on the streets of Managua, the spontaneous cries of "Freedom!" and the moral courage displayed by the editor of *La Prensa* and Cardinal Miguel Obando y Bravo —convinced me that in a free election Ortega would be voted out of office in a landslide.

What stands out most in memory about the trip isn't Ortega, a man of limited charisma and predictable views; what I remember most clearly is the agony of refugees driven across the border into neighboring Honduras. A few hours before touching down in Managua, I had been to a United Nations—run camp housing six thousand people, forced from their homes and fearful of returning to Nicaragua as long as the Sandinistas hold power. My heart went out to the little girls without shoes, the mothers without sons, the men who had farms confiscated and who now were forced to live in primitive huts—part of several hundred thousand Nicaraguans and Salvadorans made homeless by Marxist persecution. I tried to reassure the camp's inhabitants that the American people would never abandon them, nor permit a Soviet-backed regime to draw a totalitarian shade over Central America.

It's a promise I intend to keep.

One of the biggest ovations at the Dallas convention that nominated Reagan for a second term in August 1984 went to United Nations Ambassador Jeane Kirkpatrick, who told delegates about an early conversation she had with some Third World diplomats in New York. They had asked her what separated Ronald Reagan's foreign policies from Jimmy Carter's. Kirkpatrick responded, "We have taken off our 'Kick Me' sign."

Kirkpatrick wasn't the only woman spotlighted in Dallas. Convention week gave me an idea what life must be like for Margaret Thatcher's husband. A prominent columnist asked me how I'd feel about a Bush-Dole ticket in 1988.

"I'm not sure," I answered. "To tell you the truth, I don't believe I'd really be interested."

"Good," he said, "because I wasn't thinking of *you*."

I decided it was a good omen that our Dallas hotel suite was numbered 1988. Then Howard Baker did a little checking. "That room isn't registered to Bob Dole," he informed the *Washington Post*. "It's registered to Elizabeth Dole."

But there are limits even to Elizabeth's name recognition, as we found out when a woman in the Kansas delegation overheard a pair of male delegates discussing upcoming events.

"What's on the program tonight?" one of the men inquired.

"I don't know," said his friend. "The Dole Brothers are going to speak."

There's no doubt which "Dole Brother" won the orator honors that evening. The best part of my speech was its conclusion: "A legacy is a gift to the future. I am fortunate to have one of my own, and I take great pride in presenting her to you now: the Secretary of the United States Department of Transportation."

Elizabeth promptly upstaged me. "The stature of women everywhere would be diminished if a candidate for national office were supported simply because she's a woman," she declared, a month after Democrat Geraldine Ferraro's nomination for Vice President. "The idea that an election could be won on the basis of gender insults our electoral process. We are thinking women. No platitudes will buy us. No party will inherit us. No candidate will own us." Elizabeth told the crowd exactly what it wanted to hear—and stole the show. I've never been prouder of her.

While Elizabeth and I are big supporters of each other in public, we observe a strict ban on speechmaking around the house. We also allow the other his or her indulgences. Because I'm a news junkie, Elizabeth surprised me one birthday with a cable-TV hookup. She doesn't complain about the round-the-clock headline service, and I don't complain—much—about her monopolizing the closet space, even if our dog has more room for his things than I do.

The dog is Leader, a miniature schnauzer Elizabeth found at a local Humane Society shelter. Harry Truman used to say that if you want a friend in Washington, get yourself a dog. We're both glad for the chance to get outdoors and think—or not think—that comes with walking Leader around the block. But not even canines, it turns out, are immune to controversy. After the press reported that Leader had allegedly ridden in a government car, the *Wall Street Journal* had a little fun with the pet-gets-chauffeured angle. A Hays, Kansas, newspaper ran a less amusing editorial, and Leader filed a protest: "I don't mind if you criticize my owner, as you occasionally do, but when you pick on me . . . that really gets under my flea collar! To compare me with Fala, FDR's best friend who was transported around the globe on a Navy vessel, is cynically unfair. Then again, just think what my critics would say if I drove myself!"

Next to a sense of humor, life in the political goldfish bowl demands nothing more than the ability to improvise. When I led a senatorial delegation on a trade mission to the Far East in the summer of 1985, Elizabeth wore three hats on the trip. As Secretary of Transportation, she conducted some tough aviation and maritime negotiations with her foreign counterparts. As wife of the delegation's chairman, and a Reagan Administration spokesman in her own right, she never knew in advance whether she would be called upon to give a toast to Deng Xiaoping or answer questions about U.S. railroads. And as host to senatorial spouses, she got in as much socializing as a crowded official itinerary would permit.

In some ways, the journey was a metaphor of our lives together. Not exactly relaxing, but full of memorable experiences. One Sunday morning Elizabeth slipped away at seven o'clock with Pat Moynihan and Pete Domenici to attend services in a Beijing cathedral. It was a special moment for her, finding a church overflowing with worshipers despite a torrential rainstorm, in the capital of Mao Tse-tung's officially Godless state.

Closer to home, one of Elizabeth's most meaningful birthdays was spent with some of Washington's large homeless population. A friend had told her about Sarah's Circle, a church-sponsored organization that ministers to and houses street people. She decided that instead of a traditional birthday party, with people giving her gifts, she would reverse the process.

Since our birthdays are a week apart, I went in with her on decorating a local coffeehouse and choosing presents for each of the residents of Sarah's Circle. During lunch we heard from a woman named Beulah. According to her, before finding Sarah's Circle she had spent her time sitting on street corners. Now Beulah collects old clothing from area churches and sells it on the weekend to raise money for Sarah's Circle. She takes nothing for herself. "If I had some money," she explained, "I'd only want more."

At one point Beulah said she never thought she would be sitting next to a United States senator. The honor was all mine, I told her.

Two political contests were decided in November 1984. Three weeks after Ronald Reagan's forty-nine-state sweep, Republican senators met to decide on Howard Baker's replacement as Majority Leader. In the weeks leading up to the caucus, I knocked on more doors than a Fuller Brush man. In one office, I got a blank stare from a receptionist who didn't know me. Luckily, she wasn't voting.

When the fifty-three senators filed into the restored Old Senate Chamber on the morning of November 29, it was Alaska's Ted Stevens against a field that included Richard G. Lugar of Indiana, Pete Domenici of New Mexico, James A. McClure of Idaho and myself. Stevens had earned high marks as a vote-counter during his four years as Baker's deputy, but, in this campaign, preelection polls were meaningless. There was no way to predict the outcome. After four secret ballots, Stevens and I were tied with twenty votes apiece. At the end of the fifth round, Howard Greene, secretary to the Senate majority, flashed me a thumbs-up sign. A few minutes later, the official count confirmed Greene's gesture: for Dole, 28; for Stevens, 25.

I had no illusions about the Majority Leader's position or

the clout it carried within the Senate. Howard Baker once confided to me that there were days when he was sure he had the best job in Washington, but there were other times when trying to make the Senate function was like pushing a wet noodle. Personally, I think the job ought to be renamed Majority Pleader.

Unfortunately, tools of persuasion that were razor sharp in Lyndon Johnson's hands have long since been dulled. Old power bases formed on geographical or institutional allegiances have dissolved. Along with them has gone the ability of a few senior committee chairmen ("herd bulls," LBJ called them) to impose their will on deferential juniors. In this age of weakened party loyalties, any Majority Leader is part ringmaster and part traffic cop. He is an architect, building a legislative house brick by brick, commitment by commitment. Most of all, he's a juggler, keeping half a dozen balls in the air while looking down the road to see where vectors of policy and politics converge.

Despite the modern Senate's fragmentation of power, the Leader still has a few arrows in his quiver. A well-placed word from his office can help move a stalled bill through committee, or keep an unwanted one bottled up. He can assist colleagues by turning the media spotlight their way, scheduling their bills on the floor, raising campaign funds or wangling White House invitations.

A President in crafting his legislative agenda is obliged to consider the Majority Leader's reading of the political temperature on Capitol Hill. My own priorities for the Ninety-ninth Congress were spelled out plainly: to do something about the federal deficit and to write a new farm bill that would make U.S. agriculture more competitive in the world market.

I knew that each of these issues would demand more than the usual political courage from lawmakers. But the way I see it, voters send us to Washington to make things happen. Granted, when talking to most audiences about attacking the deficit I'm never sure whether all those heads out front are nodding in agreement or dropping off to sleep. But the problem is real. The deficit won't go away, or *grow* away, even with a robust economy.

When I became Majority Leader, the fastest-growing program in Washington was interest on the trillion-dollar national debt—an economic deadweight fast approaching $200 billion a year. Now, I know that all those zeroes can begin to lose their meaning after a while, but consider them from another angle: think what we could do in this country with an extra $200 billion. We could invest in an educational system to help us better compete with Japan and other technologically advanced countries. We could target additional tax cuts in ways that would distribute prosperity more widely and salvage the growing underclass of Americans who are hungry, homeless or destitute.

We could bolster funding of President Reagan's Strategic Defense Initiative, intended to shield the West from Soviet blackmail and put an end to the forty-year-old nuclear nightmare. We could also give more assistance—military and humanitarian—to democratic forces around the globe. Or we might even pay off some of our $2.4 trillion accumulated debt. Not much chance of that, but it was worth thinking about then and still is.

Beginning in January 1985, Senate Republicans were determined to do more than nickel-and-dime the deficit. For weeks, Pete Domenici and others on the Budget Committee struggled to come up with a plan acceptable to the White House. But when the President's men dug in their heels on the issue of military spending, the ball was back in our court.

As a rule, I don't like meetings. Half of the people show up late; the other half never come at all. You're lucky to get a meeting of minds without a knocking together of heads. But I'd rather play the game than umpire, so that spring I turned my office into Budget Central. More than a hundred meetings produced a deficit-reduction package with teeth.

We hoped to realize $135 billion in savings over three years by freezing most government outlays at current levels, limiting the Pentagon to an increase covering only inflation, and deferring for one year scheduled cost-of-living adjustments on entitlement programs. No one on Social Security would forfeit any current benefits. Instead the ax would fall on fourteen federal programs that had outlived their usefulness.

It was a bold plan, affecting virtually every American and

containing something to offend just about every senator. Passage hung on the vote of Pete Wilson, a freshman Republican from California who was taken to the hospital and operated on for an emergency appendectomy thirty-six hours before the final vote. Had it been anyone but Wilson, a former marine, I would have accused him of not being sick at all, just hiding out.

President Reagan couldn't give us much help, either, but for entirely different reasons. He was five thousand miles away, visiting European allies. That left Vice President Bush, who returned from a trip out West after being advised by White House chief of staff Don Regan that the Republican plan had the President's approval. Bush would be on hand to break a tie. Problem was, to get a tie we needed Pete Wilson.

On the morning of May 9, with Wilson in a recovery room at Bethesda, I called his doctors. Could he physically withstand a trip to Capitol Hill? I asked them. If the answer was yes, then how long could he remain in the Capitol? Was he sedated or sufficiently clear-minded to take part in a roll-call vote?

Wilson's doctors didn't want their patient jostled over the six miles of road from Bethesda to Capitol Hill. The Senator overrode their objections. Pete Wilson may have lost an appendix, but obviously he'd kept his backbone.

Late that Thursday night, Republicans met in S-230 to see where we stood. I knew we would lose at least four, maybe five from our ranks. Partly to compensate, we had Nebraska Democrat Edward Zorinsky, who was bucking his party's leadership with the same courage Wilson displayed in leaving his hospital bed. Assuming Zorinsky held firm and we suffered no more GOP defections, we'd have our tie.

"We'll give it a shot," I said.

Outside the Capitol, an ambulance siren announced Pete Wilson's arrival. Clad in pajamas and a robe, and hooked up to an IV tube, Wilson was taken out on a stretcher, then transferred to a wheelchair for the short ride to an anteroom off the Senate floor. It was nearly two in the morning when the junior Senator from California was wheeled into a hushed Senate Chamber, to be greeted by a bipartisan standing ovation. The cheers turned to appreciative laughter when Wilson jokingly asked the presiding officer, "Now, Mr. President, what was the pending question?" and then without waiting for an answer cast his aye vote.

At the end of the roll call, the Vice President in his traditional role broke the tie. In a moment for the record books the Senate demonstrated its capacity to govern. We didn't appoint a study commission. We didn't buck the decision to future Congresses, or to future generations.

"We had a pretty close call, Mr. President," I informed Reagan in a predawn transatlantic phone conversation. "But I think you'll agree, $135 billion is worth staying up all night for."

Unfortunately, the story didn't end there. Whenever you bite a bullet you run the risk of having it explode in your face. That's what happened to me a few weeks later when the White House cut a separate deal with some House Republicans and Tip O'Neill. Together, they decided to play it safe by going ahead with the cost-of-living increase in federal entitlement programs. In doing so, the Administration not only scuttled the Senate's package but also destroyed any prospect for significant action on the deficit. And it left most Senate Republicans standing on a trap door.

Our efforts weren't a complete waste, though. The momentum that was built up in the spring of 1985 led Congress later to adopt the Gramm-Rudman-Hollings formula to eliminate the deficit by 1991. Time has shown that it will take more than Gramm-Rudman or reforms of the budget process to do the trick. The problem isn't procedural, it's political. Quite simply, are we willing to curb our appetite for government benefits? Can America's leaders develop policies based on her future needs rather than on a reading of the latest polls?

I leave the question to you.

"Those who labor in the earth are the chosen people of God," wrote Thomas Jefferson.

Americans have always had a love affair with the land. For much of our history we have made our living as an agrarian nation. Long after the farmer and the rancher won the West, the life of sun and seed and soil still has a strong hold on our collective imagination. City folks dream of owning a little house in the country, and politicians since Jefferson have praised the self-reliant farmer as the backbone of an independent, land-owning citizenry.

As a senator from Kansas, my concern for agriculture goes hand in hand with representing the interests of my constituency. There's more to it than that, though. Growing up in Russell, I learned that if you take the farmer out of a rural community you might as well roll up Main Street. He's the one who comes into town to spend money and create jobs. And when the farmer has a bad year, so does just about everyone else.

For nearly fifty years, my father depended for his income on farmers who sold him their sour cream, grain and eggs. Today's food chain creates an even longer job chain than in Dad's time. Just over two million farmers are responsible for nearly nineteen million jobs in grain elevators, farm implement factories, processing plants and export houses.

If you don't eat, you don't need to worry about the farmer. Otherwise, his problems are at least in part your problems, too. Thanks to the productivity and efficiency of this country's farmers, Americans spend less of their disposable income on food than any other Western nation. There are those who object to federal efforts aimed at stabilizing farm income in a fluctuating world market. When a farmer gets a check from the government, they call it a subsidy. In reality, it's an indirect subsidy to the American consumer, who has the best food bargain in the world.

Why should the farm economy be the center of national attention? The simplest answer is that agriculture is America's most basic industry, indispensable to our standard of living and economic growth. We *must* have a reliable food supply. We *need* to export large quantities of wheat, feed grains, soybeans and other agricultural products to help balance U.S. trade with the rest of the world.

Farming also isn't like other businesses. A farm family can work themselves ragged and then have their crops wiped out in thirty minutes by hailstorms or floods. Even with all the advances of twentieth-century technology, we can't completely protect against the threat of disease, insects and weather.

As if the farmer didn't have enough to worry about from nature, he also has to deal with the whims of Congress. Having spent twenty-seven years on the House and Senate Agriculture Committees, I can tell you there isn't a more popular vote for some on Capitol Hill than the one cast against a farm bill. To urban congressmen it's a chance to score points with consumers at the expense of farmers, and latter-day populists see almost any proposal as open season on the family farm.

Things weren't so bad during the 1970s, when a boom in farm exports kept prices and income levels high. Then came Jimmy Carter's 1980 embargo on grain sales to the Soviet Union, bracketed by double-digit inflation and crippling interest rates. Foreign markets shrank as a strong dollar and stiff competition from Argentina, Australia and much of Western Europe threatened to do to the American farmer what Japanese workers have done to the American electronics industry.

By the early eighties, rural America was reeling, with many farmers forced to abandon their livelihood, and young people in search of job opportunities compelled to look elsewhere. Against this backdrop, taxpayers and lawmakers alike were increasingly upset over federal farm programs whose costs had quadrupled in less than a decade to $18 billion in 1985. As Congress deliberated over a new farm bill early that year, I had to contend with two diametrically opposed schools of thought.

The White House sought substantial, immediate cuts in farm income and price supports. Essentially, the Administration wanted to go the free-market route overnight. In an ideal world, one in which other countries don't subsidize their farmers, we could all compete on a level playing field. American productivity and know-how would triumph. And the Administration's theories would be vindicated.

But as long as other nations refuse to play the game by free-market rules, it is unrealistic and unfair to pull the rug out from under U.S. farmers. Recognizing this fact, most farm-state legislators assailed the Administration's 1985 plan and argued instead for a four-year freeze of income-support payments at existing levels. A few went even further, calling for a return to mandatory controls over farm production—a modern variant on former Secretary of Agriculture Henry Wallace's planned scarcity of Dust Bowl days.

In my view, neither idea addressed the underlying need to restore the competitiveness of U.S. agriculture, so that farmers could earn more from the market than from the government. We burned the midnight oil in search of a workable compromise, one that would satisfy White House cost concerns and still achieve both these objectives. It took eleven months and countless hours of debate, but the final product was worth the effort. Weighing in at thirteen pounds, the 1985 farm bill included a two-year freeze on federal target price supports, followed by gradual annual reductions. This combination would help us cushion farm income during the ensuing transition period.

George Anthan of the Des Moines *Register* summarized the delicate legislative minuet that led up to the Senate's 55–38 endorsement of the final bill. To the audience of National Public Radio's *Morning Edition* Anthan described the several hats I wore. As Majority Leader, he said, I had a responsibility to support the Reagan Administration; as a senator from Kansas, I represented a constituency whose interests differed markedly from those of the White House; finally, the Senate itself needed guidance, and the fragmented coalition of various farm groups required strategic leadership.

"If it hadn't been for Dole," said Anthan, "I doubt if there would be a farm bill now. . . . He was the dealmaker. The Democrats from the farm states, who have certain demands, could go to Dole, and he can get things done for them."

I look at the 1985 farm bill as a high point of "getting things done." It's not a perfect piece of legislation. Perfect bills don't get written, except by columnists and economists. But if politics is the art of the possible, the farm bill will justifiably be seen as a real achievement. Things have improved in rural America in the two years since. But we shouldn't deceive ourselves. A lot of folks are still hurting. The day we stop caring about their needs or turn a deaf ear to their appeals will be the end of Jefferson's dream. American consumers will suffer, but no more than the American character.

ELIZABETH

At the age of eighty-eight, Oliver Wendell Holmes took a train trip. Unable to locate his ticket, Holmes searched his pockets as a conductor looked on.

"Don't worry, Justice Holmes," the conductor reassured him. "You don't need a ticket. You'll probably find it when you get off the train, and I'm sure the Pennsylvania Railroad will trust you to mail it back later."

"My dear man," Holmes replied, with some irritation, "that isn't the problem at all. The question is not, where is my ticket? The question is, where am I going?"

Before 1980, U.S. railroads were going nowhere. They were victims of declining patronage, poor management and stiff competition from the trucking industry. Adding to their problems was excessive government regulation. The Interstate Commerce Commission denied individual carriers the right to tailor services to specific shippers' needs. It was a policy of uniformity at the expense of economic dynamism, and as a result the world's largest rail system was on its knees, with a quarter of all U.S. track in bankruptcy.

Too many rules meant too much risk of companies unable to earn the capital to maintain aging tracks and cars. You could end up with service that was unsafe as well as unreliable. Congress recognized the problem in 1980, when it passed the Staggers Act, which partially deregulated the rails. Eight years later, rail shippers have signed over fifty thousand individualized contracts, agreements formerly prohibited under regulation. Increased competition has cut shipping costs and improved on-time deliveries. Railroads have become more profitable. And 1986 was the safest year in rail history. The industry's accident rate has declined from over 10,000 a year in the late seventies to 2,760 in 1986—the lowest ever.

The trucking industry has also been partially deregulated.

What used to be a closed market has been thrown open, and crazy-quilt rules—permitting some rigs to carry milk, for example, but not ice cream—have been thrown out. To graphically illustrate the absurdity of government regulation, I once testified before a Senate committee in support of legislation to complete trucking deregulation with a bowl of Orville Redenbacher's popcorn on my left and a bowl of Jiffy Pop on my right. Why, I asked committee members, did the ICC require truckers to file rates with the government for one brand but not the other?

The implications go far beyond the price of popcorn. Since transportation on average accounts for roughly 25 percent of a delivered product's cost, and government regulation tacks on another 20 to 40 percent, it's obvious that further deregulation will help U.S. businesses in their struggle to remain competitive.

Government deregulation is an acknowledgment of the superiority of individual enterprise and ingenuity. Remember the thrilling flight of the Voyager aircraft? The world held its breath in November 1986 as pilots Dick Rutan and Jenna Yaeger rode the tail winds of a Pacific typhoon and kept a watchful eye on their seventeen fuel tanks as they circled the world non-stop.

Voyager was not created by government experts. It began as a doodle on a restaurant napkin and was built with the life savings of its crew. In the deregulated, entrepreneurial climate of the Reagan years, the plane's creators had to fill out only two pieces of government papers: an application for airworthiness and a request for a tail number.

I began my government career promoting the rights of American consumers and arguing for economic deregulation. Twenty years later, those themes have been picked up by advocates in both major parties and in countless institutions, public as well as private. I hope that any temporary difficulties that may affect an economy in transition will not prompt lawmakers to pine for the imagined glories of reregulation.

A democracy—especially an economic democracy—cannot stand still. Anyone hoping to turn the clock back might just as well stop the world from spinning or the human mind from pursuing its quest for transportation that is faster, safer and more affordable. It's as simple as that.

"Deregulation" is a long word for a simple process. So is "privatization." By putting business back into the hands of the people, privatization reverses a century of collectivism and centralized planning by the state. As British Prime Minister Margaret Thatcher has said, "The wealth of a country is the efforts of its people, and effort depends on incentives."

I've twice had the pleasure of meeting with the Prime Minister. Both times we had plenty to talk about, because Thatcher's Britain has been in the forefront of privatization. Since coming to power nine years ago, she has almost single-handedly converted what Napoleon called a "nation of shopkeepers" into a nation of shareholders. State-owned firms like Jaguar, British Airways and Rolls-Royce have switched to private ownership—and over 400,000 British workers now have a personal stake in the companies that employ them.

In France, a conservative government is undoing the nationalization of banks, insurance companies and travel agencies. West Germany is divesting its holdings in Volkswagen. Italy has sold Alitalia, the state-owned airline. Japan has put its national railroad on the auction block.

The trend isn't limited to democratic countries or free-enterprise economies. Modern China permits some tenants to own their own homes. Socialist governments in Africa have dissolved agricultural monopolies. Even Mikhail Gorbachev's Soviet Union is experimenting with economic reforms that promise to reward individual effort and send Lenin spinning in his red granite mausoleum.

In this country, the flagship of privatization has been Conrail, the federally chartered railroad fashioned from the wreckage of Penn Central and a half dozen other Northeastern lines. Long before Penn Central's 1970 bankruptcy, structural changes in the region's economy, not to mention the Interstate Highway System and the eighteen-wheel trucks that use it, had sharply diminished rail traffic by traditional clients like steel, auto makers and coal shippers.

Reversing all this was a bit like ordering an avalanche

uphill. Congress tried anyway, establishing the passenger railroad Amtrak in 1971 and Conrail five years later. Having racked up $1.6 billion in red ink during its first four years, Conrail was given a fresh round of concessions in 1981, including exemption from state taxes and an easing of the way toward abandoning unprofitable routes and commuter services. The line was also granted a federal bailout on its labor-protection costs, worth $325 million in the first year alone.

For all this, and despite the new deregulated climate of the eighties, Drew Lewis could see Conrail's fragility. By breaking up the company, Lewis hoped to get back at least some of the taxpayers' multibillion-dollar investment. Opposing him was the railroad's chairman, L. Stanley Crane, a rail industry veteran who was just as determined to keep intact what he liked to call "my railroad."

By the time I replaced Lewis, Congress had ordered DOT to begin a process leading to Conrail's sale, without specifying its own preference between a public stock offering and merger with another company. One might easily question the depth of Congress' commitment, since few if any governments in recorded history have voluntarily reduced their size or their authority, and the return of Conrail to private ownership would slice off a considerable chunk of federal turf.

When I arrived in 1983, the New York investment banking firm of Goldman, Sachs had already been selected to advise the department. I ordered the financial experts to work closely with Federal Railroad Administrator John Riley in an aggressive campaign to market Conrail. More than a hundred corporations were approached.

Throughout the summer and fall of 1984, we narrowed the list of fifteen bidders to six and then to three. I wanted a good up-front price, of course, but to assure Conrail's long-range viability and make certain the federal government didn't find a destitute railroad back on its doorstep in a few years, I also insisted on a series of protective covenants.

One of the requirements was that the line's new owners invest heavily in capital improvements over a five-year period. Another placed strict limits on dividend payments. A third would insulate Conrail from the effects of any sudden economic downturn by maintaining half a billion dollars in cash reserves.

In February 1985 I accepted the best offer, which came from the Norfolk Southern Corporation. In addition to $1.2 billion in cash, the company promised to buy out employee-owned stock and to restore wage cuts imposed by Stanley Crane as part of his corporate down-sizing efforts. Most important of all, Norfolk Southern committed itself to the protective covenants. To blunt criticism of the deal on competitive grounds, NS also accepted in principle a Justice Department plan to divest some of its current holdings and thereby allow rival railroads to break out of their regional isolation.

When a snag developed, it came in one of the most unlikely places. To schedule a Senate vote on the Norfolk Southern proposal, I went to the Majority Leader. You think it was an advantage being married to the Leader? Think again. Had Howard Baker still occupied S-230, I could have easily called him and said, "Howard, this one's important. I want my bill up now." But Baker was never questioned about his wife's role in determining the Senate calendar. Bob Dole was, and it was enough to make him cautious.

"Bob," I said one evening, "you're bending over backward to be fair. And that's fine. But, my gosh, you're bending over so far you're about to fall off the chart. Meanwhile, I can't get even one issue up for consideration on the floor."

Not until December 1985 did the Conrail bill finally reach the full Senate, where it promptly ran into a filibuster. Opponents of the Norfolk Southern deal warned of the consequences of a rail merger. But they aimed most of their fire at another merger—mine and Bob's.

"The fix is in," Michigan Democrat Don Riegle declared. "It has been for a long time."

Riegle didn't know what he was talking about. John Chaffee leaped to my defense, denying, as he put it, "that the Secretary of Transportation has a grip on us."

"I wish she did," interjected Democrat Fritz Hollings of South Carolina.

The Senate finally approved the deal, 53 to 39, a margin

sufficient to move the bill to the House but not large enough to impress John D. Dingell, the powerful chairman of the House Energy and Commerce Committee. With typical candor, Dingell opposed the sale of Conrail to Norfolk Southern because of the threat he believed it posed to rivals of a merged railroad. Given the industry's history, and the nineteenth-century railroad oligopolies that once set prices and defined service, Dingell's concern had a surface validity. But Commodore Vanderbilt was in his grave. In the modern rail era, the danger is less one of monopoly than of extinction. By divesting some of its own lines and strengthening Conrail's long-range prospects, Norfolk Southern would enhance, not diminish, rail competition. For the first time in decades, two long-haul railroads would be competing from the Midwest to the East Coast.

The most outspoken opponents of the deal didn't care about the divestitures and disliked the protective covenants. At heart, they didn't want to sell the railroad, especially not in the summer of 1986. Dingell in particular knew that if Democrats managed to regain the Senate in November, he might get a more favorable hearing for his plan to reregulate the railroads. So critics of Norfolk Southern dug in their heels. With the advantages of seniority and entrenched positions in the House hierarchy, the opposition was confident it could stop the deal dead in its tracks.

If everyone in Washington allowed political differences to get in the way of personal friendships, this would be a pretty lonely town. When reporters began writing of a Dole–Dingell feud, I called up the Congressman, whose love of the outdoors was legendary, and invited myself to go fishing with him while I was out in his home state, Michigan, on a speaking engagement. At first taken aback by the request, Dingell promised to check his schedule. He later begged off, claiming that the muskies weren't biting just then. (Dingell doesn't know how grateful he made my staff. Aware of my fondness for all living things, they weren't looking forward to taking me down to the Potomac and teaching me how to bait a hook.)

Before long, anti–Norfolk Southern forces in Congress moved to take matters into their own hands. NS chairman Robert Claytor was summoned to a private Capitol Hill meeting, where he was handed a prewritten press release announcing the company's withdrawal from the Conrail bidding. The congressmen misjudged the businessman. Instead of pulling out, Claytor came straight over to DOT and a hastily assembled war council of NS officials, investment bankers and departmental experts. After listening to ten minutes of talk that was going nowhere, I pulled Claytor out of the room and took him next door. When we came out fifteen minutes later, Claytor had agreed to ask his board to consider raising Norfolk Southern's offer to $1.9 billion.

I wasn't the only one taking heat on the proposed sale. Norfolk Southern critics in the House came under pressure from restive congressmen, among them Subcommittee Chairman James J. Florio of New Jersey. Florio had questions of his own about Norfolk Southern. But he also had vivid memories of Penn Central's final hours, when the dying company continued paying dividends out of an empty cash box. Knowing that the protective covenants I had in mind were intended to spare Conrail from a similar fate, Florio kept an open mind on the Norfolk Southern offer.

Then, suddenly, a couple of seemingly unrelated legislative actions transformed the atmosphere on Capitol Hill. Passage of the Gramm-Rudman Act caused everyone in Washington to look around for ways to whittle down the federal deficit. And a sweeping overhaul of the nation's tax laws led Norfolk Southern to withdraw. The next-best plan was a public offering of Conrail stock. This was acceptable to me, as long as the protective covenants were intact and not linked to railroad reregulation.

The climactic vote came on September 17, 1986, in an Energy and Public Works Committee room packed with lobbyists and reporters. Prowling on the edge of the crowd was DOT's Capitol Hill liaison, Rebecca Range, whose persuasive gifts had earned her the title "that woman" from some resentful committee members. Resourceful as ever, Rebecca latched on to a key congressman and steered him into an adjoining room for a last-minute telephone conversation with me. DOT's position prevailed by a single vote—"that woman" had done her job brilliantly.

Six months later, I stood on the floor of the New York Stock Exchange as frenzied bidders snapped up sixty million shares in the largest first-time industrial stock offering in U.S. history. Seventeen years and billions of dollars after its bailout by the American taxpayer, Conrail was again in private hands, assured of long-term viability and the option to merge with another company in as little as twelve months. And the federal deficit was reduced by almost $2 billion.

Our success on Conrail prompted a public thank-you from hundreds of private-sector groups that had banded together to form the Coalition for Privatization. At the Washington dinner held to salute DOT's efforts on the sale, there were generous speeches and toasts. Best of all, the dinner produced a scholarship allowing a student from Hine Junior High School in an inner-city neighborhood to attend George Mason University.

DOT had already "adopted" Hine, tutoring students, taking them on board Coast Guard cutters, and inviting them to departmental functions. I delivered the commencement address at their graduation ceremony. How appropriate it was that when Conrail went private, free-market advocates showed their gratitude by funding a youngster from a neglected neighborhood to study privatization and other economic issues. An evening like that makes all the hassles of policy-making worthwhile. It's enough to demonstrate that you *can* make a positive difference in the lives of others. And that's a feeling of satisfaction hard to describe.

Two people in particular have played key roles in Conrail; exceptionally able and totally dedicated to making that difference for people, Jim Burnley and Jenna Dorn have helped make my years at DOT not only productive but highly enjoyable. They represent the finest in public service. They're also like family.

Sometimes public policy is made in the most private places. My next effort to get the federal government out of business, so to speak, started with a bit of pillow talk between Bob and me. Why should Uncle Sam operate a pair of airports, Washington National and Dulles International? Why subject a local, nonpolitical function like airport management to congressional oversight?

Bob quickly brought me down to earth. His Capitol Hill colleagues had personal reasons for opposing any transfer, he pointed out. For one thing, they appreciated National's proximity to downtown Washington—just ten minutes from committee room to boarding ramp. Did I really expect Congress to surrender control of both airports in return for vague assurances of future improvements? The idea was a nonstarter.

Bob rolled over and went to sleep. As far as I was concerned, the gauntlet had been thrown down. I reached for a bedside notepad and began sketching the outlines of a strategy to prove him wrong. Certainly Bob had history on his side. Administrations of both parties had attempted eight times since 1949 to move National and Dulles Airports out of federal control, without winning in either house of Congress. What made me think I could succeed where they had failed?

Three reasons: Deregulation. Decay. Deficits.

Because of the increase in air travel brought on by airline deregulation, Dulles International had become America's fastest-growing airport. To accommodate still heavier passenger traffic in the future, money was needed to implement a host of changes. To the south, National Airport was an embarrassingly shabby gateway to the capital of the free world. Dulles' awkward sister was badly in need of repairs. But in a period when federal deficits were causing a general belt-tightening, that kind of money—$700 million—simply wasn't available.

Finding an alternative source of cash involved a three-year process of persuasion, during which I mingled appeals to reason with old-fashioned horse-trading. We wouldn't get anywhere without support from airport users, key congressmen and the three government jurisdictions affected—Virginia, Maryland and the District of Columbia. To get it, I appointed an advisory commission, chaired by former Virginia Governor Linwood Holton. At the group's first organizational meeting I delivered some bluntly worded instructions: "Don't tell me whether to transfer these airports. Tell me how."

In the second week of June 1986, the Senate adopted the

commission's plan to create an independent regional authority to run and rehabilitate both facilities. As with Conrail, the strongest resistance to change came in the House, whose members thought of Dulles and National—especially National—as *their* airports. I could go up to the Hill and talk myself blue in the face about why it was a philosophical contradiction for Congress to supervise an airport. It didn't matter: Adam Smith had never been stuck in rush-hour traffic while trying to make a plane that was taxiing down a runway thirty miles from his office.

A few Congressmen who had were astonishingly candid. "I don't care about the merits of your case," one member told me. "I don't really care very much what you think is right. What's it going to do to my flight back home?"

By the time a final vote was scheduled, two weeks beyond Congress' original adjournment date, I was already booked into an extensive campaign tour for House and Senate candidates. Over the weekend, with the help of White House operators, I tracked down dozens of congressmen, including one in a hospital where his wife had just given birth to a baby boy. To California's Ed Zschau, locked in a tight race with Senator Alan Cranston, I said I'd do an extra West Coast event for him if he would round up votes for the airport bill back in Washington. Zschau readily agreed, as did several other candidates for whom I was scheduled to campaign out West.

On the night of October 15, I spoke at a Las Vegas temple with Senate candidate James Santini. Upon returning to my hotel room at eleven-fifteen, I found an urgent message: the House was about to take a final vote. On the other end of the telephone hookup was my deputy, Jim Burnley, who kept a running tally. "We need 218 to win," Burnley said. "One ninety ... 205 ... 210 ... 215 ..." As we went over the top, there were cheers and shouts on both ends of the line. It was after midnight, Las Vegas time. A new day had dawned, in more ways than one.

The Cabinet is often called the President's official family, and like most families it has its disagreements. Ronald Reagan encouraged open debate among his Cabinet members, the more candid the better. During Reagan's first term a proliferation of Cabinet councils made it difficult for members to participate in a meaningful way. I myself was on seven of the eight panels. For the second term, the number of these sub-Cabinet decision groups was slashed to just two—Economic Policy and Domestic Policy. Even so, Cabinet members had to be prepared several times a week to discuss issues outside their bailiwick.

Secretary of Commerce Malcolm Baldrige was a warm, unpretentious Yankee from Connecticut. He was my seatmate at Cabinet meetings until his tragic death in a rodeo accident in July 1987. I used to look over Mac's shoulder as he doodled away. His mind was as active as his hands were restless. He was particularly forceful in pressing the Administration to take a tougher stance on foreign nations that were guilty of unfair trade practices.

I lined up with Mac on that one, but later I found myself in competition with him. The issue was which of our departments would oversee the development of a private U.S. space industry based on expendable launch vehicles (ELV's), rocket boosters used only once to send satellites into space. Mac and I went head to head. After we made separate presentations to the Cabinet, the President concluded that DOT was the logical partner to work with the private sector in commercializing space. With his usual professionalism, Mac closed ranks and argued just as loudly as I against NASA's space monopoly and its 40 percent subsidy to users of the space shuttle, an incentive which effectively crippled the development of a private industry.

One day I went to the Commerce Department for a strategy session. Mac had just received a new lariat, and he was happy as a kid on Christmas morning.

"Hold on, Elizabeth," he said when I was ten feet from his desk. "I'll bet I can lasso you from here."

He did exactly that, with the grace and enthusiasm of a natural cowboy. Afterward, we huddled over ways to do a little bureaucratic lassoing, by convincing NASA to surrender its control over the launching of routine commercial satellites.

We argued for three years—at Cabinet meetings, in the National Security Council and with members of Congress—

that America could not afford to put all her eggs into one basket by relying on the shuttle alone. Instead of launching satellites for private businesses, NASA should be free to perform more exotic missions like a space station, the Strategic Defense Initiative and planetary exploration. I emphasized that private industry, eager to tap a growing market, was far better equipped than government to build and launch satellites at competitive prices.*

The debate became quite intense. Satellite customers who received government discount fares weren't that eager to pay open-market prices, while some NASA officials regarded the vastness of space as their bureaucratic private property.

Then, in January 1986, seven of the nation's most daring explorers lost their lives when the space shuttle Challenger crashed into the sea off Cape Kennedy. The Challenger tragedy left the United States with no ready access to space. It stranded dozens of NASA customers with unlaunched payloads. Foreign rivals moved in: Europe's Ariane, China's Long March; even the Soviets hoped to get a piece of the action with their massive Proton rocket.

In the aftermath of the Challenger disaster, officials saw with new eyes the wisdom of space diversification. We had nothing to lose and everything to gain by moving routine commercial satellites off the shuttle and onto expendable launch vehicles. All that private manufacturers needed was a signal from Washington. The skies were already filled with satellites that improved our telecommunications, weather and crop forecasting, and search-and-rescue capabilities. From there it was only a short leap of the imagination for me to envision a high-flying utopia in which privately launched satellites gave us additional breakthroughs, locating fuels, detecting pollution and manufacturing space-based pharmaceuticals.

---

*Among the greatest benefits of space exploration are the countless scientific and technological spinoffs that the program has generated. DOT has its own space by-product: Alan McArtor, a former member of the Air Force's high-flying Thunderbirds and chairman of my private-sector committee on space before his appointment as head of the Federal Aviation Administration in July 1987.

With all that potential, who would have expected that among DOT's first launch applications was one giving a whole new twist to the idea of cradle-to-grave government? Literally. Space Services, Inc., wanted to turn the heavens into a celestial cemetery. That is, they proposed to send aloft individual capsules full of cremated human remains ("cremains," in high-tech talk). The pitch to earthbound mourners was that they could look up and see Aunt Tilly whenever they wanted. Through all eternity, presumably. Environmentalists objected that Aunt Tilly and her companions would clutter up space. The media adopted an approach to the whole scheme that was anything but funereal. "Orbit for the Departed" ran the *New York Times* headline.

Eventually I gave the go-ahead for Aunt Tilly to rest in space. More important, in August 1986 President Reagan gave the green light to private manufacturers ready to enter the commercial launch market. Even as the President ordered a new orbiter to replace the ill-fated Challenger, he invited free enterprise to help relieve the taxpayer and meet the challenge of foreign competition.

"We must always set our sights on tomorrow," the President said in announcing his decision. "NASA will keep America on the leading edge of change; the private sector will take over from there. Together, they will ensure that our country has a robust, balanced, and safe space program."

Almost exactly a year later, I witnessed the initial signing of contracts and gave preliminary government approval for the first private-sector launch in the nation's history.

We must always set our sights on tomorrow. For the girl from South Fulton Street whose mother once rode in a horse-drawn rig courtesy of the Cathey Buggy Company, it was like coming full circle.

BOB

Nineteen eighty-six will be remembered as the Year of Tax Reform. Before revising the tax code, the Senate adopted a not unrelated change in how it conducts its business. For years Howard Baker had argued that we should follow the House and allow television cameras to broadcast our deliberations. I picked up where he left off, with the result that tax reform hit the Senate floor at about the same time TV technicians hit their lights.

The ensuing debates over IRA's—individual retirement accounts—and sales-tax deductibility posed no ratings threat to *General Hospital,* but they did give millions of viewers a first-hand look at Congress in action. Television also nationalized the issue, making lawmakers think twice before delaying or amending the bill simply to satisfy local demands. Few senators wanted to tamper with the top individual rate of 25 percent (later raised to 28 percent); fewer still dared to in front of the viewing, voting public.

Television coverage may have been historic, but not the speeches it has spawned. Like it or not, the days when Webster, Calhoun and Clay filled the halls of Congress with great oratory have gone the way of spittoons and snuffboxes. Americans today prefer their eloquence in thirty-second sound bites. Even so, millions of people are tuning in to the Senate—quorum calls, filibusters and all.

Shortly after coverage began, a faithful viewer in Boise, Idaho, approached me and said she was a bit uncertain about my exact role in the daily drama. "But you must be good," she added. "They call on you a lot."

She had plenty to watch before the Ninety-ninth Congress passed into history. In addition to tax reform, the Republican Senate confirmed President Reagan's Supreme Court nominations of William H. Rehnquist and Antonin Scalia, thereby extending the Reagan legacy long after the sun sets over Rancho del Cielo. We passed a tough new immigration law that increased control over our borders. Antidrug legislation was enacted to attack both problems of supply and demand. The Superfund that pays for cleaning up the nation's toxic-waste sites was renewed for five years at five times the previous level of funding.

Thirty-seven years after it was first submitted, a treaty to outlaw genocide was finally approved. So were the MX missile and $100 million in aid to democratic resistance forces in Nicaragua. After the April 1986 bombing raid on Qaddafi's Libya, I suggested changes in the War Powers Act to make it easier for a President to move against state-sponsored terrorism. Congress can criticize foreign policy, but only the President can create it. After all, how many businesses could survive a management structure that required the front office to consult with 535 directors on every decision?

In the atrium of the Hart Senate Office Building there is an enormous sculpture by Alexander Calder. Rearing up from the marble floor is a jagged metal mountain; overhead revolves a bank of stylized clouds. Passing by the work nearly every day, I used to wonder why the artist had made his clouds so black. On November 4, 1986, I found out.

Nationwide, GOP Senate candidates that day actually improved upon the party's aggregate vote compared with the 1980 landslide. But the distribution of support followed a different pattern. Six years earlier, we had won almost every close contest. In 1986, we lost enough of these to ensure that at the start of the One Hundredth Congress Minority Leader Robert Byrd and I would switch places.

We had no excuses, and no need for any. In six short years we had rewritten the Washington rule book, redefined the role of American government and ended the national identity crisis rooted in our Vietnam involvement. Thirteen million new jobs had been created, rekindling the spirit of American enterprise. (Contrary to what some people say, we are not on our way to becoming a nation of hamburger flippers. According to the White House Council of Economic Advisers, 60 percent of all new jobs in this country pay $20,000 a year or more.)

Political majorities ebb and flow. Chairmanships change hands. Offices rotate. But history will record that it was a Republican President and Senate who reversed America's decline and dispelled any doubts about the GOP's ability to govern. Beginning January 1987, I had fewer soldiers on my side of the aisle. We weren't going to win every fight, but we sure wouldn't duck any.

According to Elizabeth, living with a senator takes a certain amount of forbearance. "Ask him to take the trash out, and you get a filibuster." On the other hand, being married to a Cabinet officer has its own set of demands. One difference between the executive and legislative branches is that Elizabeth had a bigger organization than I. Besides that, her organization usually did what she told it to.

On the last day of March 1987, I went to the White House for a regularly scheduled meeting between the President and Republican congressional leaders. The Secretary of Transportation was already there—on hand, I discovered, to reinforce Reagan's appeal for votes to sustain his veto of an $87.5 billion highway bill.

Under the circumstances, my range of options was limited.

"This is what you call being caught between a rock and a hard place," I remarked to Reagan, who quickly corrected me.

"I may be the hard place," he said, "but Elizabeth's a gemstone."

When the Founding Fathers gave Congress oversight responsibilities, they must have had something other than potholes and parking lots in mind. I like roads as much as anyone, but, coming from Kansas, I can smell pork a mile away. I've never seen a better case for the line-item veto, giving Presidents the same budgetary authority now enjoyed by forty-three state governors. But that's another fight. Just then my hands were full trying to round up enough Republicans to sustain the President's veto.

On April 1 the Senate did exactly that, with one vote to spare. Bob Byrd got his chance to shout April Fool when he dug into parliamentary procedure and came up with a second roll call the next day. This gave Byrd and others in the Democratic cloakroom twenty-four hours to lobby North Carolina freshman Terry Sanford, whose defection had provided Reagan with his original margin of victory. When Sanford switched his vote under the harsh glare of the national media, it sealed the fate of the veto—unless one of thirteen Republicans who had defied the White House underwent a similar change of heart.

The chances of that happening were remote, I told the President on the morning of April 2; at best, one in ten. It didn't matter. Reagan had his Irish up. In a combative mood, he personally came to Capitol Hill for a hastily called meeting of GOP senators.

When the President arrived at the Old Senate Chamber, a few minutes after noon, he got a standing ovation. Unfortunately, that's all he got. At a second meeting in my office, I raised the possibility of all thirteen switching their votes as a bloc. Half a dozen members were willing to walk the plank, but no one wanted to be pushed.

"You're not going to get a vote out of here," someone finally called out.

He was right. On the final roll call, precisely two thirds of the Senate rejected the Reagan position. Pundits were quick to describe the outcome as a personal setback for the President. In his seventh year in office, they were still making the mistake of underestimating Ronald Reagan. Reagan may have lost on the highway bill, but the bigger loss would have been to do nothing. There are times when confrontation is better than capitulation, and this was one of them.

In rolling the dice that morning on Capitol Hill, Reagan had exercised the classic presidential leadership envisioned by James Madison's political system that was based on "countervailing interests." According to the Father of the Constitution, America was a land of conflicting groups and factions. "Ambition must be made to counter ambition," wrote Madison. Congress is the public arena where society's contentious fragments can thrash out their differences. But only a President can articulate and defend the national interest. That's what Reagan was doing in challenging the odds on the highway bill. Like any true leader, he knew that success is never final, nor defeat fatal, as long as you have the courage to act on principle and take the heat.

The Reagan years draw to their close, and the American people look for a model to guide their steps to the threshold of a new century. Instead of a shining city on a hill, maybe we could emulate a typical prairie village. As I look back on the small town where I grew up, it isn't freckled-faced boys and foxy grandpas and Norman Rockwell landscapes that I see. Instead, it's a powerful respect for individuals, not for themselves alone but for the contribution every single one of us can make if given the chance by an inclusive society.

My life has taught me that there's nothing average about the so-called average American, and that small towns have a large quota of common sense. When I was growing up in Russell, not everyone knew the name of our Congressman, but everyone knew his neighbor. We cared about one another in ways no government statistician could gauge. We didn't measure compassion with a dollar sign. We took it for granted that all people were equal in kind, whatever their differences in degree.

In short, we were a community. And of all the challenges we face in this country—trade and arms control, education and health—none is more important than regenerating the old sense of belonging to a common enterprise. The need is especially urgent in this age of high technology and an economy that often seems permanently stuck on fast forward.

Of what use are robots that can build cars if they make displaced workers feel like interchangeable parts? Where's the value of biotechnology if middle-class families cannot financially survive the impact of a catastrophic illness? Or of agricultural abundance if farmers are punished for productivity and people go hungry in the world's richest land?

Journalists always ask candidates for office to outline a vision of the future. I guess I'd put the question a little differently. Before you can know where someone wants to go, you ought to find out where he's coming from. Some of us start life near the top of the ladder, some near the bottom. Doran Dole's family scrambled just to get on the ladder. Like millions of my generation, I went off to war. I came back resolved to do whatever I could to keep future young Americans off the battlefield and out of the hospital wards.

Times change, and people change with them. I'm certainly

not the same man who came to Washington in 1961 to vote first, last and always for the wheat farmer. (I'm still voting for farmers—but my interests have broadened a bit over the years.) Once I was thought of as a political one-man band. I've long since realized that no one can take responsibility for every decision to reach a Capitol Hill office.

There's a big difference between holding a leadership position and *leadership*—and this too is something I've learned over time. It's the difference between sitting across from a committee chairman in a conference room and staring into Mikhail Gorbachev's face at a table where the future of the human race is being determined. It's a combination of background and backbone. It's knowing how Washington works, without becoming its captive.

In order to lead, you have to stay close to your roots, to the people and places and values that give you strength and that temper pride with humility. Washington is full of monuments that sometimes dwarf the individuals they are meant to inspire. I prefer warm humanity to cold marble, and my inspiration comes from the message of hope contained in the motto of my native state.

"To the stars through difficulties" is a philosophy to guide nations as well as individuals.

BOB *and* ELIZABETH

Writing a book together has something in common with marriage. If you can't decide who gets the last word, you might as well share it. Over the last couple of years, we've shared much of our pasts. During that time we've learned a few things we hadn't known about each other and learned still more about ourselves. We may not always have recalled events in the same light, but then, what married couple doesn't occasionally agree to disagree?

If you think government is full of checks and balances, you should see a dual career between people who love their work second only to each other. Our solution is simple: we share the good times as we share the sacrifices—equally. We come from different regions, backgrounds and traditions, but we both owe a lot to small-town America; to loving, supportive families, friends and allies who have given us far more than we can ever return. Whatever the future may hold, life has been generous. For that, as for so much else, we are profoundly grateful.

The words of writer Willa Cather sum up our feelings about public service: "That is happiness—to be dissolved in something complete and great."

Acknowledgments

Writing an autobiography is as much a group endeavor as running for office or crafting public policy. We've had the help of many generous friends and family members, and of the staffers who comprise our professional families, in recapturing the past. These include: Sheila Bair, Shirley Ballard, Dean Banker, George Baxter, Beth Bowers, Huck Boyd, Jim Burnley, Red Cavaney, Sheila Burke Chew, Dick Cheney, Edward Clement, Jo Anne Coe, Warren Cooksey, Margaret Cox, John and Edie Crutcher, Rod D'Arment, Bob Davis, G. B. "Bub" Dawson, Kenneth Dole, Robin Dole, Pete Domenici, Jenna Dorn, Ken Duberstein, Thelma Duggin, Harold and Faith Dumler, Charlotte Ellis, Bob Ellsworth, Tom Evans, Arthur Fletcher, LeRoy Foote, Bruce Freedman, Gladys Friesen, John Gordley, Mary C. Hanford, John Hanford III, Kathleen Harrington, Tom Idens, Harold Isenberg, Kathy Jeffries, Machell Johnson, Virginia Knauer, Tom Korologos, Melinda Ledden-Sidak, Dick Lesher, Stuart Levin, Bob Lighthizer, Kay Luther, Pat Lynch, Phyllis Buzick Macy, Bernard Marshall, Mari Maseng, Betty Meyer, Alice Mills, Rosemary Mong, Harry Morganstern, Gloria Nelson, Lyn Nofziger, Dave Owen, Tully Plesser, George Radelescu, Rebecca Range, John Daniel Reaves, Marynell Reece, Walt Riker, Pat Roberts, Wyndham Robertson, Randy Russell, Paul Russo, John Sears, Wilmer "Bub" Shaffer, Eric "Doc" Smith, Jeanne Smith, Jean Staley, Edward and Elizabeth Taylor, Janie

Townsley, Wayne Valis, Jerry Waters, Kim Wells, Ward White, J. D. Williams, John Woelk, Don and Ruth Wolfe, Lahoma Dennis Yates, Shirley Ybarra.

We owe a special debt to Russ Townsley, the indefatigable editor of the *Russell Daily News,* for his help in locating photographs and reviewing early chapters of the manuscript; and to Joe Snell and his dedicated archival staff at the Kansas Historical Society in Topeka, who ferreted out materials relating to Russell's early history and Kansas politics.

We are deeply grateful to our editor at Simon and Schuster, Alice Mayhew, and her associate, Henry Ferris, who went the extra mile to ease the strain of first-time authorship. Their patience and expert guidance were invaluable to a pair of literary neophytes. We are no less appreciative of the warm support and enthusiasm that have characterized Richard Snyder's attitude toward this project from its inception.

Richard Norton Smith—Rick to his friends, ourselves among them—has been much more than a collaborator. His historical and biographical training lent an extra dimension to our efforts to avoid the trap of many Washington memoirs, which describe the process of government while neglecting the people who govern. On paper at least, Rick helped us put our lives in order. Campaign schedulers: take note!

Index